C000065867

BEST BIRD wATCHING SITES IN SUSSEX

by
Adrian Thomas
and
Peter Francis

BUCKINGHAM PRESS

Published in 2003 by:
Buckingham Press
55 Thorpe Park Road, Peterborough
Cambridgeshire PE3 6LJ
United Kingdom

01733 561739
e-mail: buck.press@btinternet.com

© Buckingham Press 2003

ISBN 0 9533840 63
ISSN 0144-364 X

Editor: David Cromack
Design and maps: Hilary Cromack
Publisher: Hilary Cromack

About the authors: Adrian Thomas is Press Officer for the RSPB in the South East, as well as being a feature writer for magazines such as *Bird Watching* and *Times Education Supplement*. Peter Francis is a local government accountant and keen birdwatcher, who has enjoyed studying Sussex's birds since moving to the county in 1989.

Cover and black and white illustrations: John Davis
John has been painting and illustrating since the early 1980s becoming a member of the Society of Wildlife Artists in 1987. His illustrations have included work for *Finches and Sparrows*, *Birds of the Western Palearctic and Birds of America*. He also produced work for the RSPB, BBC Wildlife and Downland Wildlife, among other publications. John accepts commissions.
Address: 6 Redmoor, Birdham, Chichester, West Sussex PO20 7HS. Tel. 01243 512351.

Black and white illustration: John Reaney
John has always lived in Sussex and has a lifelong interest in the birds and mammals of the area. He originally worked in pastels but has now changed to watercolour. He became a member of the Society of Wildlife Artists in 1987 and has regularly had his work exhibited at their annual exhibition at the Mall Galleries, London. John accepts commissions.
Address: 1 Buxton Road, Brighton, East Sussex BN1 5DE. 01273 551993.

Black and white illustrations: Steve Cale.
Steve lives and works in North Norfolk and is a keen naturalist. He is a self taught artist and has had a number of exhibitions. His paintings have gone as far afield as Hong Kong and New Zealand and he is undertaking a commission at the Mareeba Wetlands Foundation in Australia later in the autumn 2003. Steve accepts commissions.
Address: Great Ryburgh, Fakenham, Norfolk NR21 7AP. 01328 829589.

Printed and bound in Great Britain by:
Biddles Ltd, Book Manufacturers, Guildford, Surrey.

CONTENTS

CONTENTS

FEATURED SITES IN SUSSEX (continued)

INTRODUCTION

IF YOU WERE TO RANK the UK's top birdwatching counties, Sussex might not quite make it into the top five. Its geographical position simply means that it cannot compete with the Norfolks, Cornwalls and Highlands of this world. Yet this sunshine coast, backed by glorious downland, heaths and countryside, is such a varied county within easy reach of so many people that it is still one of the most popular for birdwatching.

If this book helps you to get as much pleasure out of the county's birds as we do, then it will have done its job. Enjoy!

Adrian Thomas & Peter Francis

ACKNOWLEDGMENTS

WE HAVE BEEN extremely fortunate to have been able to turn to so many of today's top Sussex birdwatchers and conservationists who have generously and freely given their time and expertise to check our draft text and ensure that this book is as accurate and informative as possible. The help and support of the following has been wonderful, and we are truly grateful:

Roy Harman and David King from *Ashdown Forest Bird Group*
Mike Funnell and Robin Edwards from *Buchan Country Park*
John Smitherman from *Chailey Common Society*
Anne de Potier from *Chichester Harbour Conservancy*
Bob Edgar, Clair Kerr and all the staff from the *English Nature Sussex and Surrey team*
Roy Sanderson from *Friends of Weir Wood Reservoir*
Val Bentley from *Henfield Birdwatch*
David Mercer from *Kingley Vale NNR*
Sharon Cadman, Dan Delaney, Jonathan Fairhurst and Glen Redman from *The National Trust*
Paul Bennett from *Pagham Harbour LNR*
Martin Allison, Simon Busuttil, Tim Callaway, Chris Corrigan, Darren Fry, Steve Gilbert, Pete Hughes, Keith Noble and Chris Skinner from *RSPB*
Paul Troake and Barry Yates from *Rye Harbour Nature Reserve*

Richard James from *South Downs Conservation Board*
Emma Goddard, Jane Fuller and Megan Klaar from *South East Water*
Howard McKenzie, Tony Lloyd and Phil Bance from *Southern Water*
Richard Cowser, Dave Green, Richard Ives, Barrie Watson and Audrey Wende from *Sussex Ornithological Society*
Rob Free and Paul Bruce from *Sussex Wealden Greensand Heath Project*
Mark Monk-Terry, Alice Parfitt, Mike Russell and Steve Tillman from *Sussex Wildlife Trust*
Sam Bayley from *Warnham LNR*
Graham Roberts from *West Sussex CC*
Geoff Squire from *Arundel WWT*

And to Sebastian Anstruther, Ian Barnard, Barry Collins, David and John Cooper, Cliff Dean, Roger French, Dick Gilmore, Andrew Grace, Martin Hole, Colin Law, Owen Mitchell, Alan Perry, Steve Rumsey, Iris and Alf Simpson, Ewan Urquart and West Wittering Estate.

It is a long and distinguished list, and if we have missed anyone, our heartfelt apologies.

Finally our special thanks to Andy Cotton and Tony Wilson for gallantly taking away what seemed like half a book each to check.

WHY WATCH BIRDS IN SUSSEX ?

MOST BIRDWATCHERS can wax lyrical about the great places and birds to be found in their home county, but in the spirit of honesty we freely admit that Sussex has its downsides. There are lots of people living here, even more holiday-makers and the traffic can be a nightmare! In bird terms, Sussex has its limitations; it doesn't pack in the rarities like the east coast counties or the extreme south-west, nor is there any breeding or wintering speciality for which the county is unique.

So why watch birds in Sussex? Fortunately the list of the positives easily outweighs that of the negatives!

Passage in all directions

The long coastline and its geographical position is key to much of the birdwatching interest in Sussex. Situated on the narrowing English Channel, passage waders and wildfowl coming from further south and west in spring are funnelled past the Sussex coast on their journeys to Scandinavia and beyond. Thousands of Brent Geese, Common Scoters, Bar-tailed Godwits and terns in spring are accompanied by a whole host of exciting species, the most sought-after being the Pomarine Skuas.

Sussex is also the first landfall for many migrants arriving from the Continent in spring and is then their jettison point in the autumn. In the latter season in particular, thousands of migrants pause to refuel along the coastal strip and even a considerable distance inland.

Coastal treasures

There are some key habitats along the coast – Rye, Pagham and Chichester Harbours stand out, all satisfying the highest European statutory designation of Special Protection Area. Pagham and Chichester Harbours are the outstanding sites in the county for passage and wintering waders and they host a considerable proportion of the county's wildfowl, including thousands of Brent Geese. Chichester Harbour also regularly holds Britain's largest roost of Little Egrets, while Pagham Harbour has a habit of turning up rarities and can attract the largest congregation of wintering Slavonian Grebes in the UK.

Rye Harbour is the county's breeding stronghold for Sandwich and Little Terns, Ringed Plovers, Oystercatchers and Wheatears. It probably has as many wintering Bitterns as any other site in the UK, and they show themselves daily!

There are some large areas of coastal plain and land reclaimed from the sea, principally the Selsey peninsula, plus Pevensey and Pett Levels. Though none of these sites now hold the wetland bird populations they would once have done, Redshanks and Lapwings continue to breed and there are wintering wildfowl, Lapwings, Curlews, Snipe and Golden Plovers

Elsewhere on the coast, the promontory of Beachy Head is the county's hotspot for passerine rarities in spring and autumn, with a list of species topped only by perhaps Dungeness and Portland on the south coast. Birds such as Wrynecks, Bee-eaters and Hoopoes are annual. Commoner migrants, especially Blackcaps, pass through the rich scrub in their thousands in autumn and coasting movements of hirundines can be spectacular. The famous and beautiful white chalk cliffs, of which Beachy Head is a part, host breeding Peregrines, Rock Pipits and Kittiwakes.

Up on the Downs

Looming behind the coast, the South Downs is a surprisingly large, wild and harsh landscape with outstanding scenic value and is potentially set to become a National Park. The Downs, which retain excellent populations of farmland birds of conservation concern such as Corn Buntings and Sky Larks, consistently attract passage Ring Ouzels and Dotterels. Don't imagine the Downland sites in this book are the only ones to visit, they nevertheless represent a good flavour of birdwatching in this habitat.

Inner beauty

A mile or so north of the Downs, running parallel to it through much of West Sussex, is the Greensand Ridge. Its sandy soils mean that it was once covered extensively in heathland, good fragments of which remain and more are being recreated. In East Sussex, there is an even larger area of heath in one big block – Ashdown Forest. With such a heathland resource, Sussex's proportion of the national Nightjar population is perhaps higher than for any other species, plus there are Wood Larks, Dartford Warblers, Woodcocks, Tree Pipits, Redstarts, Hobbies, Redpolls and Crossbills

Much of the interior of the county is called The Weald. It is heavily wooded to this day and delightfully rural, rich in common woodland and farmland birds.

The main rivers that cross Sussex all have considerable bird interest, though the Arun stands out head and shoulders above the others. Here, the RSPB has turned unexceptional farmland between Amberley and Pulborough into internationally-important wetlands.

The county has a few substantial reservoirs. The pick of them are the large Bewl Water with its great visitor facilities and Weir Wood Reservoir which can be superb for Osprey. The network of gravel pits just south of Chichester can also be productive.

More than birds

It is easy to combine your birdwatching visits with all the other attractions Sussex has to offer, whether it be the history (such as '1066 Country'), walking, culture and nightlife (with Brighton at its core) or just a seaside holiday. Such beauty, variety and accessibility all add to Sussex's draw as a top birdwatching venue

A huge amount of conservation effort and expense has been incurred – and continues to be made – to safeguard the best wildlife sites in Sussex. There is much infrastructure in place to make your birdwatching visit easier and more enjoyable. We would urge you to ensure that you do your bit to support the charities and organisations that do so much for the wildlife of the county.

And remember, whatever birds you see, send your bird records to the County Recorder: John Hobson, 23 Hillside Road, Storrington, RH20 3LZ. Tel: 01903 740155. Email: janthobson@aol.com

HOW TO USE THIS BOOK

Here is a typical layout of the Featured Sites pages. Once familiar with the layout, you will be able to extract the information you need quickly and easily.

Key points: Includes time to allow on a visit, number of species you might see, opening times, facilities and terrain as well as other useful info and tips. No mention of hides means there are none. For public transport details see the 'Access' section of each site, but they are mentioned in the *Key points* where they are very good or very bad. For users of wheelchairs and/or public transport, see also the sections 'Best sites for Wheelchair Users' (page 166) and 'Best sites for Public Transport Users' (page 168)

Target species and likelihood of seeing them: Lists the important species for the site, with percentage figures to give an idea of the chance you have of seeing them if you visit the site at the right time and stay for a reasonable length of time. The calendar categories avoid the often-seen 'spring/summer/ autumn/winter' and instead refer to 'Winter' (loosely October to April), 'Passage' (loosely April-May and August-October) and 'Breeding season' (loosely April-September).

Other likely species: Lists the commoner species you are likely to see. Categories such as 'Woodland birds' and 'Gulls' are used to save space (see page 182 for an explanation of which species are included in each category), and these categories are listed before extra individual species.

Star rating: The more stars, the better the site. High-ranking sites will have, for example, more birds, more species, better views, better facilities, or a better chance of seeing scarce or charismatic species.

Title of site. Sites are listed alphabetically, and are numbered.

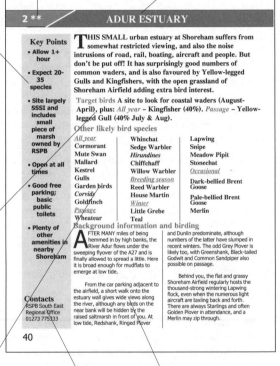

2 ** ADUR ESTUARY

Key Points
- Allow 1+ hour
- Expect 20-35 species
- Site largely SSSI and includes small piece of marsh owned by RSPB
- Open at all times
- Good free parking; basic public toilets
- Plenty of other amenities in nearby Shoreham

Contacts
RSPB South East Regional Office
01273 775333

40

THIS SMALL urban estuary at Shoreham suffers from somewhat restricted viewing, and also the noise intrusions of road, rail, boating, aircraft and people. But don't be put off! It has surprisingly good numbers of common waders, and is also favoured by Yellow-legged Gulls and Kingfishers, with the open grassland of Shoreham Airfield adding extra bird interest.

Target birds A site to look for coastal waders (August-April), plus: *All year* – Kingfisher (40%). *Passage* – Yellow-legged Gull (40% July & Aug).

Other likely bird species

All year	Whinchat	Lapwing
Cormorant	Sedge Warbler	Snipe
Mute Swan	*Hirundines*	Meadow Pipit
Mallard	Chiffchaff	Stonechat
Kestrel	Willow Warbler	*Occasional*
Gulls	*Breeding season*	Dark-bellied Brent Goose
Garden birds	Reed Warbler	
Corvids	House Martin	Pale-bellied Brent Goose
Goldfinch	*Winter*	
Passage	Little Grebe	Merlin
Wheatear	Teal	

Background information and birding

AFTER MANY miles of being hemmed in by high banks, the River Adur flows under the sweeping flyover of the A27 and is finally allowed to spread a little. Here it is broad enough for mudflats to emerge at low tide.

From the car parking adjacent to the airfield, a short walk onto the estuary wall gives wide views along the river, although any birds on the near bank will be hidden by the raised saltmarsh in front of you. At low tide, Redshank, Ringed Plover

and Dunlin predominate, although numbers of the latter have slumped in recent winters. The odd Grey Plover is likely too, with Greenshank, Black-tailed Godwit and Common Sandpiper also possible on passage.

Behind you, the flat and grassy Shoreham Airfield regularly hosts the thousand-strong wintering Lapwing flock, even when the numerous light aircraft are taxiing back and forth. There are always Starlings and often Golden Plover in attendance, and a Merlin may zip through.

Useful contacts: Phone numbers of contacts who should be able to give you further information about the site.

Background information: Generally, this section will take you through the walk, with details of the birds you might see and handy tips to help you see them. It may contain more information on points which have been briefly mentioned in previous sections.

Best time of year to visit: There may be things to see at other time of year, but the season(s) listed should produce the best results.

OS Explorer map number

Grid reference(s) of parking area(s) giving easiest access to site

Site facility symbols: (see key to symbols below)

Maps: The small thumbnail map shows the site's location within Sussex. The larger, more detailed map shows trails, hides and other key features for the site. The scale shown is in miles.

Access: Detailed directions to the parking area(s) or reserve entrance – the more difficult to find, the more detailed the description. Includes suitable bus services and nearest train stations where applicable.

Other nearby sites: Gives a selection of ideas for sites to visit in the general area of the site you have chosen. These are listed in categories of 'less than 5 miles' and 'less than 10 miles'.

SPRING/AUTUMN/WINTER OS EXPLORER 122 TQ210049

Stonechats meanwhile seem to prefer to share the reedy ditch just below the estuary wall with Reed Buntings. And keep an eye out all sides for Kingfisher.

A walk up to the old wooden road bridge, now closed to traffic, gives good views up and down the river, often over big flocks of gulls, including several hundred Common Gulls in winter.

Apart from Pagham, this is the best Sussex site for a few Yellow-legged Gulls in late summer, if your interest in birds goes that far! They are a taste of the Continent, along with the Little Egrets that can now be seen in any month.

The riverside path downstream from the east side of the old road bridge looks promising but frustratingly dead-ends. Better to retrace your steps and walk down the west bank, or drive round, to the recreation ground.

From here, cross the A259 to look over the RSPB reserve, sandwiched between Norfolk Bridge and a motley line of houseboats. Visibility is not easy - on Norfolk Bridge the traffic whooshes at your back; and from the public footpath behind the houseboats, much of the view is obscured by their variously rotting or bohemian hulls.

Access details
Free parking by the airfield: turn S off the A27 at the traffic lights opposite Sussex Pad Hotel, 1-mile E of Lancing, signed to 'Airport'. Swing L, then turn immediately R down private Shoreham Airport road. Park on the broad hardstanding bays on E side of the airfield. Never stop in the clearly restricted zone.

Recreation ground free parking: take the A259 in Shoreham W over the Norfolk Bridge and parking after 50 yards to N of road.

Other nearby sites
Less than 5-miles: Shoreham Harbour; Steep Down; Henfield Levels. Less than 10-miles: Cissbury Ring to Chanctonbury Ring; Brighton Marina; Brighton to Newhaven

41

Key to site symbols

 £ Payment required

 Refreshments available

 Parking available

 Visitor Centre

 Toilets

 Wheelchair access

Key to maps

 Water

 Sand/grass

 Mud

 Trees/scrub

T Toilets

P Parking

🌾 Marsh

〰 Reeds

↯ Viewpoint

9

THE BIRDWATCHER'S CODE OF CONDUCT

1. Welfare of birds must come first
Whether your particular interest is photography, ringing, sound recording, scientific study or just birdwatching, remember that the welfare of birds must always come first.

2. Habitat protection
A birds's habitat is vital to its survival and therefore we must ensure that our activities do not cause damage.

3. Keep disturbance to a minimum
Birds' tolerance of disturbance varies between species and seasons. Therefore, it is safer to keep all disturbance to a minimum. No birds should be disturbed from the nest in case the opportunities for predators to take eggs or young are increased. In very cold weather, disturbance to birds may cause them to use vital energy at a time when food is difficult to find. Wildfowlers impose bans during cold weather: birdwatchers should exercise similar discretion.

4. Rare breeding birds
If you discover a rare breeding bird and feel that protection is necessary, inform the appropriate RSPB Regional Officer, or the Species Protection Department at the RSPB, The Lodge, Sandy, Beds SG19 2DL. Otherwise, it is best in almost all circumstances to keep the record strictly secret to avoid disturbance by other birdwatchers and attacks by egg-collectors. Never visit known sites of rare breeding birds unless they are adequately protected. Even your presence may give away the site to others and cause so many other visitors that the birds may fail to breed successfully. Disturbance at or near the nest of species listed on the First Schedule of the Wildlife and Countryside Act 1981 is a criminal offence.

5. Rare migrants
Rare migrants or vagrants must not be harassed. If you discover one, consider the circumstances carefully before telling anyone. Will an influx of birdwatchers disturb the bird or others in the area? Will the habitat be damaged? Will problems be caused with the landowner?

6. The law
The bird protection laws, as now embodied in the Wildlife and Countryside Act 1981, are the result of hard campaigning by previous generations of birdwatchers. As birdwatchers, we must abide by them at all times and not allow them to fall into disrepute.

7. Respect the rights of landowners
The wishes of landowners and occupiers of land must be respected. Do not enter land without permission. Comply with permit schemes. If you are leading a group, do give advance notice of the visit, even if a formal permit scheme is not in operation. Always obey the Country Code.

8. Keeping records
Much of today's knowledge about birds is the result of meticulous record keeping by our predecessors. Make sure you help to add to tomorrow's knowledge by sending records to your county bird recorder.

9. Birdwatching abroad
Behave abroad as you would at home. This code should be firmly adhered to when abroad (whatever the local laws). Well behaved birdwatchers can be important ambassadors for bird protection.

(*Reprinted with permisson from the RSPB*)

FACTS ABOUT SUSSEX

THE TWO COUNTIES of East and West Sussex, now further split by the establishment of the Unitary Authority of Brighton and Hove, may be divided administratively, but are very much linked as one in people's minds and loyalties. The Sussex Ornithological Society covers it all, and birdwatchers who keep county lists tend to ignore such boundaries.

Coastline:	More than 90 miles
Human population:	1.5 million
Land area:	1,457 square miles
Highest point on coast:	532 feet (Beachy Head)
Highest point in county:	910 feet (Black Down)
Neighbouring counties:	Hampshire, Surrey and Kent

Blackcap by John Davis

R EADING a county's annual report or flicking
through the monthly reports in birdwatching magazines,
the species that are highlighted tend to be those that are
exceptional. They are the rarities that turned up out of the blue,
the migrants that appeared earlier or later than usual, the flocks
that were larger than would normally be expected.

What we have tried to do over the next few pages is give you
an idea of what is normal for Sussex, what is expected, month by
month. Whatever the date, if you are set to go birdwatching in
Sussex, turn to the relevant month and in one page you will get a
flavour of what you are likely to see. It may also help you set
your itineraries, as there are some key bird events in the county
at specific times of year that are a 'must-see' – what we have
termed our Sussex 'Highlights'.

Whichever month you choose to go birdwatching, do read the
adjacent months' accounts as well, as birds have a habit of not
strictly adhering to the calendar!

EARLY JANUARY sees plenty of birdwatchers out in Sussex, attacking their new year-list with vigour. A hundred birds in a day is possible, but requires a well-planned itinerary combining one of the best coastal locations with woodland, farmland and heath inland.

Pagham and Chichester Harbours are great for clocking up good tallies of overwintering waders, including small numbers of Whimbrels, Spotted Redshanks, Greenshanks and Avocets at both sites. The Little Stint flock at East Head is perhaps the most reliable in the country.

For wildfowl, the Arun Valley is usually best with regular counts of several thousand Wigeon and Teal and several hundred Pintails. Pulborough Brooks RSPB is great for most species, but the Bewick's Swans in the valley, which are at their peak this month, can be mobile. Arundel WWT and next-door Swanbourne Lake are better for big Pochard numbers and easy-to-see Mandarins, while triple figure Gadwall flocks are likely at Chichester Gravel Pits among the Coots.

Wild geese may turn up unexpectedly in the Arun, Adur or Cuckmere Valleys, but Scotney Court is now unbeatable, with several hundred White-fronts pulling in everything from Beans to Pink-feet to Emperors, clearly of varied origins! Scotney is also the best water on which to see rare grebes or divers, plus Scaup.

Seawatching can be a cold affair, and unproductive days are regular. Storms or cold-weather movements can, however, lead to exciting watching, with good passage of divers and auks. More accessible are the birds actually on the sea, pride of place going to Rye Bay where the Great Crested Grebe numbers can reach an impressive 500. Similar numbers of Common Scoters are also quite reliable and attract Velvet Scoters and sometimes Scaup. The sea off Hove and Worthing meanwhile often hosts several hundred Red-breasted Mergansers, while Eiders can form little flocks off places like Bexhill or Pagham.

Any of the winter semi-rarities often tend to be long-stayers that can be sought at any time over the next ten or so weeks. These might include a Great Grey Shrike, often up on Ashdown Forest, a Glaucous Gull in Pagham Harbour and perhaps an over-wintering Spoonbill in Chichester Harbour. Black Brants with dark-bellied Brent Goose flocks are now regular in Pagham and Chichester Harbours and Snow Buntings or the occasional Shore Lark at maybe at Rye or East Head.

FEBRUARY

THE WEATHER'S unpredictability is predictable! Several days of deep-freeze will cause lakes to ice over, so that Water Rails, forced out of the reedbeds, can be at their most visible. If there are snow-storms, (which isn't that often) flocks of winter thrushes and Sky Larks may move ahead of them south and west.

If the weather on the Continent is even worse however, there may be new arrivals into the county. These could include large numbers of Wigeon, a build-up in Smew numbers, often with some Goosanders, and also the possibility of Pink-footed Geese, Whooper Swans or even Barnacle Geese.

There can just as easily be warm spells, encouraging resident species into song. It can make birdwatching more comfortable and less thermal-bound, too. Pagham and Chichester Harbours are great for large numbers of dark-bellied Brent Geese, with a Black Brant or two and a few pale-bellied Brents now seemingly a regular fixture. There are plenty of other wildfowl here, Chichester Harbour being the prime spot for Goldeneyes, three-figure Red-breasted Merganser counts and an off-chance of Long-tailed Ducks.

If it's raptors you're after, Amberley Wild Brooks is tops, with a late afternoon visit likely to turn up one or more of Hen Harrier, Short-eared Owl, Barn Owl and Little Owl. Hen Harriers are also scattered across the Downs, commons and coastal plain and Short-eared Owls and Merlins are regularly seen at Thorney Deeps and Pevensey Levels.

Numbers of Water Pipits are generally at their peak in Combe Haven in what could now claim to be their UK stronghold, though in February none are yet showing any signs of the breeding plumage that makes them easier to split from Meadow Pipits.

February is a good month to see 'white-winged gulls' in the gull roost at Pagham Harbour. Mediterranean Gulls can be in double figures and there is an excellent chance of Glaucous Gull. The more urban harbours of Shoreham, Newhaven and Brighton Marina are worth a visit to find wintering Shags and Purple Sandpipers. Another urban bird spectacle worth checking out, is the huge swirling Starling flocks at their Brighton West Pier and Eastbourne Pier roosts, while a few Black Redstarts see out the winter in some of the, erm, not-so-pretty parts of the coastal strip.

Don't miss this month's highlights

- Check out Scotney Court gravel pit's big flock of White-fronted Geese, with the possibility of other wild geese species among them. Divers and rarer grebes are likely on the pit

- The Slavonian Grebe flock off Church Norton can reach 50 in some years

- Wonderful views of Purple Sandpipers are possible at places such as Newhaven Harbour

- Wintering Great Grey Shrikes tend to frequent traditional locations such as Ashdown Forest

- Seawatching can include large numbers of auks and divers on the move

- Hen Harriers, Barn Owls and Short-eared Owls can all be seen at Amberley Wild Brooks

13

Don't miss this month's highlights

- The best month for Lesser Spotted Woodpeckers at places such as Burton Mill Pond and Pulborough Brooks

- First migrants bring a taste of spring – expect Wheatears, Chiffchaffs and Sand Martins in fair numbers

- Peregrines should be on their regular nest sites, including well-known ones such as Sussex Heights in Brighton, Shoreham Power Station and Chichester Cathedral

- Brent Goose and Common Scoter passage picks up along the coast, with smaller but peak numbers of other duck species, too. The first Sandwich Terns and good numbers of divers, pass by.

- On the reservoirs, displaying Great Crested Grebes and, in places, Mandarins, can be colourful

THE FIRST trickle of migrants heralds a spring that can often seem a long time coming. Early returning migrants in the month include inevitable Chiffchaffs (difficult to tell from the over-wintering birds), Wheatears and Sand Martins, with Little Ringed Plovers, Sandwich Terns and Blackcaps soon after, but none of them yet in startling numbers.

By the very end of the month, there may be a Ring Ouzel or two on the Downs, the first Swallows, Sedge Warblers and Yellow Wagtails may have been seen, but more regular are Meadow Pipits arriving during daylight over the sea. Ultra-rarities are not a feature of the month, but on the scarce-bird front, it is a good month to find a few Firecrests at coastal locations and the handful of over-wintering Black Redstarts are bolstered by some new arrivals, too.

At seawatching sites there is more concerted birdwatching effort, though nowhere near the jostle-for-space situation experienced in early May. Mid to late March is generally the key time for Brent Goose passage east along the coast, several thousand passing the main seawatching stations. This is also peak time for the light passage of freshwater ducks, which can sometimes include an incongruous Garganey among the many Common Scoters.

Breeding activity includes Mistle Thrushes and if the recolonisation of Ravens in Sussex is successful, they should be feeding chicks, too. At Splash Point, plenty of Kittiwakes should be kicking around the cliffs, while the unabated activity at garden feeding stations, including plenty of Siskins, shows how the need to feed is still driving birds more than the need to breed.

Numbers of White-fronted Geese at Scotney Court may peak this month, but some wintering species show a marked reduction in numbers - Bewick's Swans disappear in dribs and drabs, but Smew move out quickly, with Redwings and Fieldfares also becoming much scarcer towards the end of the month.

Migrant arrivals

(Average first dates)

MARCH 1st-7th
Wheatear

MARCH 8th-15th
Sand Martin
Swallow
Willow Warbler

MARCH 16th-23rd
Little Ringed Plover
House Martin
Yellow Wagtail
Ring Ouzel

MARCH 24th-31st
Osprey
Common Tern
Cuckoo
Tree Pipit
Redstart
Whinchat

WARM WEATHER in early April can flatter to deceive. What feels like a world that should be full of summer visitors is strangely quite empty because, though the vanguard of many species have arrived, the floodgates have yet to open. Even a bird like the Sand Martin which first appeared mid March does not come through en masse until mid April.

By the end of the month however, it is difficult to know which way to turn, with warblers, hirundines, Nightingales, Cuckoos and the other birds of summer popping up overnight all over the county. Dawn choruses, while often chilly, are still at a decent hour and much easier to get up for than later in the season! You don't need to be on the coast to enjoy the arrival either - given a southerly wind and clear skies, incoming passerines pass straight over the top and drop into their breeding habitats.

Do spend a couple of hours early-morning seawatching, especially with a wind in the south eastern quarter. The passage of adult-plumaged skuas – Greats, Arctics and the first of the Pomarines – is wonderful, as is the tern passage with streams of Sandwich and 'Commics' (Common or Arctic or both) peppered with Black and Little Terns and Little Gulls towards the end of the month. All this is set against a constant backdrop of Common Scoter passage with some Velvet Scoters and Eiders among them. Red-throated Diver passage quickly abates, replaced by small numbers of Black-throateds in stunning summer plumage.

April presents the best chance of a Kentish Plover, now such a difficult bird to find in Britain – Pilsey or Rye are your best, if long, bets.

Woodcocks are well into their roding flights over the heaths, where Tree Pipits, Wood Larks and Dartford Warblers sing, yet at the same time big numbers of wintering Siskins and Redpolls still linger.

Migrant arrivals

(Average first dates)

APRIL 1ˢᵗ-7ᵗʰ
Nightingale
Sedge Warbler
Whitethroat

APRIL 8ᵗʰ-15ᵗʰ
Hobby
Little Tern
Turtle Dove
Swift
Reed Warbler
Lesser Whitethroat
Garden Warbler
Pied Flycatcher

APRIL 16ᵗʰ-22ⁿᵈ
Pomarine Skua
Black Tern
Spotted Flycatcher

Don't miss this month's highlights

- Get out to find those first returning summer visitors anywhere in the county

- A wind from the southeast holds the promise of some superb seawatching, including peak Arctic and Great Skua passage and the start of the 'Pom' season towards the end of the month. Expect plenty of terns and some Little and Mediterranean Gulls

- April through to May is the best period for scarcer species such as Kentish Plovers and Hoopoes, and is also good for short-staying Dotterels on the Downs

- Late in the month, three-figure roosts of Whimbrels build up on the Quarry at Rye Harbour, viewable at dusk as they flight over in noisy congregations of terns

15

MAY

Don't miss this month's highlights

- The joy of birdsong is at its peak, Nightingales, Turtle Doves, Grasshopper Warblers and Redstarts are perhaps some of the target summer visitors for birdwatchers

- During the first two weeks, you'll need to fight for a place at seawatch venues to see the Pomarine Skuas and associated top-class cast of passage birds, including an accelerated tern and wader passage

- May is the month of bird-races, a good indication that this really is the top month to see the greatest number of species

- Late-arriving migrants still needed for year lists include Nightjars and Spotted Flycatchers

- This is a good month for overshooting Continental migrants such as Bee-eaters

WHILE MAY doesn't quite have the rarity potential of autumn, it is surely *the* month to enjoy the richness of our common and breeding birds as they set up territories. Even at inland locations such as Pulborough Brooks, 60 species in a day is feasible.

Not that rarities aren't possible, now is the time to keep a watchful eye at places such as Beachy Head for colourful overshoots from the Continent such as Purple Herons, White Storks, Bee-eaters, Golden Orioles, Serins and Red-rumped Swallows. All are still rarities, but all are close to annual now, with Subalpine Warblers not far behind. The second week of May provides the best chance of Temminck's Stints at sites such as Pagham Harbour, though they are scarce.

It is amazing how many wintering migrants are still around in early May. Purple Sandpipers can still be found on the harbour arms and also Common and Velvet Scoters pass by at sea. There is also a determined passage of waders off the coast, birds probably from African wintering grounds zooming through in natty breeding plumage such as Bar-tailed Godwits, Sanderlings, Dunlins and Grey Plovers.

The peak arrivals of most migrant species is actually in May, with House Martins, Swallows and even Willow Warblers still piling in. By mid-month, one of the latest arrivals, the Nightjar, is back on the heaths. It is an annual pilgrimage for many to have an evening out, entertained by the heathland glamour species – Wood Larks, Dartford Warblers, Tree Pipits and Woodcocks, with Nightjars as the star turn.

But maybe all you need from May is a walk through a piece of Sussex countryside rich in birdsong and flowers. Maybe you enjoy hearing breeding Lapwings and Redshanks at places like Pulborough Brooks where, hopefully, a drumming noise will announce that Snipe is still a breeding species in the county. At Rye Harbour, Pett Level and Arundel WWT, the breeding colonies of Black-headed Gulls make perhaps the most noise of any Sussex wildlife, boosted at Rye by the Sandwich and Little Terns.

Or perhaps you want to find Nightingales - there are up to 1,000 pairs in the county, with Ebernoe Common, Pulborough Brooks, Amberley Wild Brooks, Ditchling to Ashcombe, Powdermill to Darwell and Lullington Heath being the best sites in this book.

JUNE

WITH THE RUSH to breed and raise young well underway, there is some slackening in birdsong levels as June progresses, unless you're prepared to get up at what is now a very early crack of dawn.

Now is the time to enjoy some of our breeding birds, such as the clockwork Ringed Plover chicks at Rye Harbour, with young Wheatears on the wing there, too. Garganeys, Shovelers and Teal may all have broods at Pulborough Brooks RSPB, though with summer's lushness, they tend to remain well hidden. Mandarins and Pochards at Swanbourne Lake may be equally retiring.

For those who enjoy seeing birds on the move, June is not devoid of activity. Early in the month can still be good for some birds arriving from the Continent, with a Black Kite not to be ruled out and Serins still possible. Some movement of Sanderlings and terns still continues into the first days of the month, and a late Whimbrel may move through, too.

It is then a fine line between northward passage ending and the return of the first birds, often non-breeders, first-year birds perhaps who have just tried out the migration but never attempted to breed. Green and Common Sandpipers can be back before the month is out, but it is a quiet month for waders in Pagham and Chichester Harbour.

Some birds never make the journey north, however, and it is normal to find some winter-plumaged Grey Plovers, plus considerable numbers of Black-tailed Godwits and Turnstones lazily sticking out the summer here. Similarly, a few Eiders may linger right into the summer, especially off Pagham or Chichester Harbours. Bizarrely, there can still be some Common Scoter passage through the month, with small flocks lingering off Rye Bay all summer.

Don't miss this month's highlights

- Rye Harbour's Sandwich and Little Tern colonies, the only ones in the county, are full of activity with Roseate Terns dropping in annually

- A trip onto the Downs should find Corn Buntings in full voice, with Quails possible, too

- The warm June evenings on the West Sussex commons or Ashdown Forest can be best for enjoying Nightjars

JULY

JULY IS SEEN as a bit of a lull in the birdwatching calendar. Correct that – it's a major lull. Birdsong is now all but over, a bewildering array of juvenile birds and somewhat dishevelled adults lurk in the dense foliage of bushes and woods and there are very few rarities to pep up birdwatching. And it often gets so hot that birds stick well to cover and long walks are not always desirable. Butterflies and dragonflies often provide a welcome distraction.

There's still plenty of reason to visit many of the birdwatching sites, however. In particular, places such as Sidlesham Ferry Pool, together with Ternery Pool and Castle Water at Rye, can by the month's end have a fine assortment of sandpipers, including Wood and Curlew, albeit in small numbers. On the estuaries themselves, the first Dunlins and Bar-tailed Godwits are likely to be back, too. Common Sandpiper numbers peak this month, especially on the canalised rivers such as the lower Ouse.

The reservoirs tend to be quiet, apart from the large honking herds of Canada and Greylag Geese. It is worth looking out for the first Ospreys, though, as they move back, some now choosing to linger for days or even weeks.

One obvious build-up is the numbers of Little Egrets, presumably the same post-breeding dispersion from the Continent that precipitated the first big invasion in 1989. Every wetland site is likely to have one or more. The Yellow-legged Gulls, which reach an impressive 300 or more in Pagham Harbour, presumably come from the same direction. In Cuckmere Haven, the return of Little Egrets is mirrored by that of Little Grebes onto the meanders.

You often associate seawatching with bad weather, but July is often the key month for Shearwater movement in the Channel. There are usually Manx, but try late in the month for the chance of Mediterranean Shearwaters passing by. Nearctic waders such as Least and Baird's Sandpipers have also turned up towards the end of July, so don't strike the month completely off the birdwatching calendar.

Perhaps the sound of July though, is that of Swifts screaming around the town centres and village churches. As the schools break up for the summer holidays, the Swifts are already beginning to think about getting out!

AUGUST

AUGUST IS A BUSY month in tourist terms but, for many birds summer is now quickly drawing to an end and many are getting ready to move or are already in the process of doing so.

Post-breeding congregations of Great Crested Grebes can exceed 100 at Bewl Water, while the Ringed Plover flock at the high tide roost at Pilsey can reach a couple of hundred. At Beachy Head, there can be hundreds of Whitethroats, Blackcaps and Willow Warblers, with smaller numbers of Redstarts and Pied Flycatchers. After an easterly wind, the first of the scarce Continental migrants may join them, such as Wrynecks, Melodious Warblers and Red-backed Shrikes.

This is also the month for Aquatic Warblers to turn up, though they land in mist-nets more often than in front of birdwatchers' binoculars. It is an exceptional season if the total reaches double figures. Beware of stripy-headed young Sedge Warblers though, which pass through the county's reedbeds in large numbers.

Black Terns don't match the numbers that were seen on spring passage, but the few passing through tend to afford better views as they now favour reservoirs and gravel pits. A westerly passage of Common Terns starts at the end of the month, too.

Adult waders, often still in superb summer plumage, return from the far north ahead of the juveniles. Grey Plovers and Curlew Sandpipers are especially smart, with Pagham Harbour being an ideal venue for both. The month is the peak time for Green and Wood Sandpiper passage, a chance to see several of each together at Pagham and Rye, with others regularly at sites such as Pulborough Brooks and Arundel WWT.

Of the breeding birds, most people have been to see and hear their Nightjars, but they continue to churr well into the month, and Hobbies still hunt over the dry dusty heaths. It can still be a good month for hearing Quails, and a trip onto the Downs is doubly worthwhile to try to find Dotterels on ploughed fields.

Don't miss this month's highlights

- Put on your walking boots for a Dotterel search on the Downs east of Brighton

- Birdwatchers seem to love hunting for Curlew Sandpipers and Little Stints among the wader flocks in places such as Pagham Harbour

- Dropping water levels at some of the reservoirs draw in waders such as Greenshanks and sandpipers

- There is a build-up of warblers at coastal sites, especially at Beachy Head, with Willow Warblers leading the invasion.

19

SEPTEMBER VIES WITH May and October for being the most exciting month to be birdwatching in Sussex. It's the cue for many birdwatchers to scour the scrub at what is one of the UK's prime migration sites, Beachy Head, but many of the birds that pass through are quite possible to find at many other localities including Pagham, Climping, Cissbury Ring, Lancing Ring, Hollingbury Camp, Sheepcote Valley, Seaford Head, Combe Haven, Hastings Country Park and Pett Level.

Warblers are the most abundant species in the bushes. Blackcaps gorge on berries, with several hundred a day at Beachy Head the norm rather than the exception. By mid-month, Willow Warbler numbers are dwindling fast, but Chiffchaffs are on the up, and plenty of Whinchats, Wheatears and Spotted Flycatchers are also around. Grasshopper Warblers on passage, are now easier to find than the few remaining breeding pairs in Sussex.

Given east winds, records of scarcer species such as Melodious and Barred Warblers show a peak in early September, as do Tawny Pipits and Red-backed Shrikes. Later in the month is perhaps a better time for a Red-breasted Flycatcher to put in a brief appearance.

In the skies, watch for raptors – often Marsh Harriers but sometimes Honey Buzzards and Ospreys moving south. Beachy Head is again often the place to be.

Diurnal movement of pipits and wagtails is often prominent in early morning, but hirundine passage can last all day. Ten thousand can pass in a day at sites such as Beachy Head, almost always flying into the wind, and providing one of the most dramatic sights in Sussex birdwatching.

At dusk, the hirundines often roost in reedbeds, such as at Filsham Reedbed and Thorney Deeps, as do considerable numbers of Yellow Wagtails.

Elsewhere, exciting wader passage continues at sites such as Rye and Pagham. Brent Geese begin to return to the western harbours, and there is a swift build-up in wildfowl numbers at places such as Pagham, Pulborough and the Cuckmere. This is also the month for Spotted Crakes, but you'll need either a great deal of patience or a ringing licence to find one!

OCTOBER

THE BIRDWATCHING focus in October remains firmly on migrants. The first week is a time of farewell to many summer species, with the last wave of birds such as Tree Pipits and Yellow Wagtails on the move. Wheatears, Whinchats, Chiffchaffs, Blackcaps and Spotted Flycatchers generally retain a presence and Hobbies can be seen well into the month, continuing to hawk for dragonflies or dashing after hirundines.

Though the numbers of the commoner species are now generally much lower, among the late stragglers there is the greater chance now of something much rarer somewhere in the county, such as a Radde's or Dusky Warbler. Beachy Head really is the prime location, but anywhere coastal can do the trick, including gardens.

The first two hours of daylight are the time to pick up coastal movement of Siskins, Redpolls and perhaps the best chance in Sussex to see Bramblings, though knowing their calls really helps. Indeed, the variety of species moving through can be dramatic, with big numbers of Goldfinches, Pied Wagtails and Meadow Pipits, plus more unexpected species such as Great Spotted Woodpeckers.

The first Redwings and Fieldfares arrive, and the coastal scrub becomes alive with Goldcrests and ticking Robins. One warbler to always keep an eye and ear out for is the Yellow-browed, which seems to have a love affair with the sycamores at Horseshoe Plantation at Beachy Head. This is the peak month for Firecrests and it is easy to see several in a day at Beachy Head or Pagham Harbour. Black Redstarts also arrive and are even more visible.

Other arrivals include a surge of Merlin sightings at coastal localities – indeed, this can be the best month to see this small falcon in the county, alongside the first returning Hen Harriers and Short-eared Owls.

Cetti's Warblers, Dartford Warblers and Bearded Tits tend to be on the move this month, turning up at non-breeding sites while, by mid-month, the first Bitterns are likely to have returned. The Little Stint flock should have reformed at East Head and the first Water Pipits of winter tantalise birdwatchers at Combe Haven.

Don't miss this month's highlights

- Possibly the most exciting month, with the chance of some real rarities, especially passerines

- Typical hauls at places like Beachy Head include Ring Ouzels, Black Redstarts, Firecrests and Merlins, with the chance of a Yellow-browed Warbler

- Coastal migrants can include Bramblings, Siskins and Redpolls, with the first returning Redwings and Fieldfares

- Given wild-weather conditions, watch for storm-driven seabirds such as Grey Phalaropes, Sooty Shearwaters, even Sabine's Gulls.

21

Don't miss this month's highlights

- Check Horseshoe Plantation, Beachy Head, for Yellow-browed and Pallas's Warblers

- Inclement weather and strong winds can make for good, if rugged, seawatching, with large-scale Kittiwake and Gannet passage spiced up with the chance of Sooty Shearwaters and possible Grey Phalaropes and Sabine's Gulls

- Not usually a bird to get excited about, Wood Pigeon emigration at coastal sites can be dramatic, numbering several thousand a day

NOVEMBER CAN seem a rather dark and dismal month after the excitement of October. Late Swallows, Sandwich Terns and Wheatears allow us to cling onto the tail-end of an Indian summer, but it takes something like a Pallas's Warbler flitting around the sycamores in Horseshoe Plantation to really brighten a birding day.

There are plenty of birds only now starting to make big moves back into the county for the winter. Seemingly unseasonal are the Fulmars, which can be back on their breeding ledges by the end of the month, and their circular flights out to sea confuse seawatch counts from this point on!

It is not until this month that Red-throated Divers are back in any numbers along the coast. There is often still considerable movement of Brent Geese coming in from their Waddensee staging post, and north-west winds have been proven to be the best for seeing wader passage along the coast, Dunlins predominating.

Purple Sandpipers are late back, and they are joined in Brighton Marina and Shoreham Harbour by Shags, usually first-year birds. It takes until November for the first Bewick's Swans to be back on the wintering grounds, too.

With the summer visitors gone and many tits and finches having moved into gardens, the woods and heaths can become rather birdless places. It can take a flock of Long-tailed Tits streaming through the bare branches to enliven proceedings as they drag all manner of other tits, Goldcrests and Treecreepers along with them. Jays become obvious everywhere in their blinkered search for acorns.

If there is one bird to look for moving past the coast, it is the Little Auk. It seems that an increasing number are being driven south into the North Sea each year and a few continue to blunder on desperately into the Channel and along the south coast.

DECEMBER

THE PERIOD BETWEEN December and February is perhaps the most static period in the birdwatching year. Yes, there are ins and outs as cold weather pulses across Britain and the Continent, but many species are permanent winter residents.

Perhaps the most noticeable new birds will be – if you are lucky enough – a few Waxwings, which may filter down into the county from the country's north and east coasts. The appearance of a scattering of Snow Buntings along the coast is also to be expected, but with the disappearance of the regular flock at Camber, there is now no reliable wintering site in the county. There is also a movement of Shelducks west into Sussex.

December is usually the time for the Great Crested Grebe and Common Scoter flocks to reappear off Pett level and Smew become more reliable at this time at Northpoint Pit and Rye Harbour. On the garden front, more people will have a chance to see the continental Blackcaps as they begin to turn up in gardens and dominate the birdtables.

Numbers of wading birds will have settled at their winter population levels, which will include more than 1,500 Grey Plovers and five-figure Dunlin counts in Chichester Harbour. Kingfishers are now to be found on any of the lower stretches of the rivers.

Arrivals this month are often top-ups to those that have turned up earlier. Bewick's Swan numbers build up in the Arun Valley and Bittern numbers in the county increase as the first hard frosts hit. The big roosts of gulls at Bewl Water can now top 20,000 to 30,000, though finding 'white-winged' species is more reliable at places such as Southwick Canal and Pagham Harbour.

Away from the coast, the Downs and woods are now often quite bleak and birdless. A good stubble field however, may be stuffed with Corn Buntings, Yellowhammers and Linnets. On the birdsong front, almost all may be quiet bar the sad winter lament of Robins, but Cetti's Warblers may strike up exuberantly at places such as Thorney Island and Arundel WWT. For an unusual bird location however, try a supermarket car park at dusk where the hot-air ducts attract some notable roosts of Pied Wagtails.

Don't miss this month's highlights

- Duck numbers now often peak at places such as Pulborough Brooks RSPB, with Gadwalls in three-figures at Chichester gravel pits

- Winter wader roosts can be a dramatic winter sight, in Chichester and Pagham Harbours

- A few apples slung on your lawn or wired to your trees should attract wintering Blackcaps

- Scotney Court gravel pit begins to produce good birds, worth checking for any grebe or diver species or Scaup

23

SEAWATCHING IN SUSSEX

Key points

- Allow 2 plus hours, although tailor your stay according to whether passage is good or poor

- Expect 5-40 passage species

- For facilities and access, see individual site details

- Often good for wheelchair birding

- Telescope and good tripod very helpful

- Watch the weather forecast closely in advance

- Indulge yourself! – take folding chair, warm waterproof clothing, flask and lunchbox!

- It can be handy to keep a running log of what you have seen

- Expect to join plenty of other watchers at key times

SEAWATCHING IN Sussex is primarily about the spring passage up-Channel of big numbers of divers, ducks, waders, gulls, skuas and terns, often in very pleasant conditions and often quite close to shore. Any time from early March to late May can produce some dramatic passage, with up to several hundred birds passing each hour, and with species counts in a day sometimes topping forty.

Pomarine Skuas top the list of exciting species, with Black-throated Divers, Velvet Scoters, Black Terns and Little Gulls being eagerly awaited too.

There are several key locations at intervals along the coast for watching, and certain weather and wind conditions have been shown to be the most productive. However, part of the beauty of seawatching is that there are no hard and fast rules and the unexpected can be expected. Spring seawatching has the added excitement of birds arriving from the sea, whether it be something simple yet miraculous like a flight of Swallows battling in on the final leg from South Africa, or something bizarre like a Stone Curlew pitching up on the beach. Do not rule out the possibility though, that on the day you visit, absolutely nothing may be on the move!

Outside of the exciting spring passage, the more hardy can enjoy some good winter seawatching, with auk and diver passage predominating. Increasingly good birds are also being seen on a few good autumn days and even summer has birds of interest at times.

Target birds

Percentages are not given for the target species. Reliability varies according to season, indeed often according to week, and is also dependent on weather conditions.

All year
Regular Gannet

Spring passage
Usually abundant - dark-bellied Brent Goose, Common Scoter, Whimbrel, Bar-tailed Godwit, Sandwich Tern, 'Commic' Tern. *Regular* Black-throated Diver, Eider, Velvet Scoter, Red-breasted Merganser, Knot, Sanderling, Arctic Skua, Pomarine Skua, Great Skua, Little Gull, Little Tern, Razorbill, Guillemot. *Occasional* Great Northern Diver,

Black-necked Grebe, Slavonian Grebe, Garganey, Long-tailed Duck, Avocet, Long-tailed Skua, Black Tern.

Summer passage
Regular **Manx Shearwater.** *Occasional* - **Meditteranean Shearwater, Storm Petrel.**

Autumn passage
Regular – **Brent Goose, Red-breasted Merganser, Dunlin.** *Occasional* – **Arctic Skua, Pomarine Skua, Great Skua, Sooty Shearwater, Little Auk, Grey Phalarope, Sabine's Gull.**

Winter
Usually abundant - **Razorbill, Guillemot.** *Regular* - **Red-throated Diver.**

Other likely bird species

<u>*All year*</u>	<u>*Winter*</u>	**Grey Heron**
Gulls	**Great Crested Grebe**	**Common Sandpiper**
Kittiwake		**Turnstone**
	<u>*Occasional*</u>	**Mediterranean Gull**
<u>*Breeding season*</u>	**Shag**	
Fulmar	**Little Egret**	

Top Sussex seawatching sites – west to east

Brighton Marina
See p55 for access details. Watch from West Arm, spray permitting. Toilets and facilities in Brighton Marina Village.

Selsey Bill
Watch from 'The Wall'! See p141 for access details. There is a friendly crowd of regulars who turn up from March through to May and frequently at other times too. Having parked at the Bill House, the place to sit is on the sea-side of the rather rickety wall at the top of the beach, or nearby depending on the wind.

Expect dozens of watchers at peak times. The Selsey headland suffers somewhat from being in the shelter of the Isle of Wight, which pushes a proportion of the passage too far out into the Channel to be seen, but the range of birds on offer doesn't suffer.

Worthing Beach
The regular watching venue is in the shelter opposite the Marine Gardens in West Worthing. Plenty of seafront parking available.

Splash Point, Seaford
See p147 for access details. Watch in cold or wet conditions from blue seafront shelter on promenade 50-yards before beach road ends (just before line of little beach huts). Parking usually possible directly adjacent. In fine weather, watch from 25-yards out on concrete jetty jutting out into the sea in line with end of beach road. Expect dozens of people in early May from dawn onwards.

Birling Gap, Beachy Head
See p47 for access details. Watch from cliff top at Birling Gap.

Galley Hill and Glyne Gap, Bexhill
Combe Haven map on p79 shows parking at Glyne Gap (with toilets). For Galley Hill, the small raised cliff barely 400 yards west along coast from Glyne Gap, it is a 3 mile drive round to Bexhill seafront and back along.

Watching is also quite feasible anywhere on the coastal strip between Goring and Brighton.

SEAWATCHING IN SUSSEX

Background information and birding tips

SEAWATCHING IS one of those esoteric offshoots of birdwatching that isn't everyone's cup of tea. Its overriding image in the UK is of autumn gales, sea-sickness-inducing pelagics, bone-chilling winds and sea spray kicking into your face. There are some birdwatchers for whom the prospect of sitting for several hours, eye pressed firmly against a telescope, passively letting the birds move past instead of 'hunting them down', is contrary to their idea of a good day's birding. The birds seem to pass too distantly, too quickly and too infrequently to permit any enjoyment.

We would challenge anyone however, not to be impressed on an early May morning on the Sussex coast, with a south-east wind, as several hundred birds of perhaps 20 or more species pass east each hour. From first light, there can be a constant stream of Common Scoters and 'Commic' Terns punctuated by summer-plumaged Black-throated Divers, Little Gulls and Bar-tailed Godwits. The excitement is capped by a string of Pomarine Skuas, complete with 'spoon' tail feathers, lumbering by. And almost anything can turn up, strange things from Long-eared Owls to Stone-curlews!

The key to Sussex's value as a seawatching county is its lengthy coastline and its location so far east up the narrowing English Channel. Plenty of ducks, waders and

terns which have wintered in Biscay, are on their way to Scandinavia and the Arctic. Many nip through the Channel and out across the North Sea rather than passing overland or going up the west coast of Ireland.

A huge proportion of the birds pass unseen, either mid-Channel or along the French coast. But, given favourable winds, usually between south-west and north-east and with some light showers thrown in, they pass quite close to the Sussex shore. (A southeasterly is the wind to pray for, while there is little or no passage in a northwesterly or in calm conditions.) Looking at a map of England, you would think that their route would take them closest to land at the big headlands of Selsey Bill and Beachy Head, but they seem to follow the shoreline quite religiously and can also be seen from many other points on the coast. Only those bits of coastline directly in the shadow of the headlands (eg Pagham Harbour, Pevensey Bay and Rye Bay) seem to see a much-reduced passage.

To get the most out of seawatching, you really do need a good telescope, a good tripod and a degree of patience. There can be very poor days, even when the weather seems favourable, whereas some days can be fairly good even with the

wind in the wrong quarter. Early morning is definitely best, but again it is a rule that can be broken. We've had seawatching sessions which have started poorly, only for passage to suddenly kick in at 8.00am - encouraging news for late-risers! Pomarine Skua passage in particular, can continue throughout the day and on April 24 2001, a Sussex record passage of 363 Little Gulls passed mainly in the mid-afternoon. This record was broken on April 21 2003 in the early morning!.

In terms of how to watch, different seawatchers have different techniques. Some just turn to their scopes as a back-up, scanning with their bins and naked eyes. In doing so, they pick up birds the scope-users miss, such as birds coming through high above the horizon, which can include divers, Brent Geese and Poms or also birds of prey or Short-eared Owls arriving in off the sea, or waders moving along the tideline. The scope-users however, have the advantage of steady views of difficult or distant birds, especially Manx Shearwaters and auks.

Whatever your technique, seawatching can be one of most sociable birdwatching activities there is.

The Seawatching Calendar
Spring passage starts early, with dark-bellied Brent Geese on the move by February, heading for the Waddensee on the first leg of their massive migration back to the Arctic.

Your week-by-week guide for improving your spring seawatching success

	Feb wk3	Feb wk4	Mar wk1	Mar wk2	Mar wk3	Mar wk4	Apr wk1	Apr wk2	Apr wk3	Apr wk4	May wk1	May wk2	May wk3	No. in year
Diver sp.														1000
Gannet														1500
Brent Goose														7500
Shelduck														150
Wigeon														100
Teal														100
Pintail														50
Shoveler														150
Eider														150
Common Scoter														7500
Velvet Scoter														25
R-b Merganser														400
Oystercatcher														300
Grey Plover														75
Knot														100
Sanderling														150
Dunlin														150
Bar-tailed Godwit														2000
Whimbrel														500
Curlew														75
Arctic Skua														200
Great Skua														25
Pomarine Skua														100
Little Gull														200
Sandwich Tern														2000
'Commic' Tern														6000
Little Tern														200
Black Tern														50
Guillemot/Razorbill														2000

This table is derived from Splash Point data, 1994-2001, collated by Dick Gilmore

Key

■ More than 20 birds/hour
▨ 5-20 birds/hour
▨ 1-5 birds/hour
☐ Less than 1 bird/hour
☐ Little or no passage

Large winter movements of auks and divers (probably mostly Red-throats but often a devil to identify) occur at the same time.

By March, the Brent Geese are joined by lines of Common Scoters heading for the Baltic. This is very much the 'wildfowl month', with small numbers of

Pintails, Teal and Shovelers on the move too. It is not unusual to see one or more of these species tagging onto a flight of Brent Geese. Almost all travel

27

SEAWATCHING IN SUSSEX

low over the sea, although Brent Geese more than others can rise up dramatically above the skyline. By the third week of the month, the first Sandwich Terns are passing through, and Meadow Pipits are often seen arriving on the coast.

Into April, and the passage of dabbling duck is subsiding, replaced somewhat by more frequent Eiders and Red-breasted Mergansers, and with a higher chance of Velvet Scoters amongst the Common Scoter flocks. Don't be surprised if you see a Garganey or Long-tailed Duck amongst the Scoters.

Skua passage starts in April with Arctics and Greats passing by. The passage of Common and Arctic Terns kicks in too – both species are known to pass, but of the several thousand 'Commics' that pass, no-one knows for sure in what proportions. Little Tern passage doesn't start until the third week.

The last week of April and first week of May is probably the most exciting time. Waders start passing through in numbers. A slightly different wind is best for them, namely a light north-easterly, and often in the evening. Most visible are big numbers of Whimbrels and Bar-tailed Godwits, often in mixed flocks. Some of the smaller waders – Sanderlings, Dunlins, Knots and several other species in smaller numbers – can pass right along the beach, sometimes

even pausing, although most migration now seems rather determined. The birds seem to come in quite unpredictable waves. Many of the divers that pass through now are clearly Black-throats in spanking summer plumage.

It is now that the big prize – Pomarine Skuas – is sought. Excitingly, they can move through in quite large flocks, sometimes a dozen or more, always moving quite purposefully. They too can, on rare occasions, pass right along the shore. On most days, action begins to slow by about 9am, but little sub-peaks of activity can continue throughout the day. Remember, Poms can fly high, especially in calm conditions, and they can just keep on coming right through to evening!

The tern passage is, for many, just as exciting. Up to 4000 Commics can pass in a day, with up to 50 Blacks, 100 Littles, 1000 Sandwich and a good chance of a Roseate.

Whilst watching the sea, other birds may appear. Passerines and Common Sandpipers can come in off the sea and land on the beach, hirundines and Meadow Pipits pass high over, as can raptors; finches move along the coast. *Anything* is possible; Long-eared Owl, Night Heron, Nightjar – you name it, it's arrived on a Sussex seawatch.

The number of seawatching hours put in slumps after mid-May, but

commendable watching effort in mid-summer has turned up some interesting records in recent years, including repeat showings of Storm Petrels off Selsey Bill in late May to early July. Tern passage can continue right into June, which is now known to be a key time for Manx Shearwaters, having once been thought to be regular mainly in May and October.

Early autumn passage has generally little of the excitement of spring, but can start with Curlews in late June moving west, and then August and September hold the possibility of Balearic Shearwaters. In 2001, unprecedented numbers, around 250 in total, appeared in early to mid August.

Later in the autumn, there are a few days each year to set seawatchers' hearts racing. Periods of northerly winds have been shown to often precede passage of waders (especially Dunlins) and Brent Geese, usually from the end of October through to November. But it is after storms, especially after strong southwest winds, that Sooty Shearwaters, Little Auks, and even occasional Grey Phalaropes or Sabine's Gulls can be seen. Now those sturdy tripods really come into their own!

And then its winter again, and the appearances of auks in numbers along the coast, moving backwards and forwards to the best feeding sites.

FEATURED SITES IN
SUSSEX

Roding Woodcocks can be seen in many of Sussex's woodlands and forests in summer. (John Davis)

Key points

- Allow 1-plus hour

- Expect 20-35 species

- Site largely SSSI and includes small piece of marsh owned by RSPB

- Access at all times on public rights of way

- Good free parking; basic public toilets

- Plenty of other amenities in nearby Shoreham

- Many of tracks either Tarmac or rough paving – some viewing possible from wheelchair

- Well served by bus and train

- Telescope helpful

THE ADUR ESTUARY gives some very nice estuary birdwatching, despite being a busy urban-edge site, hemmed in between houses, railways and airport. Considering the small size of the estuary, there are surprisingly good numbers of common waders. The river is favoured by Yellow-legged Gulls and Kingfishers and the open grassland of Shoreham airport adds extra bird interest.

Target birds A site to look for coastal waders (August–April), plus: *All year* – Kingfisher (40%). *Passage* – Yellow-legged Gull (40% July & Aug), Mediterranean Gull (30% spring).

Other likely bird species

All year	Common Sandpiper	*Occasional*
Waterbirds	Greenshank	Brent Goose
Gulls	Wheatear	Merlin
Garden birds	Whinchat	Peregrine
Corvids		Golden Plover
Little Egret	*Winter*	Knot
Kestrel	Coastal waders	Little Stint
Goldfinch	Teal	Curlew Sandpiper
	Lapwing	Bar-tailed Godwit
Passage	Snipe	Whimbrel
Hirundines	Rock Pipit	Mediterranean Gull
Warblers	Meadow Pipit	
	Stonechat	

Background information and birding tips

AFTER MANY miles of being hemmed in by high banks, the River Adur flows under the sweeping A27 flyover and is finally allowed to spread a little. Here it is broad enough for mudflats to emerge at low tide.

From the car parking adjacent to the Airfield, a short walk onto the estuary wall gives wide views along the river, though any birds on the near bank will be hidden by the raised saltmarsh in front of you. At low tide, Redshanks, Ringed Plovers and Dunlins predominate, though numbers of the latter have slumped in recent winters. The odd Grey Plover is likely too, with Greenshanks and

Common Sandpipers also possible on passage.

Behind you, the flat and grassy Shoreham Airfield regularly hosts year-round Sky Larks and a 1,000-strong wintering Lapwing flock, even when the numerous light aircraft are taxiing back and forth. There are always Starlings and often Golden Plovers in attendance, even a Sociable Lapwing once. A few dark-bellied Brent Geese sometimes graze here also. The perimeter fence is highly attractive to Wheatears and Whinchats on passage (oh for a repeat of 1990's long-staying Great Spotted Cuckoo!). Stonechats meanwhile, prefer the reedy ditch just below the estuary wall.

Contacts

RSPB South East Office
01273 775333

A walk to the old wooden road bridge, now closed to traffic, gives good views up and down the river. Often there are large flocks of gulls, including several hundred Common Gulls in winter. In hard weather, ducks and divers are possible. In late summer this is the best site, apart from Pagham, for a few Yellow-legged Gulls. They are a taste of the continent, along with the seemingly permanent Little Egrets.

The riverside path, downstream from the east side of the old road bridge, looks promising but frustratingly dead-ends. Better to either continue upstream to Cuckoo Corner (good for Kingfishers, and also for Little Egrets when disturbed further downstream), or retrace your steps down the west bank, or drive round to the recreation ground.

From here, cross A259 to look over the RSPB reserve, sandwiched between Norfolk Bridge and a motley line of houseboats. Visibility is not easy - on Norfolk Bridge the traffic whooshes at your back and the view from the public footpath, behind the houseboats, is partially obscured by their variously rotting or bohemian hulls.

The pedestrian bridge across to Shoreham is probably best, but is rather high-sided. It is narrow and well-used, making telescope use difficult. Aided by a high tide however, you should see plenty of wintering Snipe flushed into view on the saltmarsh and add Turnstone, Sanderling, Knot or Bar-tailed Godwit to your wader list.

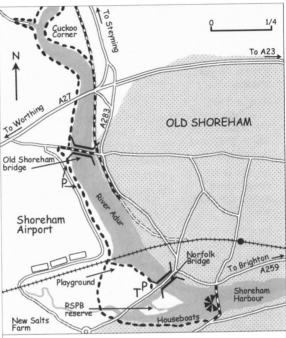

Access details
(6 miles W of Brighton)

PARKING BY SHOREHAM AIRPORT: From Worthing, take A27 towards Brighton. 1 mile E of Lancing, turn S off A27 at traffic lights opposite Sussex Pad Hotel, signed to 'Airport'. Swing L, then turn immediately R down private Shoreham Airport road (closed at night). Park on broad hardstanding bays to E of Airfield (TQ206056). Never stop in the clearly restricted zone.

RECREATION GROUND PARKING: From Shoreham town centre, take A259 W over Norfolk Bridge. Free parking is after 50 yards to N of road (TQ210049). Parking is also available behind the

houseboats in Shoreham Beach next to a small playing field (TQ212046).

BY TRAIN: 0.25 mile walk from Shoreham station.

BY BUS: Several services pass down Shoreham High Street/ Norfolk Bridge/Old Shoreham Road, but the most regular/ useful are No.2A (Steyning to Rottingdean), No.700 (Brighton-Southsea) and No.702 (Brighton-Arundel).

Key points

- Allow 2.5-plus hours
- Expect 25-40 species
- Part of Arun Valley SPA; SSSI; owned by RSPB, SWT and privately
- Access at all times along public rights of way
- Very limited parking; no other facilities – nearest in Amberley/ Storrington
- Walks generally flat, but wellies are essential
- Impossible for wheelchairs
- Late afternoon recommended in winter
- Telescope useful

Contacts

RSPB Pulborough Brooks
01798 875851

Sussex Wildlife Trust
01273 492630

THESE LARGE wet wildfowl-rich grasslands lie just downstream from Pulborough Brooks. In winter, Bewick's Swans may be present and in spring, the site holds some of Sussex's last breeding Snipe. With an 'olde worlde' atmosphere, this is the best place in Sussex to see Barn Owl, Short-eared Owl and Hen Harrier together.

Target birds *All year* – Barn Owl (60% at dusk), Little Owl (30%), Peregrine (30%), Lesser Spotted Woodpecker (10%), Kingfisher (10%). *Breeding season* – Nightingale (hear 80%, see 10%), Hobby (30%), drumming Snipe (10%), Grasshopper Warbler (at dawn and dusk, hear 70%, see 10%). *Winter* – Bewick's Swan (40%), Hen Harrier (30%), Short-eared Owl (30%), Redpoll (25%).

Other likely bird species

All year		*Occasional*
Waterbirds	Redshank	Whooper Swan
Wildfowl	Cuckoo	White-fronted Goose
Gulls	Yellow Wagtail	Garganey
Woodland birds	Garden Warbler	Merlin
Farmland birds	Lesser Whitethroat	Whimbrel
Corvids		Black-tailed Godwit
Greylag Goose	*Winter*	Golden Plover
Shelduck	Wigeon	Wood Sandpiper
Marsh Tit	Pintail	Turtle Dove
Nuthatch	Shoveler	Brambling
Treecreeper	Ruff	
	Dunlin	*Passsage*
Breeding season	Grey Wagtail	Green Sandpiper
Hirundines		

Background information and birding tips

AMBERLEY Wild Brooks cover a big sweep of the River Arun's floodplain. It consists of an expanse of rank wet grassland dissected by ditches, but with small pockets of carr woodland and flanked by woodland and fields.

It is possible to access the Brooks from Amberley, but there is no designated parking in the narrow village streets. We recommend starting in the little car park at the Sussex Wildlife Trust's Waltham Brooks reserve by Greatham Bridge and heading south. Indeed, from there you can also walk along the edge of Waltham Brooks on the west side of the river. There is always open water here, attracting wintering duck and passage waders such as Greenshanks or even Whimbrels.

Crossing Greatham Bridge for the walk through to the Wild Brooks, remember to look upstream, especially if the river is in flood - Bewick's Swans sometimes graze the wet fields. Once over the bridge, the footpath leads along the riverbank and up behind some trees that attract woodpeckers, with Lesser Spotted if you're lucky.

The track zigzags through Quell Farm and out past a little copse, again good for Lesser Spotted Woodpeckers, then down past a black barn-conversion and onto the Brooks. Winter thrushes are common here in season.

The near edge of the Brooks is slightly elevated with scattered, mature oaks, ideal for Little Owls. Barn Owls also hunt regularly. Beyond are the open and vast wet Brooks. Scan regularly for Short-eared Owls and Hen Harriers in winter as it is unusual not to see either one or the other.

The rather boggy (but much improved) track leads over an elaborate footbridge, with wet woodlands first to one side and then the other. This is a Nightingale hotspot and also good for Redpolls and Siskins. The views then open up once more and, in winter, you may see a distant herd of Bewick's Swans. Summering Grasshopper Warblers favour the tussocky sedge fields on either side.

The track on to Amberley is shin-deep with grey mud in winter. If you're feeling energetic, it is possible to walk round the top end of the Brooks through Rackham Woods, which are great for Marsh Tits and Lesser Spotted Woodpeckers. Any of the wildfowl and raptors can be scoped from here too.

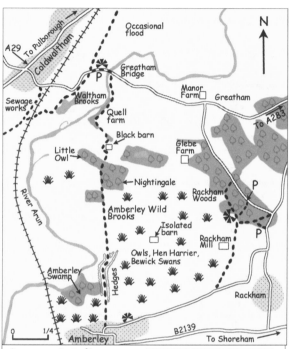

Access details
(3 miles SW of Pulborough)

FOR GREATHAM BRIDGE: From Pulborough on A29 head S. Turn E at Coldwaltham, and Greatham Bridge is after 1 mile, with small muddy car park on R just before bridge (difficult after rain). From E, access from A283 Storrington-Pulborough road, turning W just N of Parham House signed to Greatham and Rackham, and 0.5 mile S of Pulborough brooks RSPB. Greatham Bridge parking is after 2.5 miles on far side of bridge. (TQ031163).

FOR RACKHAM WOODS: turn N

off the B2139 Storrington-Amberley road to Rackham, pass the turn to Amberley, and parking is 0.5 mile further in an open sandy bay just beyond the Old School House. (TQ053143).

BY TRAIN: Just over 1 mile walk from Amberley station.
BY BUS: No.73 Amberley-Horsham is twice-hourly.

With Amberley, you get the feeling you haven't seen everything. There can often be 3,000 wildfowl and 1,000 Lapwings out there, but all can be tucked out of sight. It is this remoteness that is all part of its success.

33

Key points

- Allow 2-plus hours

- Expect 15-25 species

- Privately owned SSSI

- Access at all times

- Rough sandy parking bays; no other facilities (closest in Midhurst or Petworth)

- Paths can get wet in winter; some mild gradients

- Not suitable for wheelchairs

- Keep strictly to paths and keep dogs under control

- Fire risk high in all seasons – take every precaution not to cause them

- Insect repellent and torch needed at dusk

Contacts

English Nature, Sussex and Surrey Team
01273 476595
sussex.surrey
@english-nature.org.uk

A MBERSHAM is all about quality, not quantity. Though you won't see a mass of species here, you stand a good chance of seeing a full range of heathland species – Nightjars, Wood Larks, Dartford Warblers *et al* - often giving great views in an area small enough to be covered easily. Brilliant!

Target birds *All year* – Dartford Warbler (90%),
Crossbill (50%), Woodcock (90% when roding April-June, 10% otherwise). *Breeding season* – Tree Pipit (90%), Nightjar (hear at dusk 90%, see 80%), displaying Sparrowhawk (60%), Wood Lark (60%), Hobby (30%). *Winter* – Redpoll (50%), Tawny Owl (hear at dusk 90%).

Other likely bird species

All year	Yellowhammer	*Occasional*
Woodland birds	Reed Bunting	Hen Harrier
Buzzard	*Winter*	Jack Snipe
Stonechat	Siskin	Redstart
Nuthatch	Linnet	Great Grey Shrike

Background information and birding tips

H EATHLAND is never exactly bursting with birds, but the specialities (Dartford Warblers, Wood Larks and Nightjars are the Big Three) ensure it a place on most annual birding itineraries. As far as we're concerned, the best site in Sussex to see them is Ambersham Common. Though you could easily walk round it in an hour, we reckon you'll find enough to keep you here for three.

There are technically two commons here. The lower one, readily visible to the west of the road, is actually called Heyshott Common. The real Ambersham Common is on top of the rise behind the pines east of the road.

The following walk starts from car park A on the map. Crossing the road, a broad sandy track leads up under the pylons between the pines. Noisy Coal

Tits and Goldcrests are a constant presence year-round and winter flocks of Siskins may call from the treetops.

At the top of the rise, the land levels out and, 100 yards further on, it emerges at one of our favourite viewpoints. To your right is the scarp slope of the South Downs, while in front stretches the tracts of pine and larch that cloak the long, but less prominent, geological feature known as Greensand ridge.

This is a great place to see raptors from late February through to May. Buzzards are regular and displaying Sparrowhawks are frequently seen, though sometimes they can be little more than dots in the sky. Kestrels and Hobbies are also possible. Watch too for Crossbills, pausing in the tops of the larches, or for Wood Larks flying over.

Rather than dropping off the edge of this plateau, turn left and out onto Ambersham Common. The habitat here is wonderful, gorgeous areas of heather with random pines dotted throughout. These are loved by Crossbills, and we've had excellent close views here. Dartford Warblers zip over the short heather and, as there's little gorse for them up here, they can be all the easier to see. Stonechats and Linnets also occur and the northern edge of the common is especially favoured by Wood Larks.

From the north side of the plateau, you can drop back down and across the road onto Heyshott. Rather wetter, and with birch trees dotted about rather than pine, this is the place for Tree Pipits, Yellowhammers and yet more Wood Larks. The track running north-south through the middle of the common can literally run with water, attracting Reed Buntings and the occasional Jack Snipe. There are also Dartford Warblers on the drier edges. Hen Harriers sometimes quarter over the heath in winter.

Both Ambersham and Heyshott are brilliant for Nightjars, with up to nine pairs present. Woodcocks criss-cross the dusk sky time and again and Tawny Owls are likely to be heard as well.

One of the beauties of Heyshott is that to see or hear these species, there's no need to stray far from the car. You will still need insect repellent, but it means that dusk birdwatching can be done, if not from inside the car, then at least from the comfort of the bonnet!

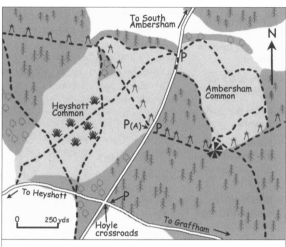

Access details

(2 miles SE of Midhurst)

Not easy to find, Ambersham Common is S of South Ambersham. From Midhurst, take A272 E towards Midhurst and Petworth. After 2 miles, turn R at a sharp bend down narrow unmarked road through a sandstone cutting. Bear L at first fork, then R towards Heyshott. Various parking opportunities after 1 mile, first on the L, and then either side of the road at 'A' (SU912193) where the line of pylons crosses the road. Alternatively, from A286 between Chichester and Midhurst, turn E towards

Heyshott, 2 miles S of Midhurst. After 2 miles, turn L at Hoyle crossroads towards South Ambersham (Heyshott Common will now be apparent on your L) and parking 'A' is after 0.5 mile.

BY TRAIN: **No direct access.**
BY BUS: **No.71 Midhurst-Graffham occasional loop-service stops at Hoyle cross roads.**

Other nearby sites

Less than 5 miles: Lavington Common.
Less than 10 miles: Burton Mill Pond, Lord's Piece, Iping & Stedham Commons.

35

Key points

- Allow 2.5-plus hours
- Expect 25-35 species
- Local Nature Reserve
- Free car park open until 4pm winter, 6pm summer
- Disabled car park and some wheelchair access
- Toilets (limited opening)
- Amenities in nearby Ardingly village
- Two hides
- Tracks can get muddy in places in winter
- Walks generally on flat; no stiles to climb
- Dogs on leads

Contacts

South East Water
01323 870810
egoddard@
southeastwater.co.uk.

THE 'KINGFISHER TRAIL' at this attractive mid-Sussex reservoir 'does exactly what it says on the tin' – gives you a great chance to get to see Kingfishers. Ospreys are annual visitors and Hobbies are frequent in spring. Waterbirds don't tend to be present in large numbers, but you should still see a fair tally of species and, being an under-watched site, maybe you will strike lucky.

Target birds *All year* – Kingfisher (50%). *Passage* – Hobby (20%), Osprey (5%).

Other likely bird species

All year	✓Grey Wagtail	*Winter*
Waterbirds	Marsh Tit	Thrushes
Wildfowl	Nuthatch	Siskin
Gulls		
Woodland birds	*Passage*	*Occasional*
Corvids	✓Hirundines	Little Egret
✓Great Crested Grebe	Common Tern	Mandarin
✓Greylag Goose		Pochard
Tufted Duck	*Breeding season*	Buzzard
	✓Whitethroat	Redpoll

Background information and birding tips

WITHOUT its dam, Ardingly Reservoir would look like the landscaped lake of some grand country house, where attractively mixed woodlands and fields slope gracefully down to the water's edge. It makes for a pleasant walk (albeit 'there-and-back' rather than circular). South East Water has worked hard to put in good paths, a couple of hides and a marked nature trail to accommodate birdwatchers and visitors.

The mixed habitats also ensure quite a varied bird list, although don't expect the reservoir itself to have large numbers of waterbirds. A bit of scanning along the margins may pick up the odd pair of Great Crested ✓✓✓ Grebes, a few dozen Mallards and Tufted Ducks and a Grey Heron ✓ or two, but other duck species are in single figures at best. Waders are infrequent too, except for a few ✓ Common Sandpipers on passage.

From the car park at the base of the dam, it is worth heading back down the road 50 yards to the outflow stream of the reservoir (Shell Brook), which regularly attracts Grey Wagtails.

Your main walk, however – the Kingfisher Trail - starts by climbing up to the crest of the dam. At the left-hand end of the dam is a small sailing club (with toilets). To the right-hand end, the footpath leads out along the east shore of the reservoir. Kingfisher Hide is just a few yards along on the edge of a little block of woodland. It affords little extra view of the reservoir than from the dam itself, so proves its worth only if a Kingfisher happens to be perched in a waterside tree.

The reservoir is 'Y'-shaped, and a 20 minute walk takes you to a causeway, which cuts off the right-hand 'arm' of the 'Y' from the rest of the reservoir. The 'arm', a private nature reserve, can be viewed from the road which crosses the causeway. There's always at least some Tufted Ducks, maybe a few Pochards and certainly some Cormorants loafing on the small tern islands. Gulls drop in here and it's a good place for Kingfishers (which breed in purpose-built artificial banks).

In the far distance, look for the impressive 'Osprey' nest platform – one day, fingers crossed, it will attract them to breed. In the meantime, May and September are the best months to see a passage bird overhead or fishing.

The footpath continues along the left-hand arm. This section of the walk is good for Marsh Tits in any of the damp woodland blocks – we have yet to fail to see them here. Beyond a 'hide-on-a-jetty', there is a final block of woodland before reaching the top of the reservoir. This is good place to check for Bullfinches and occasional Redpolls and Siskins before you retrace your steps.

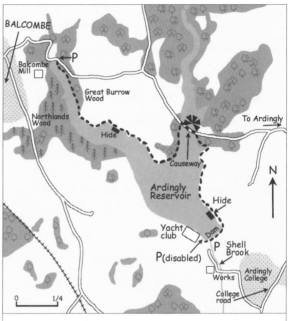

Access details

(3 miles NNE of Haywards Heath)

Head to Ardingly village, from either Haywards Heath N on B2028, or if coming down A23, turn E at Junction 10 towards East Grinstead and then turn S down B2028. In Ardingly, take road signed to 'Ardingly College and Reservoir'. After passing the imposing College, the reservoir is signed R. Access track has some punishing 'sleeping policemen', and it is a good 0.5 mile and a poorly-signed L and R turn before you reach the car park below the grassy dam wall (TQ334286). For disabled parking only, follow

road up L side of the dam to an elevated special car park.

BY TRAIN: 1 mile walk from Balcombe station to head of Reservoir.
BY BUS: 1 mile walk from Ardingly where No.82 Haywards Heath-Crawley is only frequent service.

Other nearby sites

Less than 10 miles: Weir Wood Reservoir; Ashdown Forest; Chailey Common; St Leonard's Forest; Buchan Country Park

5 ** ARLINGTON RESERVOIR

- Allow 2 hours
- Expect 25-35 species
- SSSI and LNR, owned and managed by South East Water
- Pay and display car park with height-restriction barrier and restricted opening hours
- Roadside parking at other times
- Good toilets on site
- One hide, suitable for pushchairs and wheelchairs (access via dam)
- One-hour flat circular 'Osprey Trail'
- Telescopes useful, especially for gulls

Contacts

South East Water
01323 870810
egoddard@
southeastwater.co.uk.

ALL CREDIT TO South East Water as they have ensured that Arlington Reservoir is attractive to both wildlife and visitors, even though some other reservoirs can be less than inspiring. Sometimes the water surface is all but empty of birds, but each year sees good winter duck numbers, appearances from rarer grebes and divers, breeding Nightingales and passage Ospreys.

Target birds *Spring* – Nightingale (hear 50%, see 10%). *Autumn* – Osprey (20%), Black Tern (5%).

Other likely bird species

All year	*Breeding season*	*Occasional*
Waterbirds	Warblers	Rarer grebe/diver
Gulls		Goosander
Farmland birds	*Winter*	Hobby
	Shoveler	Dunlin
Passage	Wigeon	Greenshank
Hirundines	Pochard	Mediterranean Gull
Little Egret	Lapwing	Little Gull
Common Sandpiper		

Background information and birding tips

BUILT IN 1971, Arlington Reservoir is almost circular and, with a shoreline of only just over a mile, an hour or two is adequate for a pleasantly varied round walk. Once wellies were a winter necessity for the clay ground but considerable improvements have now been made.

In front of the car park, visitors can get close to the reservoir shore where many feed the ducks. Small clumps of reeds have been planted here, just enough for a pair or two of Reed Warblers. You can also scan the whole reservoir - Great Crested Grebes should be apparent year-round, as should Cormorants on the wooden pontoons offshore.

In bad spring or autumn weather, hirundines may be forced down over the reservoir's surface in large numbers, or

Black Terns and Little Gulls may quarter the water, though all are likely to leave once the weather clears. Two Red-rumped Swallows joined the early May hirundines in 2003.

Heading out clockwise on the way-marked 'Osprey Trail', the first stretch through wildflower meadows looks down onto the gravelly shoreline. Pied Wagtails and Coots, or noisy late-summer masses of Canada Geese may be all you find, but an early morning visit during passage periods can turn up Common Sandpipers or Greenshanks. Many other wader species have been recorded but the banks are not quite muddy enough to tempt them to stay.

It is worth scanning ahead along the shoreline too, as this is where ducks often lounge, maybe only 50 or so, but expect a few Teal, Wigeon and Shovelers in winter and possibly Pintails too.

38

Also scan back down the western shoreline towards Polhills Farm. In winter, Lapwings tend to gather along here and, from July through the autumn, a Little Egret or two may be present - and strikingly obvious!

Move on through the young plantation, where Chiffchaffs, Blackcaps and Willow Warblers battle orally in spring. Nightingales have been a regular feature here too, though we only found one singing male in 2002. Just before the end of the wood, a little track leads down to a good hide at the reservoir's edge for some water-level views

It is then out onto the exposed long dam, the best spot for Common Sandpipers, with Grey Herons often sitting hunched along here. Sometimes the few diving ducks – Tufted Ducks, Pochards and, if you're lucky, a Smew or Goosander – are over this side. It's also a good place from which to view the gull roost. A good mix of Black-heads, Herrings, Commons and Great Black-backs come in from late afternoon, sometimes with numbers of Lesser Black-backs and occasional Mediterranean. The track then loops behind Polhill's Farm and back in front of the fishing lodge next to the car park.

What Arlington lacks is islands, bankside vegetation or little reedy backwaters for breeding waterbirds. But it does have a reputation for regularly pulling in the odd rare grebe, especially Black-necked.

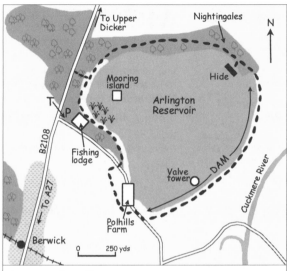

Access details

(8 miles ESE of Lewes)

From Lewes, take A27 E towards Eastbourne. After 7 miles, turn L at roundabout next to Drusilla's Zoo, signed to Berwick station (Alfriston is signed to the R). After 1 mile, ignore R turn to Arlington village – instead cross railway crossing at North Berwick, and the entrance to the reservoir car park is after 0.5 mile on R under the height-restriction barrier (TQ527074). Parking after hours is possible in a small lay-by opposite.

BY TRAIN: Excellent. Only 0.5 mile walk from Berwick station.
BY BUS: Difficult. Various Cuckmere Community Bus services do very limited services, and No.51 Alfriston-Eastbourne passes Berwick station on Sundays only.

Ospreys are also seen many times each year on passage, with May and September being favoured months. They presumably perch-up somewhere away from the reservoir though, so you will need fortune to be present just at the moment one powers in to catch a fish.

Other nearby sites

Less than 10 miles: Lullington Heath; Cuckmere Haven; Splash Point and Seaford Head; Newhaven Tide Mills.

6 *** ARUNDEL WWT

Key points

- Allow 1.5-plus hours
- Expect 25-50 species
- Reedbed is SSSI
- WWT Reserve (entrance fee for non-members)
- Opening times 9.30-5.30 (4.30 in winter)
- Excellent facilities, including good wheelchair access and free wheelchair loan
- Hides, sightings board etc.
- Excellent website with up-to-date sightings
- Flat terrain and no need for wellingtons.
- Good public transport links
- Telescope not necessary
- Hosts annual South East Bird Fair in May

Contacts

Arundel WWT
01903 883355

MAINTAINING the tradition set by other Wildfowl & Wetland Trust centres, Arundel has top facilities where plenty of wild birds slot in and around the captive wildfowl collection. The site is actually quite small, but boasts the best population of Cetti's Warblers in Sussex, wild Mandarins and terns and waders dropping in to pools where there is a noisy Black-headed Gull colony in summer.

Target birds *All year* – Mandarin (80%), Cetti's Warbler (hear 80%, see 40%), Peregrine (30%). *Winter* – Water Rail (hear 90%, see 80%), Chiffchaff (30%), Firecrest (15%).

Other likely bird species   Kingfisher, Lapwing

All year	Green Sandpiper	Siskin
Waterbirds	Common Sandpiper	
Wildfowl	Black-tailed Godwit	*Breeding season*
Woodland birds	Common Gull	Oystercatcher
Shelduck	Lesser Black-backed Gull	Redshank
Buzzard		Black-headed Gull
Pied Wagtail	Sky Lark	Common Tern
Grey Wagtail	Yellow Wagtail	
Nuthatch		*Occasional*
Treecreeper	*Winter*	Bittern
Marsh Tit	Wigeon	Bewick's Swan
	Gadwall	Osprey
Passage	Shoveler	Hobby
Hirundines	Pochard	Little Ringed Plover
Warblers	Snipe	Wood Sandpiper
		Mediterranean Gull

Background information and birding tips

UPSTREAM of the historic town of Arundel, this reserve and captive collection has the excellent facilities you would expect of any WWT centre. There is a restaurant, a gift shop, excellent toilets with baby-changing facilities, binocular hire, and an In Focus optics shop.

If you're not a WWT member, there is an entrance fee. There is level access to all areas and free wheelchair loan. Guide dogs are welcomed and, with prior arrangement, the WWT can even organise tactile exhibits.

Start looking for birds before you even get inside the Visitor Centre. Buzzards and Peregrines are recorded almost daily over Offham Hanger, the wooded bank behind the car park. In recent years Goshawks, Honey Buzzards and Hobbies have also been seen. There is also an active Rookery.

Inside, a picture window overlooks a large pool that attracts many wild ducks as well as some obviously captive ones. Mandarins are regular here, and with luck a pair or two will fly in to confirm their wild status. Most of the Shelducks are wild, as are the substantial numbers of Pochards in winter.

40

We tend to hurry through the captive pens to the boardwalk, though give a second glance to all the ridiculously tame Moorhens among the captive birds as Water Rails can be almost as confiding here in winter. Also at this time of year, numerous bird feeders tucked away in the woodland fringe here attract loads of finches, tits and Nuthatches. Wintering Chiffchaffs and Firecrests are a good possibility in the bushes.

The boardwalk is fabulous. It winds through the reedbed - one of the largest in Sussex - giving great views of the dozens of pairs of Reed Warblers in summer and every chance of glimpsing a Cetti's Warbler. At the very least you should hear one, as several pairs are usually present. Passage warblers use the reedbed, as do Reed Buntings, including a sizable winter roost.

The south edge of the site is given over completely to wild birds, with a series of hides overlooking scrapes. It's only a small reserve – indeed, it's probably only half a mile round circuit, but it packs in plenty of birds.

The Peter Scott hide overlooks a large Black-headed Gull colony which now includes a couple of pairs of Common Terns, too. Bewick's Swans use these pools regularly in winter to roost, but usually after the reserve has closed for the day!

Small numbers of passage waders use the scrapes, too. In autumn Green, Common and Wood Sandpipers are likely to be recorded, along with Ruffs,

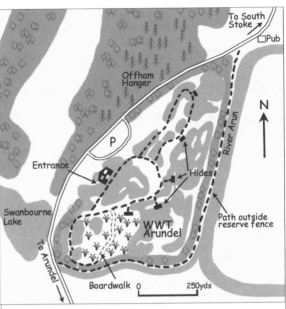

Access details

(0.5 mile NE of Arundel)

Take A27 to Arundel, and follow the brown duck signs into the town. At the roundabout just over river in town, turn NE along Mill Road, still following the duck signs. The road passes under the castle, goes over a bridge, passes the foot of Swanbourne Lake, and the entrance to the large WWT car park is another 0.25 mile on R (the first entrance is for staff only) TQ020082.

BY TRAIN: Just over 1 mile walk from Arundel station.
BY BUS: Both No.702 Brighton-Arundel and No.55 Arundel-Chichester hourly or more (not Sundays).

Greenshanks and perhaps Little Ringed Plovers. Redshanks and Lapwings are present throughout the year and some of both species may breed.

Other nearby sites

Less than 5 miles: Swanbourne Lake.
Less than 10 miles: Climping, Amberley Wild Brooks, Pulborough Brooks

41

Key points

- Allow 3-plus hours (or all day!)
- Expect 20-40 species
- SPA and SSSI, with SWT reserve
- Open access at all times
- Ashdown Forest visitor centre open weekends/ Bank Holidays (11am-5pm); weekdays April to September only (2-5pm)
- Toilets only at Forest Centre. Plenty of pubs, however, in surrounding villages
- Sandy tracks, some muddy, with some moderate gradients. Not suitable for wheelchairs

Contacts
Ashdown Forest Centre
01342 823583

A HUGE MOSAIC of open woodland and sweeping vistas of heather and gorse, Ashdown Forest is staggeringly beautiful and wild. Famous as the setting for the 'Winnie-the-Pooh' books, the forest is popular at weekends. if you get away from the car parks however,you get away from the crowds, too. You'll enter into a landscape that is bursting with Nightjars and Woodcocks, plus Dartford Warblers, Hobbies and all the other heathland specialities.

Target birds *All year* – Redpoll (60%), Dartford Warbler (40%), Woodcock (20%, increasing to 95% during breeding season), Crossbill (5%). *Breeding season* – Nightjar (90% hear, 80% see), Tree Pipit (75%), Hobby (20%), Redstart (20%), Wood Lark (20%), Wood Warbler (5%). *Winter* – Hen Harrier (5%), Great Grey Shrike (5%).

Other likely bird species

All year	Stonechat	Cuckoo
Scrub birds	Marsh Tit	Spotted Flycatcher
Woodland birds	Nuthatch	
Buzzard	Treecreeper	*Winter*
Sky Lark	Reed Bunting	Thrushes
Swallow		
Meadow Pipit	*Breeding season*	*Occasional*
	Lapwing	Brambling

Background information and birding tips

THE FOREST at Ashdown has been used by Man since pre-Roman times, but has never been cultivated. A forest in the sense of Royal hunting grounds rather than endless thick woodland, several hundred years of grazing by cattle, sheep and deer have created the random mix of heathland, woodland and scrub.

Typical views in this rolling landscape are of dry sandy paths through yellowing grass, purple heather and green and yellow gorse, with scrubby areas of birch, and distinctive clumps of Scots pine on high ground. In some areas there is mature woodland of oak and beech – and all with barely a building in sight.

Today, the Forest is managed by a Board of Conservators to ensure it remains both an amenity and an area of natural and outstanding beauty. The public has a right of access to any part of the forest, but this is a vulnerable landscape in which camping and caravanning, mountain biking and barbecues are NOT permitted and the risk of fire is very high.

On a map, it becomes clear that the Forest is really a ring of interconnected sites, served by a wonderful network of free car parks. A lot of people visit this beautiful area at weekends and no wonder, it is a stunning place. You can join them if you wish for the Alternative Ashdown pilgrimage to Pooh Sticks Bridge and the other places that

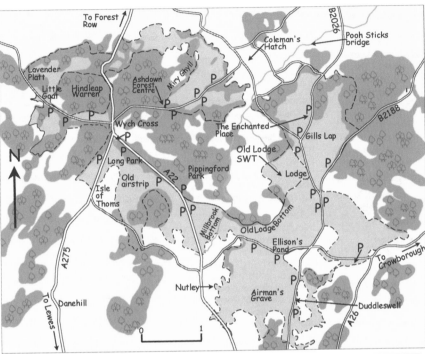

Access details

(Area within triangle of Uckfield, Crowborough and East Grinstead)

Access area via A22 East Grinstead-Uckfield or A26 Royal Tunbridge Wells-Uckfield roads. Ashdown Forest Centre is on minor road (Ridge Road) 1 mile E towards Coleman's Hatch from the traffic lights on A22 at Wych Cross (TQ431324).

Gills Lap and Old Lodge (TQ470305) are after 1 mile on the minor road SE from Colemans Hatch to the B2026.

Ellison's Pond and Airman's Grave (TQ461286) are after 0.5 mile on the minor road from the B2026 W to Nutley. The Old Airstrip is on A22, 1mile SE of Wych Cross (TQ428309).

BY TRAIN: No direct access.
BY BUS: Not easy. Best is No.270 Haywards Heath-East Grinstead via Wych Cross.

---

inspired A.A.Milne but there is also plenty of space to avoid the crowds.

In bird terms, a large proportion of the county's Nightjars breed here, and an evening walk to see them and roding Woodcocks is an essential fixture on many a Sussex birdwatcher's calendar. Also notable are Hobbies, Dartford Warblers, Redstarts (their stronghold in Sussex), Wood Larks, Tree Pipits and Redpolls, with a few Wood Warblers clinging on. Some open landscapes on the forest repeatedly attract Great Grey Shrikes in winter, the season when Hen Harriers wander widely about the Forest.

The heathland birds aren't

Continues overleaf

43

Key points

- **Dozens of free car parks, each named - the best way to navigate around the forest**

- **Good forest maps are available at visitor centre**

- **Keep strictly to paths and keep dogs under control**

- **No dogs permitted in Old Lodge reserve**

- **Between April 1 and October 31, large area of forest is fenced for grazing**

- **High risk of fire at all seasons – take every precaution not to cause them**

- **Insect repellent essential at dusk**

- **Visitor centre welcomes all bird records from the Forest**

- **Help out on Conservation Days, the last Sunday in the month**

guaranteed but, even on rather birdless trips, the scenery seems to compensate. Picnic packed, we go back again and again. Though all areas deserve exploration, the following seem to come up with the goods repeatedly:

Ashdown Forest Centre

This Visitor Centre near Wych Cross is an ideal starting point and also has the only public toilets on the Forest. There are leaflets, publications and displays to check out and the car park gives wonderful panoramas across to the North Downs.

There are some good walks from here too, especially the area of heath to the north-east of the centre, overlooking Miry Ghyll. The terrain is fairly steep, mostly of open heather with scattered birch and pine, and occasional denser clumps of trees. It can be wet underfoot in winter. This is a good area for Nightjars, roding Woodcocks and hooting Tawny Owls simultaneously - we have never been unsuccessful here. The slope on the southern side of the Ridge Road leads down to Tabell Ghyll, one of the best woodland areas on Ashdown.

Gills Lap

"And by and by they came to an enchanted place on the very top of the Forest". It brings a lump to the throat to hear A.A.Milne words again, and many people come to the Gills Lap or Piglet's car parks just for this.

Gills Lap itself is a dramatic bowl of heathland with just a few scattered pines and thick areas of gorse good for Dartford Warblers. They can be elusive, but a still sunny spring morning should entice the males to sing and

reveal themselves. The site has proved to be reliable for wintering Great Grey Shrikes. And there's always a well-stocked ice cream van in the car park!

Old Lodge LNR

This area is managed by Sussex Wildlife Trustand the reserve has a good variety of habitats, with open heath, mature pines and dragonfly pools. The circular nature trail passes close by the open grassy army training ranges of Pippingford Park and Siskins, Crossbills, Nightjars, Redpolls and Spotted Flycatchers are all possible.

It is also probably the best area on the Forest for Redstarts, Tree Pipits and Wood Larks. Even Wood Warbler is possible. The reserve is grazed by cattle, sheep and Exmoor ponies and no dogs are permitted.

Ellison's Pond to Millbrook

A great place for Redpolls, you can sometimes hear their buzzing calls in the trees around the pond from the moment you get out the car. Once again, great sweeps of open heathland ahead of you can be explored.

It is worth getting down to Old Lodge Bottom where a stream winds its way through mature trees down to Millbrook Bottom. Instead of Meadow Pipits and Sky Larks, you'll find tits, warblers and woodpeckers and also the chance of Redstarts. The slope back up to Millbrook is thick with gorse, good for Dartford Warblers.

Airman's Grave

The south slope of the Forest at Airman's Grave has some of the most open landscapes in the area, with a 40 mile panorama of the South Downs stretched out in front of you. Here, instead of beds of heather,

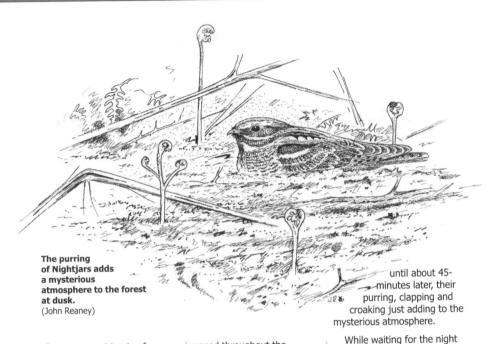

**The purring
of Nightjars adds
a mysterious
atmosphere to the forest
at dusk.**
(John Reaney)

until about 45-minutes later, their purring, clapping and croaking just adding to the mysterious atmosphere.

there are great tracts of bracken, regularly cut. Consequently Dartford Warblers and Nightjars are irregular.

However, the wet shallow valley down the centre is great for Reed Buntings and quite a favoured area for Redpolls, with even the possibility of Lapwings in the breeding season. Stonechats are common and vistas are good for spotting Hobbies. Note that it can be wet underfoot here, and a large part of the forest up towards Old Lodge Bottom and Millbrook Bottom is fenced and grazed throughout the summer.

Isle of Thorns/Old Airstrip

This area we have found to be one of the best for exciting views of Nightjars and Woodcocks in a primeval landscape (with plain evil midges). Park in Long Park car park and head south.

Woodcocks come out first, well before dusk (by about 8.30pm in midsummer) and are easy to see, the strange soft '*pfitt*' noise alerting you to another one on its way across the Forest. Nightjars aren't out

While waiting for the night birds to emerge, we have found Isle of Thorns good for Redpolls coming into roost. Indeed, they are reliable here all year. Pied Wagtails roost here too and Dartford Warblers make their churring calls until sunset. The area has also been favoured by Great Grey Shrikes in past winters and by Wood Larks recently.

Goat

This part of the forest is relatively heavily wooded, so is a good place for Nuthatches, Treecreepers, Jays and roaming tit flocks. In spring, the more open glades are excellent for Tree Pipits singing from their treetop perches. Like a lot of the forest, this site can be very muddy after wet weather.

Other nearby sites

Less than 5 miles: Weir Wood Reservoir.
Less than 10 miles: Chailey Common, Ardingly Reservoir.

45

Key points

- Allow 3-plus hours

- Expect 25-40 species (or more with seawatching)

- SSSI. Much land around Birling Gap owned by NT.

- Access at all times to public areas

- Good facilities – toilets, food and parking

- Countryside Centre at Beachy Head open Apr-Sep 10-5.30; weekends-only 10-4 in winter

- Short Peace Path disabled trail

- Rarely muddy but paths often steep

Contacts

For Beachy Head:
Eastbourne Borough Council
Downland Trees and Woodland
01323 415267
dtw@eastbourne.gov.uk

For Birling Gap:
National Trust
01323 871318

L OOKING AT A MAP, it is clear how prominent a position Beachy Head occupies, jutting out into the Channel. It is also the highest point on England's south coast with sheer chalk cliffs towering over 530 feet above the sea. With four miles of scattered shrubs along the clifftops too, it all adds up to make the area a magnet for passage warblers, chats, finches, hirundines and raptors, with rarities and semi-rarities recorded every year.

Target birds There is always the option of seawatching from Birling Gap – see pp25 for the species and timings. The main targets however are landbird migrants. *All year* – Peregrine (75%), Raven (30%). *Spring passage* – Black Redstart (30%), Firecrest (20%), Serin (5%), Pied Flycatcher (annual), Hoopoe (near-annual). *Breeding season* – Corn Bunting (40%). *August-September* - Redstart (60%), Tree Pipit (60%), Hobby (50%), Grasshopper Warbler (10%), Pied Flycatcher (5%), Wryneck (5%), Nightingale (annual), continental migrants (one of Red-

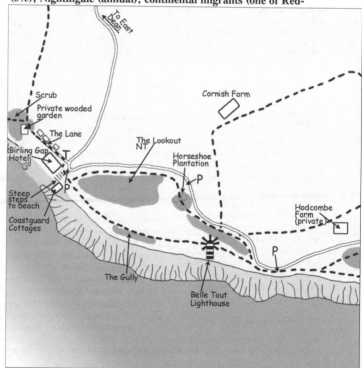

backed Shrike, Tawny Pipit, Melodious Warbler, Barred Warbler, Red-breasted Flycatcher – 5%). *October* - Firecrest (80%), Black Redstart (70%), Siskin (65%), Brambling (60%), Redpoll (60%), Ring Ouzel (60%), Merlin (60%), Short-eared Owl (5%), Yellow-browed Warbler (almost annual). *November* – Pallas's Warbler (almost annual).

Access details

(2 miles SW of Eastbourne)

Beachy Head is easy to find. From Seaford, take the A259 towards Eastbourne. The Beachy Head 'loop' road runs S from East Dean, down to the clifftop at Birling Gap, and then runs along the back of the cliffs and almost over Beachy Head itself to the B2103 into Eastbourne. Parking along the route, from

W to E, is at: Birling Gap car park (with toilets, TV555959), Horseshoe Plantation car park (TV561958), Shooters Bottom (TV575955), Raptor view point (TV584955), Beachy Head car park – pay and display with toilets (TV590960); and Whitbread Hollow car park (TV594964).

BY TRAIN: No direct access.
BY BUS: Good year-round on Sundays only, when No.713 runs between Brighton and

Eastbourne. Sightseeing services usually run in summer during the week from Eastbourne.

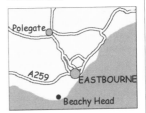

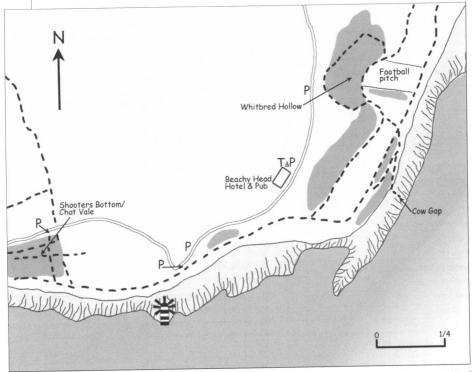

Continues overleaf

47

Beachy Head Migrant Calendar

The following chart gives a good idea of what species are seen when, and how abundant each is likely to be. Each month is split into half, with 'weeks' 1&2 shown in the first column and 3&4 in the second. Note that migrants have such an edge of unpredictability that is some years passage may fall way short or far exceed the figures shown here, or their pattern of occurrence may shift slightly left or right across the table!

	Mar 1&2	Mar 3&4	Apr 1&2	Apr 3&4	May 1&2	May 3&4	Jun 1&2	Jun 3&4	Jul 1&2	Jul 3&4	Aug 1&2	Aug 3&4	Sep 1&2	Sep 3&4	Oct 1&2	Oct 3&4	Nov 1&2
Merlin																	
Wood Pigeon																	
Stock Dove																	
Swift																	
Sky Lark			B	B	B	B	B	B	B	B	B	B					
Sand Martin																	
Swallow							b	b									
House Martin																	
Tree Pipit																	
Meadow Pipit					B	B	B	B	B	B	B	B					
Yellow Wagtail																	
Grey Wagtail																	
Pied Wagtail																	
Robin	b	b	b	b	b	b	b	b	b	b	b	b					
Black Redstart																	
Redstart																	
Whinchat																	
Wheatear																	
Ring Ouzel																	
Grasshopper Warbler																	
Lesser Whitethroat						b	b	b	b	b							
Whitethroat					B	B	B	B	B	B	B	B					
Garden Warbler																	
Blackcap						b	b	b	b								
Chiffchaff							b	b	b	b							
Willow Warbler																	
Goldcrest																	
Firecrest																	
Spotted Flycatcher																	
Pied Flycatcher																	
Brambling																	
Goldfinch																	
Siskin																	
Linnet					B	B	B	B	B	B	B						
Redpoll																	

Key

■ Daily in more than double figures	▨ Daily in single figures	B - Breeding (many pairs)
▨ Daily in double figures	▨ Regular, although not daily	b - Breeding (a few pairs)
	□ Little or no passage	

Other likely bird species (also see Migrant Calendar)

All year	Thrushes	*Occasional*
Gulls	Sedge Warbler	Osprey
Scrub birds	Reed Warbler	Honey Buzzard
Farmland birds		Wood Lark
Corvids	*Breeding season*	Dartford Warbler
	Fulmar	
Passage	Stonechat	
Cuckoo		

Background information and birding tips

A NORMAL DAY'S birdwatching at Beachy Head consists of a slow wander while you peer into every bush, patiently checking each little bird that flits in front of you. Perhaps you might sit for a while, waiting to see what emerges from choice thickets or listening for tell-tale calls and all the time you will be keeping an eye on the sky above.

For many migrants this is the first British land they see in spring but it is in autumn that things really hot up, with thousands of birds lingering to feed on the abundant berries and insects and thousands more passing overhead, especially in the first two hours after dawn. It's a great place for Wrynecks each autumn with near-annual Hoopoes, Bee-eaters, Alpine Swifts, Melodious and Subalpine Warblers, plus an amazing list of five-star rarities such as Crag Martin and Sardinian Warbler.

The table left gives a good overview of how abundant and at what time the common migrants pass through. Numbers and timings vary annually and even day-by-day, of course, but conversely it is fascinating how predictable many of the birds are. The table also shows clearly how much quieter Beachy is in spring. In autumn, a period of easterly winds is likely to boost numbers of birds such as Pied Flycatchers, Redstarts and Wrynecks considerably (highest day counts recently being 25, 85, and eight respectively).

It is in these kinds of conditions that Beachy can then turn up some exceptional rarities. Savi's, Greenish, Radde's, Dusky and Bonelli's Warblers have all been seen. Don't discount spring as a time for rarities either, particularly May. There are records of Sardinian, Greenish and Bonelli's Warblers, and several of Subalpine, some of which have hung around holding territory. Red-rumped Swallows, Alpine Swifts and Bee-eaters have also been seen on several occasions in spring. There have even been some amazing mid-summer sightings – July 9 1988 saw Britain's second Crag Martin arrive and there was a three-day Lesser Grey Shrike in 1982.

The habitat at Beachy Head is generally open downland with areas of scrub and one or two patches of trees. Much of the time, you may not be aware you are near cliffs, which is why we emphasise the dangers – the open grass sweeps up to the cliff edge, hiding several hundred feet of unfenced, sheer and actively-eroding drop. Please take great care.

Key points

- **Year-round bus link on Sundays; limited services at other times.**

- **SHEER CLIFF EDGE SHOULD BE TREATED WITH EXTREME CAUTION**

- **Plenty of birdwatchers around in autumn**

- **First two hours after dawn will seriously increase number of birds you'll see**

- **Can be exposed and windy here, adding extra danger near cliff edge**

- **This is a big area, and takes all day to cover**

- **Excellent for butterflies and downland flowers**

- **Countryside Centre at Beachy Head (01323 737273), but it's future is uncertain**

Continues overleaf

Birling Gap and The Lane

Birling Gap is the lowest point in the cliffs between the Seven Sisters and Beachy Head. From the Birling Gap NT car park, there is access to the beach via a steep wooden stairway. You can seawatch from here, but it is rather high and Splash Point at Seaford is a better venue.

From the car park entrance, a track known to birdwatchers as 'The Lane' runs northwestwards. It passes a row of bungalows with enviable sea views, and impressive garden bird lists too – at the relevant season, check the fences for Whinchats, the lawns for Wheatears and the rooftops for Black Redstarts. Serins are seen annually, but remember that these are private homes, so be careful not to trespass or cause a nuisance.

At the top of the lane, the garden of wind-stunted Scots pine is a good place to peer through the fence slats for Firecrests. The left turn brings you out onto a patch of open scrub where many Wrynecks have been seen and, in late summer, is full of butterflies including chalkhill blues and marbled whites. You can continue to follow the track over the Seven Sisters if you choose.

Belle Tout and Horseshoe Plantation to Birling Gap

A fruitful circular walk can be had from Birling Gap eastwards to Horseshoe Plantation and back along the clifftop via Belle Tout lighthouse.

Starting from Birling Gap car park, the bank of low scrub immediately east of the coastguard cottages is usually the best place for Whinchats as well as resident Stonechats. The clockwise circuit takes you parallel to the road with open farmland opposite you and a steep bank of scrub, 'The Lookout', to your right.

Fifteen minutes walk (or more if there is warbler activity in the bushes) brings you to Horseshoe Plantation. This scrap of sycamore woodland, with little more than a Great Tit and a Wren in summer or winter, is fantastic during passage. Firecrests are to be expected in October, and it is the county hotspot for Pallas's and Yellow-browed Warblers.

The warm southeastern flank of the wood in particular, can buzz with Chiffchaffs and Spotted Flycatchers. Butterflies and dragonflies also abound here, including green and white-letter hairstreaks and silver-spotted skippers.

Above the wood, streams of hirundines pass through. Sand Martins kick things off in early August and by September, House Martins and Swallows predominate, with peak days of 10,000 birds of each species. The direction of flight is usually into the wind and passage can sometimes continue for much of the day, unlike wagtail, pipit and lark passage, which peters out quickly.

By October, watch tired finch flocks pause in the treetops or a Merlin whizz through as well as Cuckoos, Green Woodpeckers and Hobbies. In November, there is a huge passage of Wood Pigeons just after dawn.

One possible diversion is to cross the road up the dry concrete track towards Cornish Farm. This looks unpromising, but it is probably as good a place as any in mainland Britain to look for Tawny Pipits in autumn. Ortolans and Dotterels have also been recorded here, and look out for Wheatears, Whinchats, Sky Larks and Corn Buntings.

Continuing east from Horseshoe Plantation, the shrubby bank to your right continues the theme of migrant Blackcaps, Lesser Whitethroats and Robins. It's a good place for Ring Ouzels too and always the chance, after favourable winds, of a Red-backed Shrike or a Wryneck.

Up above is the Belle Tout lighthouse, now a permanent private home. Belle Tout was famously moved away from the edge of the cliff a few years ago on huge rollers! Black Redstarts may patrol the walls and always keep an eye out above for Peregrines.

Walking back over the top towards Birling Gap, with fabulous views of the Seven Sisters in front of you, check out the little scrubby dip right by the cliff edge – 'The Gully' - for chats and warblers. Wheatears are also likely throughout spring and autumn passage on the open paths back to Birling Gap.

Shooters Bottom

Shooter's Bottom is a discrete block of scrub half a mile east of Belle Tout. From the roadside pull-in, a track leads along the floor of the shallow valley ('Chat Vale') towards the cliff edge. The scrub all around this area is again an ideal migrant trap. Even in spring, when migrants are fewer and don't stay for as long, we've seen Black Redstarts, Redstarts, Whinchats and Stonechats all within twenty minutes, and several Subalpine Warblers have been 'pulled in' here. On the right, the large area of gorse is ideal for watching Dartford Warblers on passage.

In autumn, this is an unbeatable spot for Ring Ouzels, although they do have a habit of nipping across to the private leafy gardens of Hodcombe Farm opposite. Now that Ravens have returned to Beachy Head, this is a reliable place to see and hear them overhead. If there are cattle grazing nearby, check for Yellow Wagtails nipping about their feet.

The open fields opposite the car park are also much loved by Meadow Pipits and, by October, flocks of several hundred are possible here. Any summer sees clouded yellow butterflies here too; in a good year it can be awash with them.

Other nearby sites

Beachy Head

Being the highest point on the headland, any bushes in the vicinity of Beachy Head act as a drop in point for birds arriving at night. These include what is known as the 'Old Trapping Area', the bushes on the 'S'-bend in the road coming up from Shooter's Bottom to Beachy Head. The migrants soon get the urge to slip away from all the tourists and find better feeding, so get in early (ie dawn) for rarities such as Red-breasted Flycatchers and Melodious Warblers, with early September to early October and an easterly wind providing your best chance of success.

Come back again mid-morning onwards to look for raptors on the move. We were privileged to be in the area for the unprecedented Honey Buzzard passage in autumn 2000. On October 1 we saw nine raptor species in about two hours, including Honey Buzzards, Marsh Harriers, and an Osprey, most of them flapping out to sea over the Head. None of us can expect such days again in the near future, but all these species are seen annually.

Whitbread Hollow, Francis Bottom and Cow Gap

Whitbread Hollow is a very steep 'bowl', dense with impenetrable bushes, but there is a network of tracks around the outside. There is a ringing programme here,

hence the records aplenty of scarce migrants such as Melodious and Barred Warblers. Lots of good birds are nevertheless seen here outside of a mist net, being particularly good, we've found, for Ring Ouzels and Redstarts. The elder bushes at the bottom of the Hollow are often the easiest to watch, but it is one rarity to every thousand Blackcaps and other common Sylvia warblers.

You can if you wish walk on further north towards Eastbourne, into the area known as Holywell, where there are more scattered bushes and trees.

We prefer however to go down towards the sea where a set of steps go down to kind of mezzanine levels of scrub and elder called Cow Gap. This is the part of Beachy Head that sticks out furthest towards France and, possibly as a result, Cow Gap has perhaps the most exciting bird list of anywhere in Sussex. We can't guarantee repeats of Crag Martins, Booted Warblers or Desert Wheatears, but Wrynecks love it here. The slope-hugging scrub can also be great for Firecrests and Redstarts and Francis Bottom, up above Cow Gap, is one of the best places on the Head for Ring Ouzels in October. There is a chance however, that this area can be empty. If so, you can always go down another steep set of steps to the beach for a paddle! Do not attempt to follow the shoreline through to Birling Gap, however – it is only possible on a very low tide, and there is no other way up the cliffs if trapped.

9 ** BEWL WATER

Key points

- Allow 3-plus hours (or 6 if doing the complete circuit)

- Expect 30-40 species

- Includes SWT reserve

- Paths open at all times; Visitor Centre open 9am-sunset except Christmas Day and July 14 (Concert and Fireworks Day)

- Good pay-at-barrier parking at Visitor Centre with all facilities, including wheelchair access

- Facilities limited elsewhere around reservoir

- One hide at SWT reserve

- Many tracks very good; just a few muddy

- Telescope useful

Contacts

Southern Water (Bewl Water Estate Office)
01892 890661

BEING THE LARGEST water body in South East England, Bewl Water is bound to attract plenty of birds. It doesn't pack in the rarities, but a good range of habitats around the 13 miles of shoreline, coupled with good facilities, make for a decent day's birding.

Target birds *All year* – Kingfisher (50%).

Other likely bird species

All year	Little Egret	Snipe
Waterbirds	Common Sandpiper	Grey Wagtail
Wildfowl	Green Sandpiper	Siskin
Woodland birds	Greenshank	
Farmland birds	Yellow Wagtail	*Occasional*
Great Crested Grebe		Diver species
Marsh Tit	*Breeding season*	Goldeneye
Nuthatch	Common Tern	Willow Tit
Treecreeper		Redpoll
	Winter	
Passage	Wigeon	
Hirundines	Shoveler	

Background information and birding tips

BEWL WATER IS almost the size of all of Sussex's other reservoirs combined so it can hardly fail to have some birdwatching interest. There are dozens of pairs of both common grebe species, while winter brings hundreds each of Mallards, Tufted Ducks, Gadwalls and Wigeon. The gull roost can be huge, with over 30,000 Black-headed and 50,000 Common and it's a fabulous reservoir for Kingfishers.

Some species though are notable by their absence: Pochards rarely top fifty, Shovelers struggle to achieve half that number and Goldeneyes can be counted on one hand. But then birdwatching at Bewl is as much for the farmland and woodland birds around its edges as it is for its waterbirds.

Unless you're on a bike, you'll be hard pushed to cover all 13-miles of Bewl's heavily-indented shoreline in one day. Try these three good access points:

1) Visitor Centre and Dam to Hook Straight

The Visitor Centre is excellent, with a big café, excellent toilets, bikes on hire etc. It is also the focus for the wide range of land and water based activities which go on at Bewl. Overlooking the deepest stretch of water by the dam and, with sailing activity concentrated here, the number of water birds is low but includes the chance of a diver in winter.

Walks from here, either along the north shore or across the dam, lead through mature woodland, scrub and farmland, with woodpeckers, Marsh Tits, Treecreepers and Goldcrests to be expected. Willow Tits and Lesser Spotted

Woodpeckers probably still occur, though they are elusive.

Hook Straight can be one of the most productive areas of the reservoir for waterfowl. Gadwalls will certainly by there, dabbling amongst the Coots, and a few Pochards and Tufted Ducks are also likely.

2) Sussex Wildlife Trust Reserve

This area is low in visitor pressure but, except for a small car park, there are no facilities. It is probably the best part of the reservoir for birdwatching and is where, incredibly, a wintering Blackpoll Warbler was found in 1994.

From the quarry car park, walk 100 yards further along the road and turn left down to a wonderful tower hide hidden in a copse at the water's edge. It gives great views over an arm of Bewl Water where fishing and watersports are not permitted. However, a telescope and a head for heights are helpful!

Along with a good range of wildfowl, including a huge herd of Canada Geese in Summer and perhaps a Bar-headed Goose or two, expect passage hirundines and summer Common Terns hunting over the water. In late summer, a couple of Little Egrets may pick along the margins. Walks north along the reservoir bank are good for hedgerow birds such as Yellowhammers, Reed Buntings and Garden Warblers.

3) Ketley Pond

The parking bay here fills quickly at weekends, a setting-off point for hikes around the

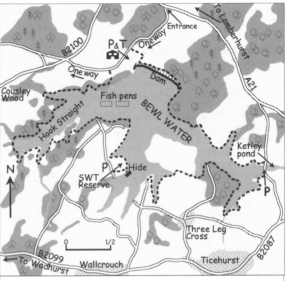

Access details

(7 miles SE of Royal Tunbridge Wells)

VISITOR CENTRE: From Royal Tunbridge Wells, take the A21 S. The entrance road to the Visitor Centre is on R, 1mile S of Lamberhurst (TQ675337).
SWT RESERVE: Travel 1 mile E from Wadhurst on the B2099. Turn L towards Birchett's Green soon after the R turn to Stonegate. After 0.5 mile, turn L at the end of a wood, and follow this narrow lane for just over 1 mile — it doubles back on itself and the little quarry car park is on R (TQ672321).
KETLEY POND: The parking

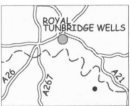

bay on the causeway between Bewl Water and Ketley Pond is half way between the A21 at Stonecrouch and the NFU Mutual building in Berner's Hill on the B2087 between Flimwell and Ticehurst (TQ700319).

BY TRAIN: No direct access.
BY BUS: 1 mile walk from Ticehurst or Cousley Wood just to reach reservoir edge.

reservoir. The birdwatching attraction is the muddy-fringed Ketley Pond, cut off from the main body of the reservoir and viewed over the hedge. Birds feed undisturbed here and it is a good spot for wintering Teal and Snipe. We've also had superb views of displaying Kingfishers. Purple Heron has been recorded here and check for migrant waders such as Green and Common Sandpipers in autumn.

53

Key points

- Allow 1-plus hours (more if seawatching)

- Expect 10-40 species

- Public access permitted to harbour arms at all times, except in stormy weather when spray dangerous

- Keep on upper level of breakwaters away from fishermen

- Site directly adjacent to Marina Village, where there are shopping/eating/toilet facilities

- Good flat walking

- Wheelchair access possible, but viewing into harbour itself difficult

- Very public site; excellent bus links

- Telescope useful

A TRIP TO Brighton Marina can be combined with a visit to the supermarket, cinema or gym - convenience birding! Essentially a seawatching site, (see p25) a short winter visit can find Shags, Purple Sandpipers and sometimes Black Redstarts and the Marina has a history of sheltering storm-driven birds such as Grey Phalaropes. Not the most glamorous of sites, but well worth a look.

Target birds Seawatching birds, plus *All year* - Rock Pipit (40%, easier in winter). *Winter* – Shag (70%), Purple Sandpiper (70%), Black Redstart (40%), Mediterranean Gull (10%).

Other likely bird species

All year	*Passage*	*Occasional*
Gulls	Hirundines	Mute Swan
Cormorant	Wheatear	Kingfisher
Pied Wagtail		Scandinavian Rock
Starling	*Winter*	Pipit
	Ringed Plover	

Background information and birding tips

A BOVE ALL other considerations, Brighton Marina is a seawatching site. The harbour arms jut into the Channel - 350 yards in the case of the west arm - bringing you that much closer to many of the auks, waders, wildfowl and seabirds passing by. The watching is good enough to entice some brave souls to come here most days.

We say brave because:
1) in winter it can be bitterly exposed.
2) the outer harbour wall is brilliantly designed to dissipate the power of waves hitting it - even in just a moderate onshore wind, the waves shoot high, right over the harbour arm. It means that, in strong winds, the harbour arms are unapproachable.

See the seawatching pages for a full description of what to look for passing by. This text concntrates on what else you might see here.

Parking is easy in the large free multi-storey car park, situated close to the west arm. As you walk out onto the arm, the small beach to your right may sometimes have a Black Redstart (October –March) or Rock Pipit on it. Check the gulls around the surf too as 'white-winged' varieties are possible in winter.

The Marina has an outer and an inner harbour, and the west arm protects the outer. On the water, Grey Phalaropes are sometimes recorded after storms, as are exhausted Little Auks. There are often gulls loafing about too, particularly late afternoon, with Mediterranean Gulls regular in winter, Kittiwakes in late summer and Little Gulls possible after autumn storms, when terns may shelter here, too.

There is a small shingle beach at the back of this sheltered water where Ringed Plovers, up to 50 or

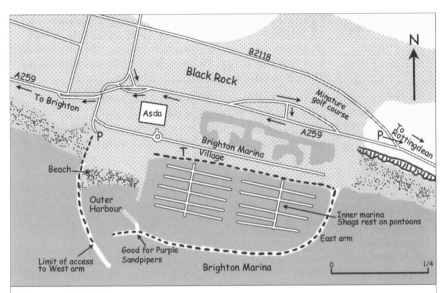

N

B2118

Black Rock

A259

← To Brighton

Asda

P

Miniature golf course

A259

P → To Rottingdean

Brighton Marina Village

Beach

Outer Harbour

Inner marina
Shags rest on pontoons

East arm

Good for Purple Sandpipers

Limit of access to West arm

Brighton Marina

0   1/4

Access details

(1 mile E of Brighton)

Clearly visible and signed from A259 Brighton-Rottingdean coast road, 0.5 mile W of Roedean School. Note, when driving E from Brighton, it is necessary to pass the Marina to your R and double back where A259 widens after 0.5mile. Then, or if coming from Rottingdean, stay in the left-hand lane to drop down under A259, swing left under the bridge and free parking is clearly signed ahead of you (TQ334032) in multi-storey car park.

BY TRAIN: No direct access.
BY BUS: Very well served from Brighton station. Eg Nos.7, 14, 21, 47, 52 & 57.

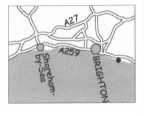

so, roost in winter and may even attempt to breed. Much of the inside perimeter however is scattered with huge puzzle-shaped concrete blocks - sea defence mechanisms – on which the two or three Shags sometimes perch, as do the Purple Sandpipers or, sadly, oiled Guillemots and Razorbills. In 1995/6, a Black Guillemot spent a lengthy winter holiday in Brighton right here.

It is only possible to walk three-quarters of the way down the western arm, but that's far enough to see along the outside of the eastern arm, perhaps the most reliable site for Purple Sandpipers and Shags on the concrete blocks. The Purple Sandpipers tend to feed around the Marina itself, and rarely stray far.

It is possible to walk right around and along the eastern arm, though it is a surprisingly long trek. From here, look for Shags within the boat-filled inner marina on the wooden pontoons. Early morning in spring may produce some fresh arrivals – Wheatears maybe, or even warblers, before they get second-wind and move up to the Sheepcote Valley. Offshore, small flocks of Eider may linger in winter, or any of the scarcer grebes, particularly towards early spring.

It is always worth checking the undercliff and the few bushes behind Asda too as a Pallas's Warbler once stayed a few November days here.

Key points

- Allow 1-plus hours
- Expect 10-25 species
- SSSI
- Clifftop and undercliff paths open at all times, though the latter are very dangerous in storms!
- Exercise caution near cliff edges
- Several free parking opportunities
- Toilets at Ovingdean, Saltdean and Peacehaven
- Some access to undercliff for wheelchairs
- Excellent bus links

THE COASTLINE between Brighton and Eastbourne is dominated by towering chalk cliffs. Despite the urban clifftop sprawl from Brighton to Newhaven, the cliffs still hold breeding Peregrines, Fulmars, Rock Pipits and Kittiwakes. Black Redstarts are also regular in winter.

Target birds

All year – Rock Pipit (60%) Peregrine (60%). *Passage* – Whimbrel (30%). *Breeding season* – Fulmar (95%), Kittiwake (Newhaven only – 80%), Corn Bunting (60%). *Winter* – Black Redstart (40%), Purple Sandpiper (15%).

Other likely bird species

All year	Oystercatcher	Wheatear
Gulls	Sky Lark	
Scrub birds	Stonechat	*Winter*
Garden birds		Meadow Pipit
Cormorant	*Passage*	
Sparrowhawk	Seawatching birds	*Occasional*
Kestrel	Hirundines	Whinchat
	Warblers	Dartford Warbler

Background information and birding tips

BETWEEN Brighton and Telscombe Cliffs, a thin strip of close-cropped grass splits the cliff-top from the busy A259 coast road. Here you will still find Sky Larks, Starlings, Jackdaws and, curiously, a few Rooks along with the odd Rock Pipit.

However, the real avian prizes come from walking the wide undercliff path which stretches all the way from Brighton to Saltdean, with another section at Telscombe Cliffs and yet another at Peacehaven. It is a world away from the traffic and houses hidden above.

Fulmars breed in places along the cliffs, especially at Saltdean and Newhaven and they are back on their breeding ledges by November. These stretches of undercliff are also popular with Black Redstarts in winter – we've seen birds on the railings right against the road at Saltdean.

They like to move onto the isolated beaches between Saltdean and Telscombe Cliffs, where there is also a small Cormorant roost on the cliffs. This is possibly the best place in Sussex to find Scandinavian Rock Pipits in March.

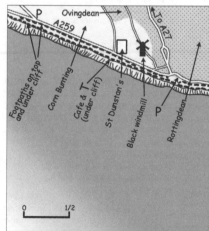

Contacts

Brighton & Hove
Countryside Service
01273 292140

For a clifftop walk without traffic or houses at your back, try the stretch between Peacehaven and Newhaven. Here the cliffs are unfenced and the drop is some 200 feet, so be very careful indeed.

There is some extensive scrub here, worth checking out at migration time. Whitethroats and Stonechats abound here, and there is a chance of Dartford Warblers in autumn.

Towards Newhaven, the clifftop path is very narrow along the edge of a ploughed field. Sky Larks and Corn Buntings breed here, while on the cliff face below are a few breeding pairs of Kittiwakes – hearing them is no problem, seeing them will need great caution! Also, keep watching for Peregrines anywhere along the whole length of the cliffs. In late summer and autumn, family parties may be in the air together.

From the Peacehaven end, you can access the beach, where you may spot Black Redstarts or one of the breeding Rock Pipits. Both these species, plus breeding Fulmars are also possible on the shingle beach next to Newhaven breakwater where there is also the chance of migrants in the undercliff scrub -a Pied Wheatear amazingly turned up here in July 1990. On the sea defences on the outside of the breakwater, wintering Purple Sandpipers are likely.

For seawatching, the cliffs tend to be generally too high to make for good viewing, but don't let that stop you from having a scan.

Access details

(Coast strip between Brighton and Newhaven)

A259 Brighton-Newhaven road runs along clifftop, very busy at rush hour. Parking at several points: Brighton Marina (free – TQ334032); Ovingdean Roundabout (turn towards Ovingdean, park on L on road verge. Walk through underpass to beach, cafe and toilets (TQ359026); Rottingdean (pay and display 50 yards W of traffic lights - TQ372022); Saltdean (free behind lido – TQ381020); Telscombe Cliffs (free behind Telscombe Tavern next to toilet block - TQ397013); Peacehaven (turn S down Roderick Avenue opposite Barclays Bank – parking on Promenade in two places); or at Newhaven West Pier (turn off one-way system in Newhaven town centre onto Riverside, drive to far end and pay at kiosk - TQ447000).

***BY TRAIN:* One mile walk from** Newhaven Town Station.
***BY BUS:* Very well served from Brighton station by Nos. 712 (to Eastbourne) and 14 (to Newhaven) along entire clifftop.**

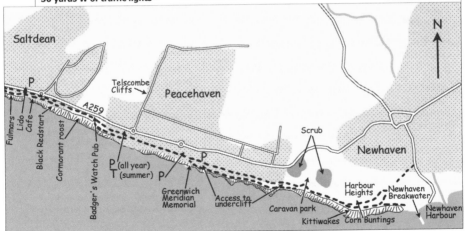

Key points

- Allow 2-plus hours
- Expect 15-25 species
- Eridge Rocks is SSSI and SWT reserve; main body of wood is privately-owned plantation
- Permissive paths into forest may be closed occasionally to allow forestry operations
- Limited parking and no other public facilities – nearest in Royal Tunbridge Wells
- Some paths can get muddy
- Not suitable for wheelchairs
- Keep dogs under close control to protect ground nesting birds

Contacts

Sussex Wildlife Trust (for Eridge Rocks)
01273 492630

THE PLANTATIONS of Broadwater Forest have such extensive areas of clear-fell that charismatic species such as Tree Pipit, Wood Lark and Nightjar have relatively healthy populations. Little-visited by birdwatchers, the commercially-managed Forest has good permissive access and, with regular Redpolls and Crossbills too, it really is quite rewarding.

Target Birds *All year* – Crossbill (5 to 30%). *Breeding season* – Tree Pipit (80%), Nightjar (dusk hear 80%, see 30%), Wood Lark (30%). *Winter* – Redpoll (40%).

Other likely bird species

All year	Nuthatch	*Winter*
Woodland birds	Marsh Tit	Siskin

Background information and birding tips

BROADWATER FOREST could so easily be poor for birdwatching. However, the influence of active commercial woodland management transforms this into something much, much better. By clear-felling big areas, a vibrant and exciting bird community can move in for up to ten years afterwards.

At the moment though, pine trees dominate much of this great chunk of woodland, dark plantations where barely a hint of daylight reaches the forest floor. Somewhere, neck-craningly high above you, the thin calls of Goldcrests and Coal Tits reveal the impoverished birdlife that is present.

Though it will extend your walk, there is no better starting point for Broadwater Forest than the SWT's reserve at Eridge Rocks. The Rocks are a rather unusual inland 'cliff', a 600-yard line of giant weathered boulders (with names such as The Heffalump!) on which rare plants grow.

The parking is good, though there are limited places. The surrounding woodland is rich and sunny with plenty of old timber. Birds such as Blackcaps, Nuthatches and woodpeckers are more numerous here than elsewhere on the forest.

Beyond Eridge Rocks, you enter a rather bird-poor sweet chestnut coppice, but keep heading west or north into a large area of the forest known as 'The Warren'. Here are those monocultural conifer plantations, but also the areas of clear-fell and replant beloved, at least in the short-term, of Nightjars, Wood Larks and Tree Pipits.

Some of the new plantations become very grassy, holding back the young conifers and extending the bird value for yet more years. These open areas are large enough for even Linnets to use, and there is still a heathiness to much of the forest, with gorse and heather valiantly clinging on along some of the rides.

The conifers inevitably draw in Crossbills and Siskins, the latter sometimes in large numbers in winter. Redpolls also sometimes gather in the pines in considerable numbers but are most usually seen in ones and twos in the scattered birches around the glades or the alders along the streams. These three species can spice up an otherwise rather bleak winter visit here – a warm sunny spring day with Wood Larks pirouetting overhead is often more fulfilling.

If you want to add a bit of variety to your day without leaping back in the car, try walking back down the lane from the Eridge Rocks car park to the A26 at Eridge Green and cross to the High Weald long-distance footpath to Eridge Old Park. The open deer park supports a range of farmland and parkland birds such as Sky Larks and Mistle Thrushes, with a chance of Little Owls too. There are views over some fishing lakes where Great Crested Grebes and Grey Herons fish and Mandarins have been seen.

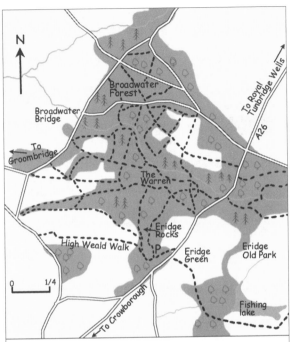

Access details

(2 miles SW of Royal Tunbridge Wells)

For Eridge Rocks, head to Eridge Green on the A26 between Royal Tunbridge Wells and Crowborough. The small lane leading to the SWT car park is immediately S of Eridge Green church – it is easy to zoom past on this busy road, so if heading N, look for the giant monkey puzzle tree opposite, or if coming S, the church is soon after the big pub on the R. The SWT car park is 200 yards down the

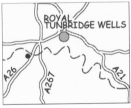

lane in front of the Rocks (TQ554355).

BY TRAIN: **1 mile walk from Eridge station.**
BY BUS: **Services Nos.228, 229 and 729 stop outside Eridge Green church.**

Other nearby sites
Less than 10 miles: Ashdown Forest

Key points

- Allow 2-plus hours
- Expect 20-30 species
- Owned and managed by West Sussex County Council
- Ponds are SSSI for dragonflies
- Good free parking (open 8am-6pm winter, 8am-8pm summer)
- Excellent toilets and Countryside Centre
- Latest sightings on notice board
- Good paths within Country Park, with some gentle inclines but allowing good wheelchair access
- Very difficult by public transport

Contacts

Buchan Park Countryside Centre
01293 542 088
01293 544 120
buchan.park@westsussex.gov.uk

WHILE RESEARCHING this book, there were several places we visited which we never expected to make the final text. This was one of them, but how wrong we were! The woods around these ornamental lakes are consistently stuffed with birds, including Crossbills, Siskins and Redpolls, and it is so difficult to believe that the birds and the scenery are only two miles from Crawley town centre!

Target birds *Winter* – Redpoll (30%), Crossbill (10%), Kingfisher (10%). *Breeding season* – Tree Pipit (40%), Redstart (5%), Wood Warbler (5%).

Other likely bird species

All year	Marsh Tit	*Occasional*
Woodland birds	Nuthatch	Woodcock
Great Crested Grebe	Treecreeper	Nightjar
Canada Goose		Lesser Spotted
Mallard	*Winter*	Woodpecker
Moorhen	Grey Wagtail	Wood Lark
	Siskin	

Background information and birding tips

BIRD NOISE HITS you the moment you get out of the car at Buchan CP. Alongside the tits, Nuthatches and Greenfinches, we've had flocks of Siskins in the tall alders here, and drumming Great Spotted Woodpeckers. Spotted Flycatchers usually breed nearby, too.

The path out of the car park leads past the Countryside Centre (weekend and peak-time opening only) with its excellent toilet block. Make sure you check the information board for the latest wildlife sightings and pick up the very good trail guide.

And then you walk out onto... wait for it... a footbridge over a dual carriageway! It doesn't bode well, you might think. But you're barely on the other side of the bridge before you're back among Nuthatches and tits.

In front of you is Douster Pond, a small lake deep among the trees, its banks dotted with fishermen. A pair of Great Crested Grebes is often here with the Mallards and Canada Geese, and Kingfishers can hang around all winter, confirming that the fishing must be good. Expect Grey Wagtails too, especially around the rather grand lake outflow that bounces down a 'turreted water cascade'. The wet woodland below is great for Marsh Tits, which we've always found easy to find in the Park.

The brilliant thing about Buchan CP is the range of woodland habitats crammed in here. There are patches of big old birches, giant larches, stands of pine, others of spruce, oak and sweet chestnut. Some nestboxes have been put up, but they are little needed because there's loads of old timber. There's no wandering through silent winter woodland here, waiting to find that roving tit flock –

Greats, Blues, Coals and Long-tails seem to be everywhere and Treecreepers are as easy as they get. No wonder the park has a history of breeding Redstarts and Wood Warblers – they are just about holding on, but with the slump in the populations of both in the south-east, you may have to get there soon to see them.

There's also a little heath – Target Hill – where a pair of Tree Pipits usually breed and where you may be lucky enough to find a Dartford Warbler. On such a small site, a hard winter may wipe out the few that make it here, but it's great that they arrived at all.

The best birds, however, are probably the Siskins and Redpolls. Barely five minutes go by in winter without hearing the twitterings of one or the other, though getting good views of these little acrobats high in the birches and alders can be difficult. With luck, you may also find Crossbills in the pines and larches – again, the call is the give-away.

In birdwatching terms, Buchan CP has plenty to offer. While you might not drop a visit to Pagham to come here, it is not a site to be overlooked either!

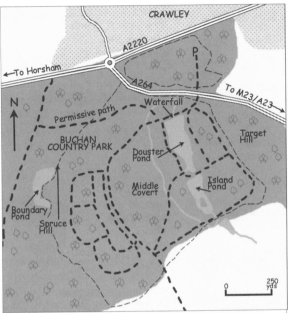

Access details

2 miles SW of Crawley town centre)

Easy to find, come off the M23/A23 at J11 (Pease Pottage) and take A264 towards Horsham. At second roundabout, the CP is signed. Turn R onto A2220, and the entrance is on R, but you need to go to the next roundabout and double back to access the entrance (TQ245346). From Crawley itself, the CP is very poorly signed, but follow the signs to Horsham, and the CP is signed at A2220 roundabout

just before the entrance.

BY TRAIN: No direct access.
BY BUS: Difficult - No.1 loop from Crawley bus station travels along past entrance but on opposite side of dual carriageway!

Other nearby sites

Less than 10 miles: Warnham Mill Pond, St Leonard's Forest, Ardingly Reservoir

Key points

- Allow 2-plus hours
- 30-45 species
- SSSI, jointly owned and managed by WSCC, Barlavington Estate, Burton Park, SDCB and SWT
- Open at all times on designated paths
- Small free car park (15 cars) but no other facilities
- Well-marked nature trail, but can get very muddy in places
- Fairly flat terrain with limited wheelchair access but steep path out of the car park
- 15 dragonfly species possible too
- Very limited bus service

Contacts

Sussex Wildlife Trust
01273 492630

THIS VERY PLEASANT walk winds its way through the wonderfully wet and mixed woods around the millponds at Burton Mill. This is possibly Sussex's top site for Siskins (winter), Marsh Tits and, most sought-after of all, Lesser Spotted Woodpeckers. The ponds too are good for wintering ducks and summer dragonflies, ensuring that there is year-round interest at this site.

Target birds *All year* – Kingfisher (25%); Mandarin (20%); Lesser Spotted Woodpecker (15%). *Passage* – Hobby (30%). *Winter* – Redpoll (20%).

Other likely bird species

All year	Marsh Tit	Pochard
Waterbirds		Siskin
Woodland birds	*Breeding season*	
Farmland birds	Hirundines	*Occasional*
Shelduck		Water Rail
Little Owl	*Winter*	Crossbill
Grey Wagtail	Gadwall	
	Tufted Duck	

Background information and birding tips

GUARANTEES AND Lesser Spotted Woodpeckers don't go together, but you've got as good a chance here as almost anywhere. Even if you don't strike lucky, this two-mile walk around Burton Mill Pond is still pleasant and varied.

From the car park, we've seen Siskins and Marsh Tits, while Grey Wagtails hang around the private old mill building and mill-stream. Up above, the road edge gives unhindered views across Burton Mill Pond. We've never failed to see a good selection of common waterbirds here, with considerable numbers of Pochards and Tufted Ducks in winter, plus a few Gadwalls and maybe Shovelers too. Reed Warblers sing in summer, the time when Hobbies hawk for dragonflies.

A public footpath leads down the western edge of the pond into what looks like Burton Mill Lodge's garden. Before you need worry that you are trespassing, the path slips into a dense birch wood, then on into an open area with mature pines. A short loop path leads to one of the few other vantage points over the Mill Pond and is well worth the detour.

The main path then leads on amongst some eerie wet alder woodland. Keep your ears open all the way for Siskins, Redpolls, Marsh Tits and Lesser Spotted Woodpeckers. Piping calls of Teal from the dense woodland reveal just how wet it is in there. There are also some creaking old sweet chestnuts here, hole-heaven for Jackdaws, Stock Doves and Little Owls, though the latter take patience to find.

The track leads you out onto a little road. Turn left through an isolated little hamlet in the woods. The road ends here but the track leads on, down into a dip and up to the north edge of Chingford Pond. We've found this a more reliable site for Kingfishers in winter than Burton Mill. Duck here include regular Shelduck, Wigeon, Gadwall, Teal. It can have muddy margins good enough for a few passage waders. Even Little Egrets and Bittern now turn up from time to time.

The outflow of the pond leads down into a swamp of huge alders. Yes, we've seen Lesser Spotted Woodpeckers here but remember, no guarantees! Their calling and drumming is very much a March thing though, as once the leaves are out, the odds lengthen considerably. Mandarins are also possible here.

Turning left, the path tracks the southern shoreline of Burton Pond, although the open water is much hidden by trees. Siskin noise is fairly constant in winter, and Marsh Tits should make themselves apparent. The trail continues through muddy woodland, out into an area of small peat bogs called Black Hole, rich in dragonflies, before looping back onto the more open and heathy area of Welch's Common.

From here, the road can be followed down the hill back to the car park, or a loop can be done around the block of mature woodland opposite. All the way, the staple woodland species should be possible, with a high probability of picking up the other two woodpeckers, Nuthatches, Treecreepers, tits and summer warblers.

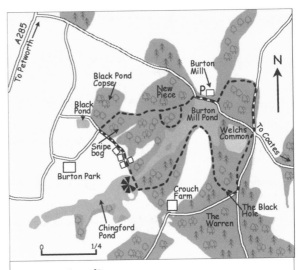

Access details

(2 miles S of Petworth)

Easiest access is from A285 Petworth-Chichester road. Turn E on minor road 2 miles S of Petworth/1 mile N of village of Duncton. The small Burton Mill car park is on L after 1mile, just before the Mill Pond opens up on the right. Alternatively, from B2138 between Watersfield and Fittleworth, turn W onto rather concealed minor road to Coates just N of small village filling station. Follow road for just over 2 miles, passing Coates Common, until the Mill Pond is unmissably on your L. At far end of Pond, turn sharp

R into car park (TQ978180).

BY TRAIN: No direct service.
BY BUS: Very difficult. No.99 Petworth-Chichester irregular service can deviate through Burton Mill on demand, but easier to alight on A285 north of Duncton and walk through to Burton Park.

Other nearby sites

Less than 5 miles: Lord's Piece; Lavington Common.
Less than 10 miles: Ambersham Common, Amberley Wild Brooks, Pulborough Brooks, Ebernoe Common.

Key points

- Allow 3-plus hours, often more

- Expect 15-30 species

- Area part NNR, part SSSI but also private farmland

- Open access at all times along public rights of way

- No facilities, nearest in Rottingdean or Lewes

- Steep climbs and long walks not suitable for wheelchairs

- Telescopes useful for scanning huge fields

- Sheep on the Downs, keep dogs under close control and obey Country Code

- Take a map, water and some nibbles

Contacts

For NNR: English Nature, Sussex & Surrey Team 01273 476595 sussex.surrey@ englishnature.org.uk

JUST INLAND from the busy Brighton to Newhaven seaside strip lies this great chunk of the South Downs, with a quite unexpected wildness and remoteness. Birds are generally scarce up here, but among 'goodies' like Hen Harriers and Corn Buntings, there is one real goal – passage Dotterels. They're far from easy or reliable, but well worth the effort should you find them.

Target birds *All year* – Corn Bunting (50%), Little Owl (15%). *Passage* – Turtle Dove (20%), Dotterel (10%), Ring Ouzel (5%). *Winter* – Peregrine (50%); Hen Harrier (40%), Merlin (10%).

Other likely bird species

All year	Wheatear	*Occasional*
Farmland birds	Whinchat	Merlin
Scrub birds	Redstart	Hobby
Stonechat		Grey Partridge
	Breeding season	Quail
Passage	Wheatear	Cuckoo
Warblers		Black Redstart
Yellow Wagtail	*Winter*	
	Thrushes	

Background information and birding tips

SUSSEX may look like the 'tame South' from the car, but this part of the Downs can make you feel quite small - don't underestimate it! It rises up from sea level to 646 feet at its peak on Newmarket Hill, and instead of being one big plateau, its core is riddled with deep steep dry valleys, miles from anywhere. Some of the valley bottoms and hill tops are planted with crops, there is some sheep grazing, and some unfertilised scrubby areas on the valley sides.

The key areas for 'trips' of Dotterels are Balsdean, Swanborough Hill and Newmarket Hill. There are three golden rules to help you find them:
1) they like recently tilled fields (where the surface is so littered with lumps of chalk it looks like Scottish mountain tops)

2) they must be the highest south-facing slopes.
3) the slope must be shallow. Then it is a case of concerted scanning.

Dotterels are possible both in spring and autumn, with peak times from mid April to mid May, and from mid August to mid September. In some years, 'trips' of up to a dozen birds stay for two or even three weeks. The problem is finding the time and energy to locate them!

Dotterel-time is also a time for passerine migration, especially in autumn. Redstarts and Whinchats may turn up in the scrub, especially somewhere like the florally-rich Castle Hill NNR. Streams of hirundines may pass over and even small bushes can temporarily host singing Willow Warblers or Chiffchaffs. Wheatear passage is so protracted that they seem to be present half the year – the occasional pair may even try to breed. Yellow Wagtails are also frequent up here, wherever cattle graze.

Something quite exceptional is the regular and well-studied passage of Ring Ouzels here. Like the Dotterels, they are not guaranteed, but they have a clear preference for the steep north-facing slopes such as Cold Coombes and there is evidence that they are faithful to these sites just like waders returning to favoured estuaries.

Each season brings different raptors to the Downs, with Hen Harriers passing through almost daily in winter and Peregrines regularly coming up from the coast. Merlins are occasional, and, on passage, Hobbies, Buzzards, and even Honey Buzzards and Ospreys are possible. The secret to seeing these is spending plenty of hours up here.

Winter stubble fields can attract Corn Buntings, Yellowhammers and Linnets, up to 100 of each. In spring, the hills are alive with the sound of, yes, music – the songs of Sky Larks, Meadow Pipits, Linnets and Whitethroats.

Other nearby sites

Less than 5 miles: Brighton-Newhaven Cliffs; Brighton Marina; Hollingbury Camp; Sheepcote Valley; Lewes Brooks.
Less than 10 miles: Adur Estuary; Chailey Common; Ditchling Beacon to Ashcombe Bottom; Newhaven Tidemills.

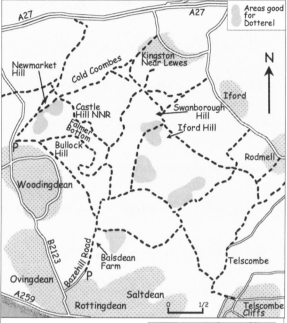

Access details

(Large area bounded by A27 (Falmer to Lewes), B2123 (Falmer to Rottingdean), A259 coast road, and the Newhaven to Lewes minor road)

Easiest access is from Woodingdean. On B2123 to Falmer there is a small rough car park with height-restriction barrier on the brow of the Downs as Woodingdean's houses end. (TQ356063). From here, *relatively* flat walks lead out over Newmarket Hill.

For Balsdean, come up through Rottingdean from the coast on the B2123, navigate the one-way loop, and turn R up Bazehill Road just after the zebra crossing on a ramp! Limited verge-side parking after 0.5 mile (TQ372033) - the road from here is private to vehicles but accessible on foot.

For Swanborough Hill (steep climb over stiles from Kingston) walk up past Kingston church, and the footpath onto the Downs is clearly signed. Roadside parking is limited in Kingston, but note there is strictly no parking in Swanborough village itself.

BY TRAIN: No direct access.
BY BUS: No.22 from Churchill Square, Brighton by far the best, stopping near car park marked at top of Woodingdean. Nos. 52 and 84 less frequent. No.123 serves Newhaven-Lewes road.

Key points

- Allow 1.5-plus hours
- Expect 20-35 species
- SSSI and LNR
- Open access at all times
- Three good sandy car parks for about 15 cars each
- No other facilities
- Some muddy paths but many are dry most of year but not suitable for wheelchairs
- Keep strictly to paths and keep dogs under control
- Heathland is at high risk of fire at all times – take every precaution not to cause them
- Grazing being introduced on some of the commons to help management

Contacts

East Sussex County Council
01273 482670

A VERY PLEASANT walk on Chailey's five wood-fringed commons can produce a nice mix of heath and woodland birds such as Stonechats, Buzzards, Nuthatches and Yellowhammers. The purring of Turtle Doves can be heard in late spring and Tree Pipits just about hang on here, too.

Target birds *Breeding season* – Turtle Dove (50%), Tree Pipit (20%). *Winter* – Redpoll (40%).

Other likely bird species

All year	*Breeding season*	*Winter*
Scrub birds	Warblers	Thrushes
Woodland birds	Cuckoo	Meadow Pipit
Moorhen	Swallow	
Kestrel	House Martin	*Occasional*
Nuthatch	Reed Bunting	Buzzard
Treecreeper		Dartford Warbler
		Spotted Flycatcher

Background information and birding tips

THE FIVE COMMONS that make up Chailey Common have a much more intimate feel than the grandness of the heathlands at Ashdown just 15 minutes up the road. With so few pines compared to the other heaths in this book, Chailey's commons have a leafier greener feel, especially in spring, and are a delight to walk around.

The site is looked after by the Chailey Commons Society working closely with the rangers from East Sussex County Council.

The Commons have areas of gorse scrub, scattered birches, some heather and a considerable amount of bracken. This is all edged with deciduous woodland, including some grand old trees. Paths wind their way around all of the commons allowing plenty of chance to explore. If this was your local patch, you'd probably be very happy indeed, with a great range of birds, particularly passerines, by which to mark the passing of the seasons.

Of the five commons, Redhouse (or Chailey) Common is the largest and perhaps has the widest variety of birds. From the top, there are views across to the distant Ashdown Forest. The

Blackbirds are common among the woodland birds at Chailey.
(Steve Cale)

northern slope is the best place we've found for Tree Pipits on the commons, though numbers are now very low, strange considering how ideal the habitat looks. The mature oak woodland at the foot of the slope is great for Nuthatches and other woodland birds. The large white windmill on top of the common is a good marker to ensure you don't get disoriented.

Memorial Common has commanding views across to the South Downs and its warm south-facing slope has large stands of old gorse, plus the most heather of any of the commons. Stonechats and Linnets are likely and it is an ideal place for Turtle Doves in spring.

Pound Common has another large area of gorse on its eastern side and, tucked away behind birches on Romany Ridge Common, are some open areas of dry grassland and boggy depressions. The fifth area of common, Lane End (to the north of Redhouse, and not on the map), is the smallest and perhaps least interesting bird-wise of the five.

In spring, wherever you are on the commons, Willow Warblers, Chiffchaffs, Robins and Whitethroats abound, with small numbers of breeding Yellowhammers and a couple of pairs of Reed Buntings. Your warbler list may be further enhanced with Garden Warblers and Lesser Whitethroats, with Blackcaps, tits and thrushes in the woodland.

It is in summer that the

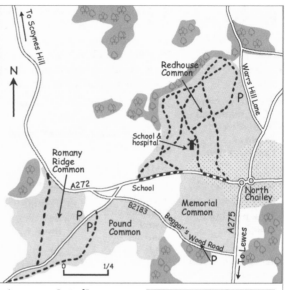

Access details

(4 miles SE of Haywards Heath)

On A275 Lewes-East Grinstead road, 0.5mile N of double roundabout (where A272 crosses A275), turn L up road called Warrs Hill. 0.25 mile on L is Redhouse Common car park (TQ391217). Good parking available on smaller commons too, especially for Pound and Romany Ridge Commons at TQ378207 and TQ376207 respectively.

BY TRAIN: No direct access.
BY BUS: No.31 Haywards Heath-Uckfield along A275 by far best service, or No.121 Sheffield Park-Lewes

commons are at their most pleasant though. They are warm and open and there is the chance of a Hobby hawking overhead, or just some House Martins and Swifts from the nearby villages. In winter, it is all rather more austere, but Redpolls and Siskins are both still possible.

Other nearby sites

Less than 10 miles: Ardingly Reservoir, Ashdown Forest, Ditchling Beacon to Ashcombe Bottom, Castle Hill to Swanborough Hill, Weir Wood Reservoir

Key points

- Allow 1.5-plus hours

- Expect 20-30 species

- Privately-owned SSSI, managed by Sussex Downs Conservation Board

- Open access at all times

- Free parking in rough lane

- No other facilities on site; nearest facilities in Petersfield

- Can get muddy but many paths dry throughout. Not suitable for wheelchairs

- Keep strictly to paths and keep dogs under close control to protect ground-nesting birds

- High risk of fire in all seasons – take every precaution not to cause them

Contacts

Sussex Wealden Greensand Heaths Project c/o Sussex Downs Conservation Board, Northern Area Office 01730 812134

HOW PLEASANTLY surprised we were when we first visited Chapel Common! So far out to the west of the county, it rarely seems to feature on Sussex birdwatching itineraries but is actually a very attractive and little-visited block of varied heathland and dry grassland, with Nightjars, Dartford Warblers and especially Wood Larks.

Target birds *All year* – Dartford Warbler (50%). *Breeding season* – Tree Pipit (95%), Wood Lark (60%), Nightjar (at dusk hear 80%, see 70%), Woodcock (at dusk 70%). *Winter* – Redpoll (20%).

Other likely bird species

All year	**Reed Bunting**	*Winter*
Scrub birds		**Meadow Pipit**
Woodland birds	*Passage*	
Kestrel	Swallow	*Occasional*
Stonechat	Swift	**Lesser Spotted Woodpecker**
Mistle Thrush	*Breeding season*	**Crossbill**
Nuthatch	Sky Lark	

Background information and birding tips

MANAGEMENT of Chapel Common was handed to the Sussex Downs Conservation Board in 1996, and they and the owners have created a wonderfully varied heathland site where the public have pretty much unrestricted access (but please keep to established tracks).

The bumpy lane where most people park is heavily wooded on the left side, with some old oaks alongside a pine plantation. Great Spotted Woodpeckers and Nuthatches are possible the moment you step out of the car. On the opposite side of the lane, the land looks open but not heath-like – on a first visit, you might wonder if you're in the right place. You are!

This open area is the first habitat segment of three. Until recently, this first block was enclosed fields, but the fences have gone and the land converted to dry grassland.

Sky Larks can be heard above the meadow at Chapel Common. (John Davis)

north-east either across the middle or along the edge of the meadow, the next habitat block is a shallow valley cutting across the Common where there is a rich mosaic of gorse, heather and rabbit-grazed grassland.

Then, beyond some pines and birch, the final block is almost wholly heather. Around the outside of it all is a thick fringe of mature birch trees, pines and oak. Indeed, there has been some considerable thinning and felling of some of these trees in the last few years, opening even more heathland.

Sky Larks sing above the meadow, and you can often hear them and Wood Larks simultaneously. The latter can be seen in and around any of the open areas. They move out in autumn, but by February are often back on territory, and the fluty song of the male is the easiest way to find them. Sometimes, however, you don't see them until they rise up calling from the path right in front of you. We've yet to fail for Wood Larks here in the breeding season.

The areas of gorse are the best for Dartford Warblers. With many of the gorse bushes being 12ft or higher, it is easy to overlook a tiny warbler, unless they too strike up song. If only they were as obliging as the Stonechats which sit around conspicuously all year!

Some of the pines are good for Crossbills in peak years, Siskins are regular and Redpolls are likely to be seen in winter

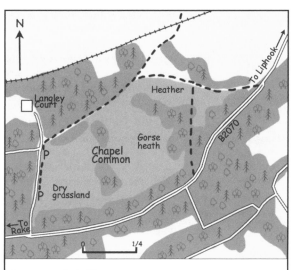

Access details

(5 miles NE of Petersfield)

Chapel Common lies alongside B2070 Petersfield-Liphook road. Just NE of Rake village look for unsigned track to N just where the road becomes a dual carriageway. This track is rather rough, but there are plenty of parking opportunities along the righthand side (SU813284). Park and walk straight out through the line of trees onto Chapel Common.

BY TRAIN: No direct access.
BY BUS: Very difficult,
Nos.294/295 Lindford-Petersfield daily only.

as they buzz over the old birches. Tree Pipits are still common, and there is always the chance of, for example, Lesser Spotted Woodpeckers around the edge or even a Great Grey Shrike in winter.

We don't have a set route here as the site is small enough to just wind your way along the many paths, circumnavigating blocks of gorse, following up interesting bird calls. There are plenty of peaty ponds to check out for dragonflies in summer, when silver-studded blue butterflies, common lizards and adders also add to the wildlife on offer.

Other nearby sites

Less than 10 miles: Woolbeding Common, Iping & Stedham Commons

69

Key points

- Allow 1.5-plus hours
- Expect 30-45 species
- Pits are private, but SOS provides tern rafts and maintains reedbeds
- Public rights of way open at all times
- No facilities, hides or designated parking
- Nearest facilities in Chichester
- Paths flat but can get muddy
- Good access by bus
- Telescope helpful but not essential
- Keep strictly to public footpaths (not suitable for wheelchairs)

NONE OF THESE 20 gravel pits on the south and east side of Chichester is very big, all are private, and many have very restricted viewing, but they are definitely worth the effort. There can be good birdwatching at any season - winter waterfowl together with passage and breeding terns are the staple species spiced up by occasional rarer grebes, ducks and terns.

Target birds Moderate numbers of wintering duck, including numerous Gadwall (95%), plus *All year* – Kingfisher (20%). *Passage* – Black Tern (10%), Little Ringed Plover (20%). *Winter* – Chiffchaff (20%), Smew (5%), Water Rail (5%), one of diver, rarer grebe or Long-tailed Duck (5%).

Other likely bird species

All year	Warblers	Shoveler
Wildfowl	Shelduck	Pochard
Gulls	Common Sandpiper	Lapwing
Woodland birds	Green Sandpiper	
Garden birds		*Occasional*
Great Crested Grebe	*Breeding season*	Bittern
Pied Wagtail	Common Tern	Goldeneye
Rook		Goosander
Goldfinch	*Winter*	Osprey
	Thrushes	Little Gull
Passage	Wigeon	Cetti's Warbler
Hirundines	Gadwall	

Background information and birding tips

THE COMPLEX of gravel pits around Chichester is the largest in Sussex and it is an ideal site to combine with somewhere like Pagham. Indeed, it is worth a quick drop in at any time.

With some pits having no public access whatsoever, especially those muddy new diggings so beloved by waders, many good birds must slip through unnoticed. Mercifully, a public footpath intersects the main group of mature pits south of Chichester and allows adequate viewing. Parking is a problem, though, limited to little more than a couple of small rough lay-bys. Keep to the footpaths, as other tracks around the pits are private.

Ivy Lake is the pit not to miss. It's the biggest but seems to be good ecologically too. In winter, it is often carpeted with a thousand or more Coots, and impressive numbers of Gadwalls associating with them. Lower numbers of Shovelers, Pochards, Wigeon and Tufted Ducks are usually present too, plus plenty of Mute Swans and both common grebes. Ivy Lake occasionally produces Slavonian or Black-necked Grebes as well, with several records of long-staying Long-tailed Ducks.

In spring, migrant hirundines shoot low over the water, then throughout the summer Common Terns fish here. They breed very successfully on rafts maintained by Sussex Ornithological Society on one of the less-accessible lakes. In autumn, Black Terns are regular, with White-winged Blacks having occurred on several occasions.

Beyond Ivy Lake are the West and East Trout Lakes with yet more Gadwalls, Coots and Tufted Ducks. In spring, Reed Warblers defend territories in the flimsiest strips of reed while, where the lakes are thickly edged with willows and hawthorn, we've seen wintering Chiffchaffs. Green and Great Spotted Woodpeckers, Tits and finches are also frequent.

The track then reaches the quiet Peckhams Copse Lane. In front of you but behind the trees and very difficult to see, is New Lake, also known as Scrapyard Pit. Runcton and Vinnetrow lakes, with somewhat better viewing, are reached by turning left along the Lane. They are perhaps better than Ivy for turning up the odd Smew. Cetti's Warblers may also occur from time to time in the waterside bushes.

Away from this group of pits, try Westhampnett Pit to the northeast (not shown on map). An active windsurfing club means disturbance is high, but birds still turn up. Rutland Way is the best vantage point but suffers from obscuring bushes. When water levels are low though, you should be able to see a shingle bar that attracts roosting Lapwings and migrant waders such as Common Sandpipers and Greenshanks.

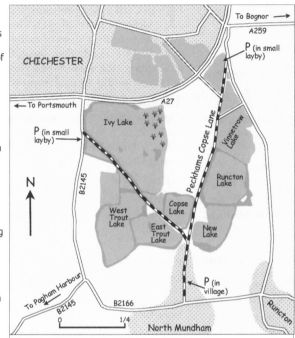

Access details

(1mile S of Chichester city centre)

For Ivy Lake: Turn S off A27 Chichester Bypass at roundabout onto B2145 to Selsey. Indicate L immediately, and in barely 100 yards, pull into lay-by on L used by fishermen/ dog walkers. There is space here for only about 6 cars (SU868034). Alternatively, another layby is at SU877038, or park considerately in North Mundham playing field car park (SU876025).

For Westhampnett Pit: Turn N off A27 at the huge roundabout E of Chichester in front of McDonalds signed to

Westhampnett. Take dual carriageway 0.5 mile to next roundabout, double back and, just before rejoining A27, swing sharply into Rutland Way and park on roadside (SU877057).

BY TRAIN: 1.5 mile walk from Chichester station.
BY BUS: No.51 Chichester-Selsey and No.60 Bognor-Midhurst pass by Ivy Lake and stop nearby.

Key points

- Allow 3-plus hours

- Expect 40-70 species

- Part of Chichester & Langstone Harbours SPA and SSSI; Nutbourne Marshes LNR on west side

- Public rights of way open at all times

- Very restricted parking and no other facilities directly on site

- Good pub in Chidham village – "The Old House at Home"

- Some muddy paths, but terrain generally flat and good

- At Cobnor, car park and toilet for the disabled and path suitable for wheelchairs

- Telescope useful

Contacts

Chichester Harbour Conservancy
01243 512301

THE CHIDHAM peninsula is a far less-watched part of Chichester Harbour than Thorney Island or East Head, but offers excellent views of many of the harbour's waders and wildfowl. In addition, the quiet narrow lanes, farmland and estuary-side walks have a rural timelessness that makes for a wonderfully tranquil escape.

Target birds

Wildfowl and waders, plus: *All year* – Peregrine (40%), Grey Partridge (30%), Corn Bunting (20%). *Passage* – Whimbrel (25%), Osprey (5%). *Breeding season* – Turtle Dove (40%). *Winter* – Goldeneye (70%), Avocet (40%).

Other likely bird species

All year	Wheatear	Golden Plover
Waterbirds		Knot
Wildfowl	*Breeding season*	Black-tailed Godwit
Coastal waders	Sandwich Tern	Bar-tailed Godwit
Gulls	Common Tern	Curlew
Farmland birds		Rock Pipit
Little Egret	*Winter*	Grey Wagtail
Sheluck	Thrushes	
Pied Wagtail	Brent Goose	*Occasional*
Stonechat	Wigeon	Hobby
	Pintail	Ruff
Passage	Red-breasted Merganser	
Hirundines	Avocet	

Background information and birding tips

BIRDWATCHERS who like to escape the crowds will find Chidham is a venue with much to offer. A four-hour ramble here can rack up 70 species of bird but far fewer fellow humans. Be aware though that there are no facilities, except a small car park and a great pub!

The birdwatching experience at Chidham mirrors that at Thorney to the west, but without the military presence! Two great fingers of water, the Bosham Channel and the Thorney Channel, cut up either side of Chidham creating a two-mile long peninsula.

From the car park, a permissive footpath leads out east to the water's edge. The village of Bosham is opposite and the yacht-filled channel should hold Little Grebes and Red-breasted Mergansers. Except at high tide, waders such as Curlews and Redshanks are likely out on the mud, so a telescope really does help.

Heading south, there are some brackish pools and ditches inside the seawall, which attract Redshanks over from the estuary and the odd Green Sandpiper. The fields nearby are grazed by Brent Geese in winter.

After half a mile, the footpath

winds around the back of the private Cobnor Activities Centre, enabling you to see some garden bird species. It passes a little car park reserved for the disabled (reached by driving on from the main car park). You then emerge right onto the muddy shore on the 'Cobnor Footpath for the Disabled', with gloriously close and unimpeded views of the muddy shore. Here some of the waders can be seen up close – Grey Plovers, Turnstones, Curlews – usually with Little Egrets too and Brent Geese in winter.

The Disabled Path ends after a few hundred yards, and the path from here is more of a scramble along the shingly shore. It is worth making the effort in order to have views across the Nutbourne Marshes LNR, a huge area of inter-tidal mud owned by Chichester Harbour Conservancy. Ahead of you stretch the linear (and inaccessible) North and South Stakes Islands, the remains of a failed 19th Century seawall now used by nesting Ringed Plovers and sometimes by terns and gulls.

It is a long haul up the west side of the peninsula, with birds very distant at low tide. The most reliable area for birds is the bay north of Chidham Point, where gulls, waders and wildfowl gather, including Pintails and Black-tailed Godwits. Scan inland where the fields still hold Grey Partridges and Corn Buntings.

Footpaths then cut back across the neck of the

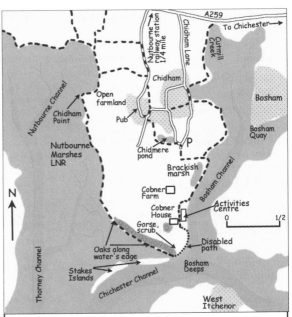

Access details

(4.5 miles W of Chichester city centre)

From the E, turn off A27 at the A259 roundabout just W of Chichester towards Fishbourne and Emsworth. After 3.5 miles, turn L down Chidham Lane onto the Chidham peninsula (just W of 'The Bosham' pub). From W, follow A259 from Emsworth for 3 miles, turning R down Cot Lane just after L turn to Nutbourne station. Chidham and Cot Lanes form a loop road around the top of the peninsula. Follow either Lane just more than a mile to Cobnor Farm Amenity Car Park on sharp bend (SU793034).

There is 1.9m height barrier.

BY TRAIN: 1 mile walk from Nutbourne station to estuary edge.
BY BUS: Not easy – No.700 Brighton-Southsea passes along A259 at half-hourly intervals, with subsequent walk. No services to Chidham itself.

peninsula to complete the circuit, or you can walk the quiet lanes back to the car park via the pub and Chidmere Pond.

Other nearby sites

Less than 5 miles: Thorney Island.
Less than 10 miles: Chichester Gravel pits, Kingley Vale, Pagham Harbour.

Key points

- Allow 2-plus hours

- Expect 20-35 species

- Both Rings are SSSIs

- Public rights of way open at all times

- Parking at either end of walk

- No other facilities

- Some mud possible, and steep climbs difficult to avoid

- Not suitable for wheelchairs

- Birdwatch as part of a long walk

THIS FIVE MILE walk takes you from one side of the Downs to the other, with the ancient forts of Chanctonbury Ring and Cissbury Ring at either end. With a broad range of woodland, downland and farmland birds and, with Cissbury attracting migrants, on a good bird day it can be productive. Whatever the birds you find though, make sure you enjoy the sense of glorious openness and freedom.

Target birds *Breeding season* – Corn Bunting (65%), Turtle Dove (50%).

Other likely bird species

All year	*Passage*	*Winter*
Woodland birds	Hirundines	Gulls
Farmland birds	Warblers	Thrushes
Buzzard	Yellow Wagtail	
Red-legged Partridge	Tree Pipit	*Occasional*
	Redstart	Peregrine
Stonechat	Whinchat	Merlin
Marsh Tit	Wheatear	Grey Partridge
Nuthatch	Spotted Flycatcher	Quail
Treecreeper		Ring Ouzel
	Breeding season	Firecrest
	Lapwing	Pied Flycatcher

Background information and birding tips

THE DISTANCE between the northern scarp slope and the southern edge of the South Downs gets progressively narrower the further east you get and here, north of Worthing, it is only about three miles across. Chanctonbury Ring, at the top of the northern scarp slope, is some 175 feet higher than Cissbury Ring, but it does not rise above the surrounding countryside in quite the same dramatic 360° way as Cissbury does.

Cissbury, being the last high ground before the Channel, becomes the focus for migrants dropping in on their journeys north and south, as well as providing a guideline for migrants 'coasting' east and west.

If starting at Cissbury we

recommend an early start in autumn to get the best of the migration. It is quite a steep climb up to the Ring itself, which is a mile-round oval of ancient fortifications. Within the Ring are patches of gorse, good for Stonechats, chalk grassland, where Green Woodpeckers collect ants, and a considerable amount of berry-bearing scrub. It is here in autumn that warblers such as Blackcaps, Whitethroats and Chiffchaffs gather, often for several days. It can be exceptional too for Spotted Flycatchers.

Inevitably, there are often smaller numbers of other migrants in among them, including Pied Flycatchers, Redstarts, Garden Warblers, Lesser Whitethroats and Ring Ouzels, with always the chance of something rarer. Activity is at its height in the

Contacts

Sussex Downs Conservation Board
01273 625242

Access details

(Area 5 miles N of Worthing)

FOR CISSBURY RING: On A24 in Findon Valley, 1.5 miles N of A27, parking for Cissbury Ring is clearly signed. Turn into Maytree Avenue, then L into Storrington Rise. There is good parking for 15 cars 100 yards up where bungalows end (TQ129077). Walk straight ahead up hill to Cissbury. Alternatively, 1mile N of here, turn E off A24 at roundabout, go through Findon village, parking is 1mile beyond village under north scarp of Cissbury Ring (TQ138085).

FOR CHANCTONBURY RING: on A283, 3 miles NW of Steyning, the Ring is clearly signposted up a very narrow lane opposite the turn to Wiston. Sussex Downs Conservation Board car park for 20 cars on L after 0.75 mile (TQ145124).

BY TRAIN: No direct access.

BY BUS: Cissbury Ring – Nos.1 and 2 from Worthing to Midhurst and Horsham, respectively pass through Findon; Chanctonbury Ring – Steyning-Pulborough No.100 stops at bottom of Chanctonbury Ring Road.

first hours of daylight. This is the time too for Tree Pipits, hirundines, wagtails and finches to pass overhead – anytime between late August and early October should be fruitful.

From Cissbury, a farm track leads north to Chanctonbury across the downs. It is blissfully isolated – no roads, no houses. Don't expect lots of species on the open downs though, but nevertheless the skies should be full of Sky Larks from

February onwards. Corn Buntings sing from about May and species such as Yellowhammers and Red-legged Partridges are year-round. You need luck these days to find Grey Partridges though, indeed you're more likely to see something like a Peregrine hurtling through.

In winter, elegant streams of Common Gulls wander across the sheep pastures. Fieldfares and Redwings can also be expected, but the Corn

Buntings, which flock-up out of the breeding season, take some finding.

If parking at the foot of the north scarp, near Chanctonbury Ring, the steep walk up through Chalkpit Wood is good, if a little muddy - Nuthatches and Marsh Tits are frequent. Chanctonbury Ring itself, encircled by stark windswept beech trees, is not the migrant magnet that Cissbury is, but watch for Buzzards sweeping over the scarp slope.

75

Key points

- Allow 3-plus hours

- Expect 35-45 species

- Dunes are SSSI and part LNR

- Open at all times

- Good pay car park 1st March-30th Sept, but it is busy with holidaymakers throughout this period; limited free roadside parking in winter

- Café and toilets at Littlehampton West Beach

- Small café and toilet at Climping Beach in summer only

- Keep strictly to public footpaths

- Flat site, but some walking on shingle and some mud

- Not suitable for wheelchairs

THE BIGGEST STRETCH of coastline to have escaped the 30-mile urban sprawl from Pagham to Brighton, is near the village of Climping. It can provide some rewarding birdwatching from autumn through to spring. Sanderlings and other waders ply the tideline, there are farmland birds right behind the beach and the bushes, particularly around Littlehampton's golf course, attract migrants.

Target birds

Coastal waders and passerine migrants, plus: *All year* – Grey Partridge (30%). *Passage (autumn)* – Hobby (35%), Firecrest (20%). *Winter* – Kingfisher (on the River Arun - 5%).

Other likely bird species

All year	Brent Goose	Brent Goose
Gulls	Red-breasted	Sanderling
Farmland birds	Merganser	Curlew
Cormorant	Common Scoter	Grey Wagtail
Great Spotted Woodpecker	Sandwich Tern	
	Wheatear	*Occasional*
Stonechat		Red-throated Diver
	Breeding season	Little Egret
Passage	Reed Warbler	Jack Snipe
Hirundines		Snipe
Warblers	*Winter*	Tawny Pipit
Great Crested Grebe	Coastal waders	Pied Flycatcher
Gannet	Thrushes	Snow Bunting

Background information and birding tips

FROM THE CAR PARK at Atherington, the walk west along the beach towards Middleton-on-Sea leads to some little woodland ponds, which attract autumn migrants – flycatchers, warblers etc – with Pallas's Warbler possible in November. In winter, the shingle beach between the groynes is good for Rock Pipits. Stonechats and Corn Buntings are possible on the open stretch towards Middleton, where the path eventually passes some extensively wooded gardens at Poole Place. This good for yet more migrants.

Most birding interest is had,

however, by walking east from the car park. From the top of the seawall, you can watch the sea and beach in one direction and the farmland behind. On the sea, Great Crested Grebes and maybe a Red-throated Diver may be seen in winter and some spring's big passage of wildfowl and waders will be visible. The concave coastline however,, means the birds rarely pass close by except in ideal south-easterlies.

Of greater interest, is the sandy tide-edge that attracts a good mix of waders throughout the winter. Likely are Ringed Plovers, Oystercatchers, Redshanks, Dunlins, Turnstones and Grey Plovers. The key species though is Sanderling, with a regular

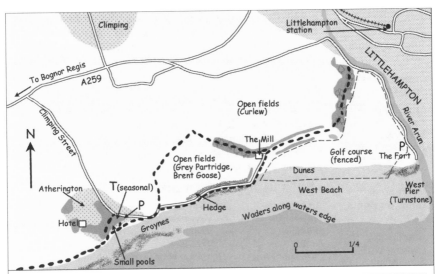

Access details

(4 miles ENE of Bognor Regis)

For Climping Beach, take the A259 either E out of Bognor or W from the Littlehampton bypass. Turn south on the road signed Atherington. Follow this road 1mile to beach. Parking in summer is in grass fields either side of end of road; in winter park considerately on roadside (TQ005008).

BY TRAIN: 1.25 miles walk from Littlehampton station. *BY BUS:* Not easy. No.63 Elmer-Bognor gives 1mile walk east along beach to site.

flock of more than fifty. At high tide, the waders sometimes use the open fields to roost.

Here too are regular Grey Partridges, plus occasionally Brent Geese. Curlews, Linnets, Greenfinches and Sky larks can also be expected.

A narrow road runs behind the seawall. This is flanked by hawthorn, blackthorn and tamarisk bushes, which hold migrants in autumn, with Firecrests reliable by October. The bushes are especially good where the road turns inland to some cottages.

The road is private and the public footpath runs alongside the golf course, which itself is adored by Wheatears and Whinchats. Given a run of easterly winds in September, Tawny Pipit records can match those at Beachy Head.

The public footpath cuts along the back of the golf course. The further you go, the better it gets, leading into a gem of a wooded corridor teeming with Blackcaps in autumn. This is a great spot to try for anything from Red-breasted Flycatchers to Yellow-browed Warblers and you could be the finder, with the few enough birders that are here.

The track suddenly emerges on the road down to Littlehampton West Beach car park. For an enjoyable circuit, walk down to the beach on the banks of the urban River Arun looking in winter for Grey Wagtails and Kingfishers.

Turnstones use the breakwater at the river's mouth and the walk back along the shore under the dunes (used by naturists), is good for Stonechats, passage Wheatears and winter flocks of Greenfinches. There are also annual records of Snow Buntings and even a Rustic Bunting in 1991.

77

Key points

- Allow 2.5-plus hours
- Expect 30-45 species
- Filsham is owned by Hastings Borough Council and leased to SWT
- Open at all times on rights of way
- Good free parking with 6' 6" height restriction barrier
- No facilities on site, but everything nearby in Bexhill/St Leonards/ Hastings
- Can be very muddy but terrain flat
- Not suitable for wheelchairs
- Well served by buses
- Telescope can help with Water Pipits

Contacts

For Filsham Reedbeds: Sussex Wildlife Trust 01273 492630

BEGINNING inauspiciously in a playing-field car park, this walk leads into a pleasant rural valley next to Sussex's largest reedbed. As well as breeding Bearded Tits and plenty of passerine migrants, Combe Haven's claim to fame is that it is the best place in Sussex – if not the country – for wintering Water Pipits. But be warned, they can be shy!

Target birds *All year* – Bearded Tit (40% in still

weather), Water Rail (hear 60%, see 5%, lower in summer), Cetti's Warbler (hear 30%, see 5%). *Passage* – Tree Pipit (autumn flyover 30%). *Breeding season* - Hobby (50%). *Winter* – Water Pipit (80%), Redpoll (25%), Kingfisher (20%).

Other likely bird species

All year	Little Egret	Meadow Pipit
Waterbirds	Green Sandpiper	
Wildfowl	Common Sandpiper	*Occasional*
Gulls	Tree Pipit	Bittern
Farmland birds	Yellow Wagtail	Marsh Harrier
Woodland birds	Grey Wagtail	Lesser Spotted Woodpecker
Stonechat		
	Winter	Whinchat
Passage	Shelduck	Ring Ouzel
Hirundines	Lapwing	
Warblers	Snipe	

Background information and birding tips

INITIAL APPEARANCES can be deceptive. As you pull into the car park, with a caravan site to your right, playing fields to the left and a mountain of a tip, heaving with Herring Gulls, ahead of you, you'd be forgiven for thinking of turning back. Resist the urge!

Take the track (sometimes a mud bath) up the left-hand side of the stream, with the static caravans on the opposite bank. After about 300 yards, the caravans end, a reedy area opens to your left and the bushes thicken on the far bank. Especially in spring and autumn, birds such as warblers, tits and crests should be apparent.

Cross the well-made footbridge, turn left and then right onto the new boardwalk, erected in winter 2002/3. It's fabulous - or at least we anticipate it will be - as it leads right into the heart of Filsham Reedbed, a Sussex Wildlife Trust reserve and the largest reedbed in Sussex (though that doesn't mean it's huge!).

Don't expect Marsh Harriers, but this reedbed does have breeding Bearded Tits, large numbers of Reed Warblers, plenty of squealing Water Rails. There are elusive, but regular, wintering Bitterns, Cetti's Warblers (more in autumn), loads of Reed Buntings and big autumn roosts of Swallows, Sand Martins and Yellow Wagtails. The boardwalk ends at a viewing platform with reedscreens.

Retracing your steps along the boardwalk, turn right up the riverbank. At the next footbridge, the beauty of the valley unfolds. It is no more than a green marshy valley flanked with woods, but it's a world away from the unseen coastal conurbation only a mile to your left - a Haven indeed.

The public footpath leads just a short way up the Haven before crossing the river towards the tip. It affords enough views, however, of more swamp to the right of the river with attendant Reed Buntings, and Stonechats along the path edge.

It is the meadows on the southern side, half underwater in winter, that are the real focus though. This is the place to look for Water Pipits. They need effort – they are shy, and often tantalisingly fly up before you get onto them, only to then disappear a mile up the valley. But, with patience, we have had stunning views, though a telescope can be essential to firmly ID such a difficult bird. And don't imagine that any pipit is going to be Water - Meadows can be just as common!

Combe Haven has one more trick up its sleeve – migrants. The valley is a well-used flight line by migrants in autumn – Tree Pipits overhead, the odd Ring Ouzel or Firecrest or even rarer (Radde's Warbler for example) in the bushes; even Honey Buzzards are annual. So while there is no guarantee here of a bird-filled visit, more often than not something is seen to make it worthwhile.

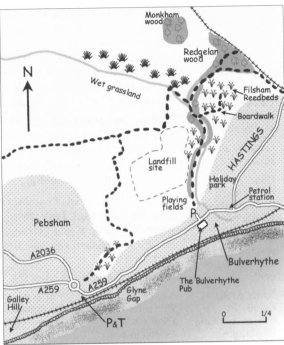

**Access details
(2.5 miles W of Hastings)**

Access from A259 in Bulverhythe, half way between Bexhill and Hastings.
Travelling E, 1 mile after the big roundabout at Bexhill trading estate, look for The Bulverhythe pub on R, then turn into playing field car park on L just before a red pillar-box.
From Hastings, go under railway bridge at W end of seafront, straight on at lights, pass Murco petrol station, and turn R is after 200 yards just after phone box. There is a 6'6" height-restriction barrier.

The car park itself is a bit of rough gravel behind some orange cabins (TQ775087).

BY TRAIN: 2 mile walk from Bulverhythe station.
BY BUS: Very good - numerous services (eg Nos.97, 98, 303, 710) between Hastings and Bexhill stop nearby along A259.

Other nearby sites

Less than 10 miles: Fore Wood RSPB, Pevensey Levels, Hastings Country Park.

Key points

- Allow 2.5-plus hours

- Expect 40-60 species

- Country Park with SSSI status

- Open at all times

- Good visitor centre with restaurant/ toilets

- Good pay & display car park with ice-cream van!

- Some paths muddy in winter; walking on shingle necessary to get to beach

- Limited wheelchair access pedestrian track gives good wheelchair access down east side of valley

Contacts

Sussex Downs
Conservation Board
(Seven Sisters Country
Park Office)
01323 871095
east@
southdowns-aonb.gov.uk

CUCKMERE HAVEN is where the River Cuckmere breaks through the famous sheer cliffs of the Seven Sisters and Seaford Head. The area and its picture-postcard scenery are very popular. The heavily canalised river holds back the tides from the wet meadows and disconnected river meanders. The range of birdlife is great, with waders, Little Egrets and wildfowl and the chance of a rarity.

There are plans which, if approved, will return the valley over the next decade to what it once was – a tidal estuary. Timings are uncertain but, if and when it happens, the birdwatching is likely to improve and the walks will remain just as, if not more, beautiful.

Target birds

Small numbers of waders and wildfowl, plus: *All year* – Rock Pipit (90%), Peregrine (80%), Kingfisher (50%, higher in winter), Little Owl (5%). *Passage* – Whimbrel (spring - 30%). *Winter* –Mediterranean Gull (10%).

Other likely bird species

All year	Warblers	*Occasional*
Waterbirds	Greenshank	White-fronted Goose
Wildfowl	Yellow Wagtail	Brent Goose
Coastal waders	Wheatear	Red-breasted Merganser
Gulls	Whinchat	Merlin
Farmland birds		Osprey
Little Egret	*Breeding season*	Knot
Greylag Goose	Lesser Whitethroat	Curlew Sandpiper
Stonechat	*Winter*	Black-tailed Godwit
House Sparrow	Great Crested Grebe	Short-eared Owl
	Wigeon	Black Redstart
Passage	Golden Plover	Raven
Hirundines		

Background information and birding tips

THE A259 COAST road cuts across the valley of the River Cuckmere via an old Roman road at Exceat Bridge. The river valley has escaped being built on, so it is a glorious mile-long rural walk down to the sea along the canalised tidal river and past the famous meanders, known by geography students worldwide but now disconnected from the river flow.

The valley is designated as a Country Park, and consequently ramblers, families and dog walkers proliferate, especially on sunny weekend afternoons (though in the main they stick to the metalled paths and of course the beach!).

In view of the unsustainability of trying to maintain the artificial river wall, the Environment Agency proposes to return the valley to

Access details

(6 miles W of Eastbourne)

The winding meanders of the River Cuckmere are unmissable below the A259 between Seaford and Eastbourne. The Seven Sisters Country Park car park is on the E side of the floodplain on S side of road (TV518994). Extra parking is on N side of road behind Visitor Centre. Do not confuse parking with that at Exceat Bridge which is for Golden Galleon pub only.

BY TRAIN: No direct access.
BY BUS: Very good - Brighton-Eastbourne service Nos.712 & 713 stop right by Visitor Centre.

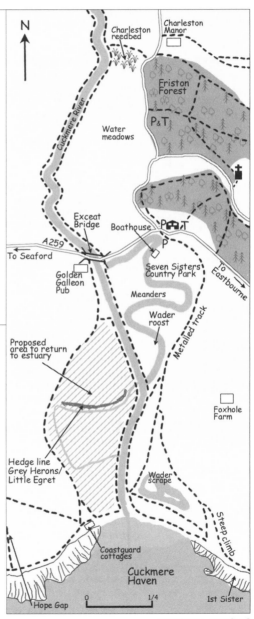

being a tidal estuary. Reversion to the west of the river would happen first (as marked on the map), with the eastern side later. A couple of riverbank footpaths would be lost, but new permissive footpaths would compensate. The proposed changes would benefit most birds, particularly waders. However, the official go-ahead has not yet been given, so the descriptions below outline the birdwatching pre-change!

Golden Galleon to the sea

From the Golden Galleon pub (please only park here if you are actually patronising the pub), you can currently do a lovely circular walk down to the sea along the west edge of the valley and back via the riverbank, or vice-versa.

Just beyond the pub car park, a horse field to your left (partly

Continues overleaf

81

Key points

- **Steep gradients up onto cliffs, although entirely flat long walks are possible**
- **On good bus route, including Sundays**
- **Telescope not essential**
- **Plenty of sightseers to contend with!**

submerged at high tide) is good for Chaffinches, House Sparrows and especially migrant Wheatears. At the next gate, carry straight on through to an overgrown avenue of berry-bearing shrubs and trees, great for tits and warblers, including Lesser Whitethroats.

The wet ditches to the left of the track, hide Wigeon and Teal in winter, and the prominent hedgeline running across the meadows is often crammed with Grey Herons and double-figure counts of Little Egrets. On the grass are sure to be Lapwings, Shelduck and Curlews, perhaps with Golden Plovers. It's also a loafing spot for gulls with lots of mean-looking Great Black-backs. If the Lapwings take sudden flight and climb high, look for the Peregrine buzzing them.

As you approach the sea, the track climbs towards the Coastguard Cottages and the famous views of the Seven Sisters (this is the border with the 'Splash Point-Seaford Head' site, page 146). The track in front of the cottages leads down to the beach and river.

Fording the river is not advised – the currents are dangerous – and there is no bridge. Instead head back along the riverbank, enjoying the reverse views back across the wet grassland, keeping an eye out for Kingfishers, Redshanks and Dunlins along the river and listening for the 'fissst' calls of Rock Pipits.

Fancy a drink after all that? Well there's the Golden Galleon at the end of the walk!

If all goes to plan, the ailing river wall on this west side will be breached and the wet grassland will flood with the tides, turning quickly to mudflats and saltmarsh. All the birds mentioned are still likely to be present, but now joined by a host of other passage and wintering waders, all living with the natural ebb and flow of the tide. A new permissive path up on the western valley flanks, will permit a new circular walk with elevated views of the estuary to compensate for the lost paths.

North of the A259

Just east of Exceat Bridge, a path leads along the riverbank upstream. One of our favourite short circular walks is upstream the mile to Charleston Reedbed, across to the minor Litlington road and back.

Bushes by the riverbank and on the opposite side can hold good migrants. In late autumn, we've seen Ring Ouzels here, and Reed and other warblers are likely. This is also a good spot to watch for the blue flash of a Kingfisher zipping by.

The wet meadows to your right are good for wildfowl. Big Canada Geese flocks can be joined by White-fronted or tundra Beans, while little drying pools are perfect for Temminck's Stints in May, the season when Red-footed Falcons have been seen twice. Check out the gulls too as this is a good spot for Mediterranean.

At Charleston Reedbed, listen for both Reed Warblers and Reed Buntings. A muddy path leads behind the reedbed to the road, from where you can follow the verge south with views back across the meadows. It's a chance in winter to check Friston Forest car park for Bramblings. Be mindful of the traffic as you walk along the road and eventually you will reach the main road near the pay and display car park.

East side of the river down to the sea

We prefer to avoid the crowds here and head out the back of the car park and past the boathouse. Always look across the water to the bushy hedge that obscures the road – it's a prime Kingfisher perch.

Following the muddy meander edge (trusty wellies time again), Wigeon, Canada Geese, Little Egrets, Lapwings and Cormorants should be obvious, as will double-figure counts of Little Grebes. The meanders here are probably the best area in Sussex for this little diving favourite of ours.

This first meander leads onto the main visitor track on the east side of the valley. From here another big meander loops away towards the distant riverbank and back again. Its far bank is where the small numbers of waders in the valley tend to roost, probably because it is one of the least disturbed areas. Best then to observe from a distance. Redshanks, Dunlins and Ringed Plovers are the most frequent species and in autumn check for Curlew Sandpipers and Greenshanks.

Half way down the valley, the embanked river and metalled track almost meet, before they veer away from each other again. Escape the crowds here by walking along the top of the rough riverbank all the way to the beach. Bushes on the left side of the bank hold Stonechats and Reed Buntings, while the salt marsh to the right in the channel, will have more and more Rock Pipits in winter the nearer you get to the sea.

Behind the beach is the 'Wader Scrape', although the birds on it tend not to be waders! We joke if we see one here, though to be fair we have noted Avocets, Bar-tailed Godwits and Knots in recent years. More usually it is just the haunt of gulls and numerous Little Egrets.

Between the scrape and the beach is a quiet shingle-and-scrub walk, ignored by all those bee-lining for the beach, but irresistible at migration time for Whinchats, Stonechats and Wheatears.

After dipping our toes in the sea (it's our ritual!), we scan for birds. Gannets, auks, Great Crested Grebes, indeed any seawatching species are possible, although Cuckmere Haven is in rather a bay and seabirds tend to be distant. On one sunny but freezing March morning here however, we watched two seemingly curious Red-throated Divers get closer and closer until they were within ten metres of us, showing how birds can occasionally be more obliging here. From the beach, it is also worth checking the face of the towering Seven Sisters cliffs for Fulmars and especially Peregrines, both are almost guaranteed.

Walks are possible up and over the cliffs here, towards Birling, or else you can retrace your steps and follow the riverbank all the way up to opposite The Golden Galleon. Relatively quiet, the river's muddy edge can have tame Dunlins and, from your bank-top vantage point, there are great views back onto both the meanders and also pools in the wet meadows. Spring waders can include Greenshanks, Temminck's Stints or even Wood Sandpipers.

Mediterranean Gulls can occasionally be found in the wet meadows alongside the Cuckmere River.
(Steve Cale)

Key points

- Allow 4-plus hours

- Expect 15-25 species

- SSSI; Ashcombe Bottom is National Trust; Ditchling Beacon is SWT reserve

- Open at all times

- Good NT car park at Ditchling Beacon (50p charge, NT members free); limited roadside parking for Ashcombe

- No other facilities

- Some very steep slopes; some tracks muddy

- Impossible for wheelchair users

Contacts

Sussex Wildlife Trust
01273 492630

National Trust
c/o Alfriston Clergy House
01323 871318

DITCHLING BEACON to Ashcombe Bottom is a walk of contrasts. Starting at East Sussex's highest point on the exposed South Downs, it takes in both the steep cold north scarp and the rich hazel woods on the shallow warm dip slope. Summer is best, when the birds range from ridge-top Corn Buntings and thermalling Buzzards to woodland specialities like Nightingales, Turtle Doves and Marsh Tits.

Target birds *Breeding season* – Turtle Dove (hear 70%, see 30%), Nightingale (hear 40%, see 5%), Corn Bunting (30%).

Other likely bird species

All year	Marsh Tit	*Winter*
Scrub birds		Thrushes
Woodland birds	*Passage*	Common Gull
Buzzard	Wheatear	Meadow Pipit
Kestrel		
Red-legged	*Breeding season*	
Partridge	Cuckoo	

Background information and birding tips

STARTING FROM DITCHLING Beacon car park, you'll probably first want to soak in the stunning view, which basically stretches the width of Sussex, top to bottom. A good display board helps you get your bearings.

Ready for your walk, the South Downs Way leads off east and west along the ridge. If time is limited, head west to the SWT's Ditchling Beacon reserve. About 200 yards along the scarp top, a steep track angles down the northern slope. 'The Slype', as it is known, leads into a small wood and above some scrubby overgrown quarries. In winter, the sun barely makes it down here and it is quite cheerless. Better to visit in spring when the Nightingales are singing and there are Yellowhammers, Linnets and Whitethroats in the scrub. Once through the wood, the track turns sharply back up to

the top of the slope but be warned, this is a scramble.

If you have more time and energy, we recommend the walk east from the car park. The Ditchling Road needs careful crossing, then it is a two mile walk along the scarp edge to Ashcombe Bottom, although the crowds from Ditchling thin out well before that. In midwinter, much of the walk along the top can be quite bleak and birdless, but in summer Sky Larks serenade you and Corn Buntings try their best to! Red-legged partridges are frequent on the arable fields and Buzzards, Sparrowhawks and Kestrels are all possible over the scarp edge.

It takes forty minutes or so to reach the sign marking the National Trust 'Blackcap' reserve ('Blackcap' is the hill-capping spinney of pines in front of you). Down the grassy slope to your right is Ashcombe Bottom, a charming wood of ash and hazel. A small gate leads into the wood,

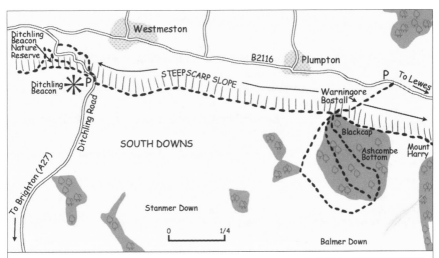

Access details

(5 miles NNE of Brighton)

For Ditchling Beacon car park:
Coming S on B2112 from
Haywards Heath, where road
veers R just S of crossroads in
Ditchling village centre,
continue straight on along
Beacon Road. Car park on R in
2 miles having climbed steep
winding road up scarp. Best
access from A27 - turn off at
Hollingbury junction (1st jnctn
E of A23). Turn N sharply onto
Ditchling Road, car park on L
after 2 miles across top of
Downs (TQ332130). The

Beacon car park can be very
busy at weekends, with cars
spilling out dangerously onto
the road edge.

For Ashcombe Bottom: From
Lewes, head N on A275 for 2
miles. Turn W on B2116 for
1½ miles towards Plumpton,
and there is rough parking on
the N side of the road, on quite
a steep edge overlooking fields
(TQ378130). A gated track
leads up Warningore Bostal
opposite.

BY TRAIN: 2 mile walk from
Cooksbridge Station to
Warningore Bostal.

BY BUS: No.79 from Brighton
station goes to Ditchling
Beacon in summer season,
Sundays only in winter.
Limited service Lewes-
Haywards Heath No.166 Mon-
Sat passes through Plumpton.

where we haven't yet failed to
see Marsh Tits, even on winter
days when all else seems quiet.
In May and June, however,
Turtle Doves and Nightingales
are likely to be heard. In
addition, Bullfinches seem to be
everywhere and warbler,
woodpecker and tit populations
are good.

Ashcombe Bottom can be
more swiftly reached by
climbing the scarp from the

Plumpton Road up the
Warningore Bostal (a 'bostal'
is an ancient drover's track).
Once again, winter can be
quiet bar a few Robins, but as
the spring sunshine arrives, so
do Yellowhammers, Linnets,

Song Thrushes etc. and the
chalk grassland is wonderful for
butterflies and orchids in
summer. Given the habitat,
we've a sneaking suspicion Ring
Ouzels may pass through too
but we've still to prove that!

Other nearby sites

Less than 5 miles: Hollingbury Camp.
Less than 10 miles: Brighton Marina, Brighton-Newhaven Cliffs, Castle Hill
to Swanborough Hill, Chailey Common, Henfield Levels, Lewes Brooks,
Sheepcote Valley

85

Key points

- Allow 2-plus hours
- Expect 35-55 species
- Part of Chichester & Langstone Harbours SPA, Ramsar site and SSSI
- East Head is owned by National Trust
- Open access at all times on foot to public areas. Car park opening times vary (contact West Wittering Estate Plc on 01243 514143)
- Good car parking, with toilets and seasonal café

WE ARE RARELY disappointed on a trip to the sand-dune spit of East Head and the neighbouring area around the mouth of Chichester Harbour. Perhaps the most reliable wintering Little Stint flock in the UK can be found here and this is always the top attraction for visiting birdwatchers. Brent Geese and Golden Plovers gather, sometimes in high numbers, and with terns, big flocks of waders, regular Slavonian Grebes and passage migrants there's always something to enjoy.

Target birds *All year* - Cetti's Warbler (hear 60%, see 10%), Grey Partridge (25%). *Breeding season* - Little Tern (60%). *Passage* – Osprey (30%), Turtle Dove (25%) *Winter* – Large flocks of Brent Goose and Golden Plover at close range (80%) with occasional Black Brant (5%), Ruff (70%), Greenshank (60%), Spotted Redshank (60%), Little Stint (50%), Red-breasted Merganser (40%), Water Rail (30%), Slavonian Grebe (10%).

Other likely bird species

All year	*Passage*	Sanderling
Waterbirds	Warblers	Snipe
Coastal waders	Gannet	
Gulls	Bar-tailed Godwit	*Occasional*
Farmland birds	Wheatear	Divers
Little Egret	Whinchat	Eider
Shelduck	Spotted Flycatcher	Long-tailed Duck
Stonechat		Merlin
	Winter	Short-eared Owl
Breeding season	Great Crested Grebe	Firecrest
Sandwich Tern	Wigeon	Snow Bunting
Common Tern	Knot	

Background information and birding tips

EAST HEAD, a highly dynamic sand and shingle spit, is constantly evolving in response to the variable influences of wind, tide and wave. It would only take about half an hour to walk around the Head non-stop, but birdwatching is so distracting it can take four times as long!

On the east side of the dunes, there is a sheltered saltmarsh bay to your right – Snowhill Creek. At low tide, a few dozen waders such as Redshanks and Oystercatchers disappear in among the creeks and vegetation, but as the tide rises, they are pushed up and made more visible. The wintering Little Stint flock, frequently into double figures, often doesn't move out of this area, but again they can be easier to see as high tide approaches. They tend to stick together in their own flock and can be quite approachable.

Moving to the tip of East Head,

Contacts

Chichester Harbour Conservancy
01243 512301

The National Trust
01243 814554

For parking and maps
www.westwitteringbeach.co.uk

you are looking north (hence the light is good) into the body of the harbour. In the distance is Pilsey Island LNR RSPB reserve, over half a mile away, with Thorney Island behind it. Even at low tide, there is plenty of navigable waters in front of you, with Great Crested Grebes and Red-breasted Mergansers in winter, but also the chance of Slavonian Grebes, too.

A few Eiders are often present, even in summer, and don't rule out Long-tailed Ducks in winter. From April through to October, there will be terns here – Sandwich, Common and Little.

Birding excitement comes as waders are displaced from the harbour's mud by that all-important rising tide. They pour south – rivers of Dunlins with some Knots, Grey Plovers, Oystercatchers and Ringed Plovers - and then split down each side of the Head. Many pass by very close, sometimes landing on the beach in front of you in dense clouds.

This is one of the best Sussex sites to see Bar-tailed Godwits, especially on passage. Unfortunately they are often disturbed by the many visitors who can swarm over the Head on sunny days, or by the yachts which frequently haul up on the beach.

The waders' ultimate goal is a high-tide roost round on the east side of East Head, so be careful that it is not you who disturbs them when walking back to the car park. At high tide, it is often best to use the boardwalk along the top of the narrowest section of dune ('The

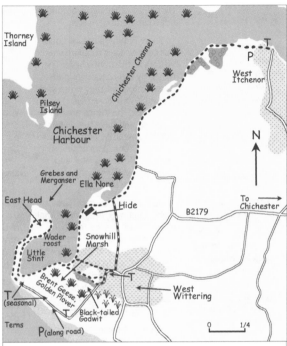

Access details

(7 miles SW of Chichester)

From A27 S of Chichester, turn S on A286 to Birdham, and there veer R at roundabout following brown tourist signs to West Wittering Beach. In village, keep following these signs to car park entrance. Coins are needed when the paybooth is unmanned. Car park is open dawn to dusk all year. Parking is then right along a 0.5 mile stretch - park anywhere along the grass here (it can get a bit boggy in winter) but the far end

(SZ765984) gives immediate access out onto East Head.

BY TRAIN: No direct access.
BY BUS: Regular Chichester-The Witterings services Nos. 52 & 53.

Other nearby sites

Less than 10 miles: Pagham Harbour, Chichester Gravel pits, Selsey Bill and West Fields

continues overleaf

Key points

- **Conditions generally good underfoot, with *some* good viewing from wheelchair**

- **Telescope useful but not essential**

- **Dangerous currents at Harbour entrance**

- **Very busy with holidaymakers/dog-walkers from Easter throughout summer, and even mid-week in fine weather**

Hinge') as other paths around the edge can be underwater.

Snow Buntings are infrequent but nevertheless regular winter visitors to the dunes here. There may only be a couple of birds each winter, but they often stick around if they do arrive. Otherwise, the dunes are Sky Lark-rich and have the odd Reed Bunting, Meadow Pipit and Pied Wagtail. Stonechats often move onto the Head in winter and make themselves readily visible on the fence palings.

Back in the car park, you can look inland over grass fields that in winter are grazed to a zero crop by Brent Geese. There are herds of them and they are often approachable. In recent years, there has been a Black Brant among them, which has subsequently returned with apparently hybrid youngsters.

The short sward also attracts large numbers of Golden Plovers, 1,500 or more, with some Lapwings, Dunlins and Ruff often among them and occasionally, even the Little Stints move here out of the harbour.

It is possible to walk the length of the car park, finding passage Wheatears, or Red-legged Partridges strutting along the back edge of the fields. Being a well-made track, it's great for wheelchairs, too. There is a seasonal café and plenty of toilets right behind the beach, though often only the toilets nearest the tollbooth are open in winter.

Walk out of the car park entrance and back down the lane, to an area of reeds on the right where Reed Warblers breed.

Directly opposite, what looks no more than a little muddy field is actually quite good for Black-tailed Godwits, Moorhens and Water Rails. This is the start of a long strip of wet ground called Snowhill Marsh, much of it hidden from view at this point.

If you continue into West Wittering village, the bushes around the church and along the little lanes, particularly the loop around Roman Landing, are recommended by local birdwatchers for passerine migrants, especially in autumn.

Alternatively, a little leafy lane (Coastguard Lane) leads along the trees and bushes on the north side of Snowhill Marsh. Only residents have vehicular access but you are welcome to walk.

We've seen Firecrests and Cetti's Warblers here in autumn, as well as the inevitable flushes of Chiffchaffs, Blackcaps and Willow Warblers. Tits, thrushes and finches boost your bird list as the lane leads through to some delightful coastguard cottages, though the narrow marsh itself is well hidden behind vegetation.

Beyond the houses, a grassy green opens up, and from its southern edge you can look back onto wetter parts of Snowhill Marsh. The light is often in your eyes, but nevertheless Shelduck, Grey Herons, Little Egrets, Mallards and Redshanks are likely all year, with Teal, Wigeon, Snipe, Black-tailed Godwits and in particular Greenshanks and Spotted Redshanks throughout the passage and winter periods. From here you can also look across to the high tide roost on East Head but you'll need a telescope.

The track heads left over a little bridge with a crabbing pool and back along some bushes to the East Head end of the car park – circuit

Large flocks of Brent Geese can be seen at close quarters near East Head.

completed, with maybe a Whinchat or Stonechat added to the list.

If you're feeling really energetic, why not walk right up the east side of Chichester Harbour towards West Itchenor? One mile from the car park you get to the little shingle promontory called Ella Nore, where Ringed Plovers and even Oystercatchers try to breed. Ella Nore is also one of Chichester Harbour's important wader roosts. It can be watched, without causing disturbance, at high tide in winter from the hide at the observation point on the coastal footpath.

The shoreline around Ella Nore also has some stretches of waterside oak trees, which make much of the edges of Chichester Harbour so attractive. In autumn, these can be good for Spotted Flycatchers, Goldcrests, Firecrests, warblers and Redstarts.

Even where the oaks thin out, the estuary-side farmland can be good for finches and both species of partridge. The area around Ella Nore is a good spot from which to see Ospreys too, which seem to favour the Thorney area of the harbour just across the water.

It's a long but pleasant walk through to West Itchenor along the harbour edge, giving you a sense of how big Chichester Harbour is and how many birds are out there. There's then little choice but the same route back unless you turn inland.

Alternatively, we've been known to relax for an afternoon on the sandy beach with screeching terns passing wonderfully close along the tide's edge in summer, maybe some Gannets out on the open sea beyond, and for us the exciting memory of an exhausted Leach's Petrel picked up on the tideline.

Key points

- Allow 2.5-plus hours

- Expect 25-35 species

- NNR, SSSI, and SWT reserve

- Open at all times

- Small free car park; no other facilities, and none nearby

- Many paths can be very very muddy, and hence slippery

- Not suitable for wheelchairs

- No public transport links

- Telescope definitely not needed

- There is a real risk of getting lost, and you won't meet many people to help you — maps, rations and a good sense of direction are useful!

A COMMON WITH a difference, Ebernoe is actually a huge woodland of towering trunks and beds of wild daffodils. There is a full suite of common woodland birds including Nightingales, the chance of Lesser Spotted Woodpeckers and Mandarins, to provide that exotic edge!

Target birds Common woodland birds plus *All year* – Mandarin (50%), Lesser Spotted Woodpecker (5%). *Breeding season* – Nightingale (hear 70%, see 10%).

Other likely bird species

All year	Coot	*Winter*
Woodland birds	Marsh Tit	Thrushes
Farmland birds	Nuthatch	Grey Wagtail
Mallard	Treecreeper	
Buzzard	*Breeding season*	*Occasional*
Moorhen	Garden Warbler	Siskin

Background information and birding tips

EBERNOE IS NOT exactly what you might think of as a Common. Rather than open heath or grassy land, the commoners' rights here were to graze their cattle underneath a woodland canopy of giant trees. When the wood was threatened with destruction in the 1970s, the Sussex Wildlife Trust came to the rescue and have recently acquired further land to create more woodland.

The car park is next to an unusual and isolated red-brick church in the woods. From the

moment you get out of the car, woodland birds should be heard, if not necessarily seen. Birdwatching at Ebernoe is best done by ear! From the car park, tracks lead down either side of the church.

Taking the right-hand route drops you straight down to Furnace Pond, a reedmace-edged pool in the trees, created 500 years ago for the iron industry. A few Moorhens, Coots and Mallards are likely, but scan the branches hanging low over the water for a splash of Mandarin colour. Grey Wagtails often use the pond's sluice.

The larger track down the left-hand side of the church branches half-way

Song Thrushes are common in the woods and open areas of Ebernoe Common.
(Steve Cale)

Contacts
Sussex Wildlife Trust
01273 492630

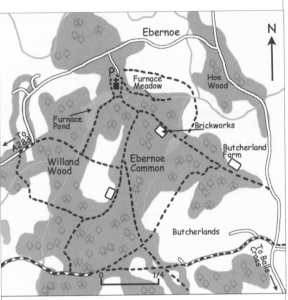

down the slope, with the side track signed left into Furnace Meadow. Still part of the reserve, it is an uncultivated scrubby meadow with breeding Linnets, Whitethroats and Yellowhammers. There's the chance of Buzzards overhead as you enjoy a sunny summer's afternoon listening to Nightingales.

Describing where to go beyond Furnace Pond or Meadow is the difficult task of putting into words a series of paths that twist and turn through the wood randomly. There are few landmarks to help orientate yourself (see the map for the key ones), the wood doesn't butt up to any main road and the little enclosed meadows within the wood all look rather similar. We once came across two visitors (ie about a day's total!) who had genuinely been lost for hours. Our advice? Take a map, allow extra time and remember the route you have taken. Oh, and take wellies.

One birdwatching rule applies pretty much throughout the Common - patience. In autumn and winter, there can be seemingly hours of birdwatching-nothingness that are then enlivened with a few minutes of fevered activity as a large tit flock comes through with attendant Treecreepers, Goldcrests and Nuthatches. In spring through to summer, birds spread themselves out more, with Chiffchaffs and Blackcaps arriving to join the clamorous residents.

Blackbirds, Robins and Great and Blue Tits are perhaps the

Access details

(4 miles N of Petworth)

Easiest access from A283 Petworth-Guildford road. 4 miles N of Petworth, turn R (or 2 miles S of Northchapel, turn L) onto minor road signed to 'Balls Cross' and 'Ebernoe'. After 1.5 miles, turn R after a red phone box down a single-track lane marked 'Holy Trinity Church – Ebernoe'. Park in wide bay in front of church (SU975278). Please respect church users during services. Visits by groups should advise

Sussex Wildlife Trust in advance on 01273 492630.

BY TRAIN: No direct access.
BY BUS: Not without a long walk!

most obvious birds, but pairs of Marsh Tits seem to be everywhere too and Nuthatches, Song Thrushes and Jackdaws are all plentiful. Nightingales prefer the

coppiced areas. It looks a perfect wood for Lesser Spotted Woodpeckers, but we have yet to be successful here - you may have to satisfy yourself with Great Spotted and Green.

Other nearby sites

Less than 10 miles: Burton Mill Pond

91

Key points

- Allow 1.5-plus hours
- Expect 15-25 species
- RSPB reserve, part SSSI
- Open at all times
- Very limited parking and no other facilities
- Take car on walk up road from village hall parking as thre is not footpath in places
- Don't park in front of wood entrance gate
- Conditions can get very muddy indeed
- Not suitable for wheelchairs

Contacts

RSPB South East Office

01273 775333

IF YOU LIKE a walk through glorious woodland, among carpets of spring flowers, with all the staple woodland bird species around you, then Fore Wood is worth a visit. Even though Nightingales may have vanished and Hawfinches are now rarely seen, such are the vagaries of woodland birds in the South East these days.

Target birds *All year* - Woodland birds.

Other likely bird species

All year	*Breeding season*	Redwing
Moorhen	Swallow	
Stock Dove	Whitethroat	*Occasional*
Marsh Tit	Garden Warbler	Mallard
Nuthatch		Kingfisher
Treecreeper	*Winter*	Lesser Spotted
Rook	Fieldfare	Woodpecker

Background information and birding tips

MAPS OF the Wealden countryside around the historic town of Battle are half green, showing that the area is still dominated by woodland. All of these ancient woods have been used and altered by Man in some way, and many are now little more than conifer plantations, but some are still rich in birdlife and wild flowers.

One of the largest deciduous woods remaining is Fore Wood, south of Battle near the village of Crowhurst. In 1976, the RSPB bought half of it and set about restoring some of the neglected coppice. Very soon, Nightingale numbers began to climb, while in the areas of high forest, which includes to this day some grand old hornbeams, Hawfinches and Lesser-spotted Woodpeckers continued to be recorded regularly.

Everything was done that should have made the woodland even better for birds than it was. But things are happening to a

suite of woodland birds in the South East, the reasons for which are not yet understood. The populations of Nuthatches, Marsh Tits, Lesser Spotted Woodpeckers and Hawfinches are all slumping. In Fore Wood, the three former species cling on today, but any record of Hawfinch is newsworthy indeed. Maybe it is climate change - new research will hopefully tell us.

Meanwhile, Nightingales are changing their game plan too. Though doing well in population terms, they seem to be abandoning coppice and moving into waterside locations. It means that Fore Wood has effectively lost its big draw species, and birdwatchers are not the feature here they used to be. No worries - it means you get the wood to yourself, except for a few local dog walkers.

The walk in through the main entrance of the wood is straight into lush verdant woodland (and straight into mud in winter). Barely 200 yards in, the track dips, and under the dip flows a stream that then falls over a shady waterfall into a deep ghyll (a ravine cut into the sandstone) - take care if you are tempted for a closer look over the edge. It is quite a dramatic little feature and here lies the SSSI interest, because the damp dark recesses hold mosses and plants more usually associated with the West Country.

Beyond the ghyll, turn left along the nature trail marked with coloured arrows. Circling clockwise around the wood, it leads through a sweet chestnut coppice down to some mature oaks near a little pond. This area is good for Marsh Tits and Nuthatches, and the pond has Moorhens and even occasional Kingfishers. There are some sunny rides, where silver-washed fritillary and white admiral butterflies can be seen in season and where the woodland plants are wonderful.

The tracks are gloriously winding, which can seem a little disorientating, but the wood is not so large that you can get totally lost. The trail returns to the wood's entrance via some more mature woodland, including some imposing hornbeams that were once such a draw for the Hawfinches and where you may still be lucky.

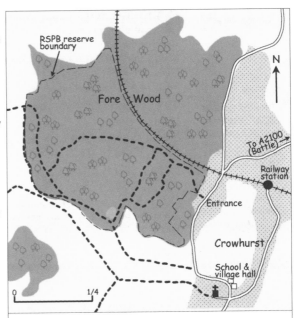

Access details

(4.5 miles NW of Hastings)

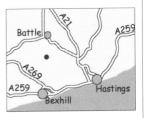

From Hastings, take A2100 N towards Battle. After 2 miles, turn L on minor road to Crowhurst. Parking for Fore Wood is currently very difficult, though improvements may be on the cards. If space allows, there is an arrangement with Crowhurst village hall (next to the primary school and opposite the church) to park there (TQ758123). Then walk up the lane, pass Forewood Rise on the left, and the wood's entrance and exit is another 200 yards up the lane on the L through a five-bar gate, clearly marked as the RSPB reserve.

BY TRAIN: 0.5 mile walk from Crowhurst station.
BY BUS: Very difficult, on limited Battle-Little Common No.395.

Other nearby sites

Less than 10 miles: Combe Haven and Filsham Reedbeds, Hastings Country Park, Pevensey Levels, Powdermill & Darwell Reservoirs.

93

Key points

- Allow 2.5-plus hours
- Expect 30-50 species
- Much of area is SSSI; applying for LNR status
- Open access at all times
- Small Visitor Centre with limited opening
- Good toilet facilities
- Conditions underfoot generally good but steep climbs down into glens
- Limited wheelchair access
- Access to beach at Fairlight Glen hazardous
- High risk of fire at all seasons - take every precaution not to cause them
- Early morning visits essential in autumn to see migration

Contacts

Hastings Borough Council Countryside Ranger Service

01424 813225

THOUGH NOT forming a headland like Beachy Head, the crumbling ochreous cliffs between Hastings and Pett Level still act as a major flight route for migrants. Backed by a huge and beautiful Country Park complete with wooded glens, scrub, heath and grassland, there is a rich variety of birds to be seen, including Peregrines and Dartford Warblers.

Target birds *All year* - Peregrine (40%), Dartford Warbler (10%). *Passage (autumn)* - passerine migrants including Redpoll (40%), Ring Ouzel (25%), Black Redstart (20%), Firecrest (15%), Brambling (15%).

Other likely bird species

All year	*Passage*	
Gulls	Hirundines	Wheatear
Woodland birds	Warblers	Siskin
Farmland birds	Thrushes	Reed Bunting
Garden birds	Tree Pipit	
Cormorant	Yellow Wagtail	*Breeding season*
Moorhen	Grey Wagtail	Fulmar
Stonechat	Redstart	
Treecreeper	Whinchat	*Occasional*
		Honey Buzzard
		Osprey
		Serin

Background information and birding tips

IMMEDIATELY to the east of Hastings, five miles of dramatic sand and clay cliffs stretch along the coast to Pett. Their face is a treacherous series of mudslips however, but from the highest ground, on a clear day, you can see to France.

Three deep wooded glens cut through the cliffs to the sea. West to east, they are Ecclesbourne Glen, the well-known Fairlight Glen, and Warren Glen. Together with areas of scrub and grassland in between them and farmland further inland, they form the large Hastings Country Park, which can take you a whole day to cover.

Of the resident target species, the Dartford Warblers stick to the big block of gorse beyond the coastguard cottages known as The Fire Hills. They are very difficult to see, and you may only find Stonechats, Linnets, Yellowhammers and Whitethroats. The 'clifftop' here is also a good vantage point to see patrolling Peregrines.

The steeper sections of cliff such as at Rock-a-Nore and Lovers' Seat support breeding Fulmars, Jackdaws and even Stock Doves. Cormorants sometimes breed on the cliffs too.

If you come to look for passage migrants, the best locations for watching birds overhead are East Hill, North Seat car park, or near the quarry or coastguard cottages at Coastguard Lane, Fairlight. Wherever you choose, early morning is essential.

The action is mainly concentrated in autumn when, from August onwards, small numbers of Tree Pipits and Yellow Wagtails may be

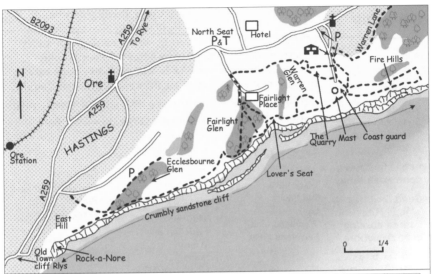

Access details

(1-3 miles E of Hastings)

For Rock-a-Nore and East Hill, park near the lifeboat station at the E end of Hastings seafront and climb the steep Tamarisk Steps. You will probably be too early to take the East Hill cliff railway.

For Ecclesbourne Glen, follow A259 inland at E end of seafront, and, in 0.5 mile, turn R onto Harold Road. In 0.5 mile, turn R onto Barley Lane, and parking is just before Shearbarn Holiday Park (TQ837105).

For Fairlight, continue on A259 up hill to Ore on NE outskirts of town. In Ore, turn R on minor road signed to Fairlight. The road climbs steeply almost 1mile to the North Seat car park, with toilets, at TQ847116. For Fairlight Coastguards, continue another mile, turning R just before church. There are toilets and parking immediately on your L, but parking with a view is another 0.5 mile down the access road just beyond the little visitor centre (TQ860115).

BY TRAIN: 1 mile walk from

Hastings station; 1mile walk from Ore station. *BY BUS:* No.344 Northiam-Rye-Hastings passes hourly along Fairlight road. Plenty of services if willing to walk from Hastings.

seen alongside bigger movements of hirundines. In October, finches and thrushes increase.

Your list of birds on the move may include raptors, Crossbills, all three wagtails, Reed Buntings, even Jackdaws or Great Spotted Woodpeckers. By late autumn, most obvious should be large numbers of Wood Pigeons and Stock Doves.

Not all the time needs to be spent sky-gazing though. The vegetation can hold plenty of birds, such as warblers, Redstarts and Spotted Flycatchers. Favoured places include the trees and scrub found down Warren Lane (also good for Bullfinches), the quarry to the west of the Coastguard Lane car park, and the tops of each of the glens. Among the commoner migrants, there are frequent Firecrests and Ring Ouzels to reward your early start.

Other nearby sites

Less than 5 miles: Pett Level. Less than 10 miles: Rye Harbour, Combe Haven and Filsham Reedbeds, Fore Wood, Powdermill Reservoir.

Key points

- Allow 2.5-plus hours
- Expect 25-40 species
- Woods Mill is Sussex Wildlife Trust HQ and reserve
- Public footpaths open at all times
- Good facilities at Woods Mill; limited parking only elsewhere
- Best for birds after heavy rain but paths can be deep in mud or deeper in water!
- Many walks are through fields with inquisitive livestock - keep dogs on leads
- Not suitable for wheelchairs

THE RIVER ADUR above Upper Beeding may be heavily embanked but its floodplain becomes wet most winters, sometimes very wet! In such conditions, the valley attracts moderate numbers of wildfowl. Sussex Wildlife Trust's headquarters at Woods Mill provides a good base on the edge of the valley, with facilities and Nightingales on site.

Target birds *Breeding season* - Nightingale (60%), Turtle Dove (30%). Winter - Kingfisher (20%), Bewick's Swan (10%), Short-eared Owl (5%).

Other likely bird species

All year	Shelduck	*Occasional*
Waterbirds	Redshank	White-fronted Goose
Wildfowl		Pintail
Gulls	*Winter*	Peregrine
Woodland birds	Thrushes	Shoveler
Farmland birds	Little Egret	Golden Plover
	Wigeon	Common Sandpiper
Passage	Snipe	
Hirundines	Green Sandpiper	

Background information and birding tips

THE RIVER ADUR between Henfield and Upper Beeding is very much like the Arun ten miles to the west. They are both fairly small slow-flowing rivers, in what would once have been an active floodplain, but now with their heavy embankments, the surrounding flat fields flood much less frequently and are dry in summer.

What the Adur lacks compared to the Arun is a 'Pulborough Brooks', ie a big chunk of land where water levels are kept high for winter wildfowl and summer waders. It means birding interest on the Henfield Levels relies on heavy winter rain, after which the valley can be very good indeed, drawing in Wigeon, Teal, Lapwings and Bewick's Swans. But if rainfall has been low, there can be little standing water and very few waterbirds. There is generally something to see however and walks along the river are a good way to 'get away from it all', albeit through some of the muddiest conditions in Sussex.

The best route out onto the Levels is the Downs Link footpath along the dismantled railway, though being elevated doesn't mean it's not muddy! The trackside is heavily hedged so gateway vantage points have to be used to the full.

From Henfield, the Downs Link leads north to Betley Bridge and south to Stretham Manor (with even better views from a parallel footpath a few yards to the right). Walking the river bank between the two makes for a good (but long) circular walk, or there are several footpaths back into Henfield along the way, shortening the circuit.

The river can be good for Kingfishers, especially in winter, when wintering Green Sandpipers are possible, while in summer, Reed

Contacts

For Woods Mill:
Sussex Wildlife Trust
01273 492630

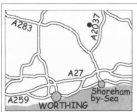

Access details

(10 miles NW of Brighton)

**Area best accessed from A2037
Upper Beeding to Henfield road.
Woods Mill is 1 mile N of Small
Dole on R, well-signposted
(TQ217137). For Downs Link
footpath in Henfield, turn W
down Church Street in Henfield
village centre. Parking is
immediately after The Old
Railway Tavern on R
(TQ204162). The Downs Link
leads off immediately N from
here, or for the walk S to
Stretham Manor, walk down
Station Road to join path. Walks
also possible from parking in
Upper Beeding 100 yards either
side of river.**

BY TRAIN: No direct access.
BY BUS: Best services are
No.100 Pulborough-Henfield
(via Woods Mill) or No.107
Horsham-Brighton via Henfield.

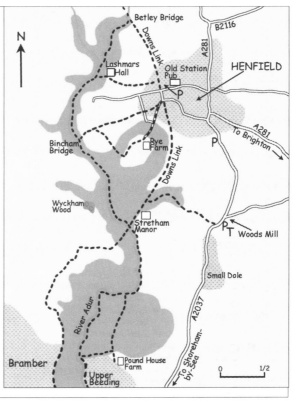

and Sedge Warblers sing
incessantly. Fieldfares and
Redwings love the old
hawthorn hedges and damp
pasture, and Song and Mistle
Thrushes are plentiful.

Hotspots include wet rough
ground on either side of the
river near Lashmars Hall, with
breeding Reed Buntings and
wintering Snipe, Green
Sandpipers and Teal. The areas
around Rye Farm, down to
Stretham Manor and under
Wyckham Wood, tend to flood
regularly and are frequent
venues for Bewick's Swans and

occasional White-fronted
Geese. Records of Common
Cranes, White Storks and
Cattle Egrets show the
potential of the area. A scrape
to the west of Rye Farm can
be particularly productive.

Another good area is that
east of the river directly north
of Upper Beeding, big enough,
open enough and rough
enough to attract Short-eared

Owls in some winters. Again,
the paths here can be muddy.

The most comfortable base
for your walk onto the levels is
Sussex Wildlife Trust's Woods
Mill headquarters near Small
Dole, where there is good
parking, great loos, and a
lovely little reserve complete
with a reed-fringed pond,
meadows and a wood with
Nightingales in season.

Other nearby sites

Less than 10 miles: Adur Estuary, Shoreham Harbour, Steep Down to
Lancing Clump: Cissbury Ring to Chanctonbury Ring, Ditchling Beacon to
Ashcombe Bottom.

97

Key points

- Allow 1-plus hours
- Expect 25-30 species
- Hollingbury/ Wild Park is LNR
- Open access at all times
- Free parking of mixed quality
- Toilets in Wild Park, but not always open
- Incredibly steep climb if you park at Wild Park, but generally not muddy
- Not suitable for wheelchairs
- The first two hours after dawn are crucial
- Urban fringe site with many dog walkers
- Be considerate to golfers

Contacts

Brighton & Hove
Countryside Service
01273 292140

WHAT MAKES Hollingbury Camp more than a ring of gorse in the middle of a golf course is its elevation - this site is all about migration. Each autumn birds such as Firecrests, Pied Flycatchers and Ring Ouzels occur. If you're nearby at the right time and enjoy birds on the move, this site is for you.

Target birds *Autumn* – Passerine migrants, including Tree Pipit (50%); Redpoll (20%); Firecrest (20%); Pied Flycatcher (10%).

Other likely bird species

All year	*Passage*	*Occasional*
Woodland birds	Hirundines	Buzzard
Corvids	Warblers	Hobby
Kestrel	Whinchat	Ring Ouzel
Goldfinch	Siskin	Dartford Warbler
Linnet		Brambling

Background information and birding tips

BIRDS ARRIVING from the Continent in spring make landfall along the Sussex coast and a few pause at the highest points before launching themselves onwards again. In autumn, before making the Channel crossing, this high ground close to the sea attracts even more, which stay if there are feeding opportunities. And when Swallows and martins are heading along the coast into the wind, they often pass close by these little summits.

Hollingbury Camp, as the highest point for miles – offers top views, literally! In spring, early Swallows pass over, maybe by the end of March. Wheatears, warblers and even Ring Ouzels make landfall here but their stays are always brief in spring.

Autumn is rather better, with more migrants staying longer. Spotted and Pied Flycatchers, Whinchats, Redstarts and are all possible at this season, with September being the prime month. They are inevitably outnumbered by Blackcaps, Chiffchaffs and Willow Warblers. Even Reed and Sedge Warblers, are possible.

There can be some impressive flights of hirundines over the top, along with a few Tree Pipits, Meadow Pipits and Yellow Wagtails. Tawny Pipits have also been recorded, but you need to be very familiar indeed with your bird calls to make the most of all these little brown jobs against the sky.

By mid-October, passage overhead has turned more to finches, with Chaffinches and Goldfinches predominating, but Siskins, Redpolls and Bramblings are all possible. Robins and Goldcrests now dominate the scrub and Firecrests are a real possibility.

Both spring and autumn can also be good for seeing raptors, with Sparrowhawks most frequent.

Buzzards, despite not breeding close by, are quite regular with Red Kites, Ospreys and Hobbies all seemingly now annual.

The Camp can be reached via the steep ascent from Moulsecoomb Wild Park, if you are feeling fit. The woods here are rich in Robins, Blackbirds and other common woodland birds, which can add a pleasant dawn chorus to proceedings.

Timing is absolutely crucial. The first two hours after sunrise are by far the best for two reasons. Firstly because migrants that arrived overnight will be making short flights looking for good cover and feeding and secondly because dog walkers are out early too!

Access details

(2 miles NNE of Brighton city centre)

For Wild Park, parking is off A270 (Lewes Road into Brighton) on R when travelling S, 0.5 mile S of A27. If coming N, turn into Park 0.25 mile after passing under railway (TQ323083). Limited parking on trackside near café.

For shorter climb to Hollingbury Camp, take Ditchling Road from A27 into Brighton. Come off A27 at the first junction E of the main A23/A27 junction, drive along minor road for 200 yards parallel to A27, passing a L turn to Ditchling Beacon, and turn immediately R back over A27. A rather isolated lay-by is

0.5 mile up on L (TQ323083), or join the dog-walkers' cars on a little pull-in at the top of the recreation ground at the entrance to the golf club (TQ315077).

BY TRAIN: 0.5 mile walk from Moulsecoomb Station.

BY BUS: Good – many services pass up Lewes Road from Brighton (eg 24,25,28, 729) with No.79 travelling up Ditchling Road on Sundays.

Other nearby sites

Less than 5 miles: Brighton Marina; Brighton-Newhaven Cliffs; Castle Hill to Swanborough Hill; Ditchling Beacon to Ashcombe Bottom; Sheepcote Valley.
Less than 10 miles Adur Estuary; Shoreham Harbour

99

Key points

- Allow 2-plus hours

- Expect 15-25 species

- SSSI, LNR and SWT reserve

- Open at all times

- Limited parking with height restriction barrier; no other facilities

- Paths are sandy and can get waterlogged making wheelchair access difficult

- Keep strictly to paths and keep dogs under close control

- Heathland is at high risk of fire in all seasons

- Insect repellent needed for dusk visit

Contacts

Sussex Wildlife Trust
01273 492630

Sussex Wealden Greensand Heaths Project
c/o Sussex Downs Conservation Board, Northern Area Office
01730 812134

IPING AND STEDHAM Commons, managed to perfection by Sussex Downs Conservation Board and Sussex Wildlife Trust, are excellent examples of lowland heathland and home to some wonderful plant and animal life. At the right times of year, you should see most of the typical bird species of this habitat, including Nightjars, Dartford Warblers and Wood Larks.

Target birds *All year* – Dartford Warbler (80%).

Breeding season –Nightjar (hear 90%, see 50%); Woodcock (85%); Tree Pipit (75%); Wood Lark (50%); Hobby (35%).
Winter – Redpoll (20%)

Other likely bird species

All year	Buzzard	*Occasional*
Scrub birds	Stonechat	Great Grey Shrike
Woodland birds	*Winter*	Crossbill
Corvids	Siskin	

Background information and birding tips

THESE TWO COMMONS sit side by side and effectively form one continuous site. The series of winding tracks across the heaths can be a bit disorientating but, as neither heath is that large, you shouldn't be lost for long!

In terms of where to go, the best advice is just to explore. All the key species are spread widely across the site and, by simply covering the ground, you are likely to come across them.

The habitat appears primeval - open swathes of heather are interrupted by quite dense stands of birch and gorse, and the site is fringed by pine trees.

A still sunny morning is the best time to visit. From as early as February, the Dartfords and Wood Larks start singing. The former are often readily visible on the patch of open heather just out the back left-hand corner of the car park. Just beyond here is some wetter ground with pond scrapes – these are great for dragonflies.

For Wood Larks, February to June is the best time – listen out for their melodic '*toolooeet*' calls, often from the tops of the scattered birches. To see Nightjars and roding Woodcocks, choose an open vantage point at sunset, and bring some old fashioned patience and plenty of insect repellent! The likelihood is that you will have to wander from the car to see them so a torch is also useful.

The sandy terrain ensures the tracks remain dry for most of the time, though it can get muddy after periods of wet weather. The downside of sandy tracks is that wheelchair access is difficult, though there are no stiles to negotiate here.

Over on the Stedham side of the road (take care crossing as you are quite unsighted for the traffic) you may come across the small herd of cattle keeping the invasive birch at

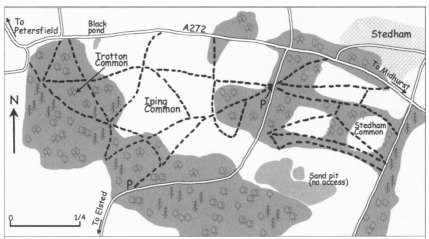

Access details
(2 miles W of Midhurst)

**Easy to find from A272
Midhurst to Petersfield road.
2 miles W of Midhurst/ 1 mile
E of Trotton, turn S on minor
road to Elsted. Sandy car park
on R after 200 yards under
very narrow and low entrance**

bar (SU852220). Alternatively,
there is some parking another
400yds further S underneath
some pine trees on the R
(SU844215).

BY TRAIN: No direct access.
BY BUS: Only regular service is
No.91 Midhurst-Petersfield.

bay. There is also more deciduous woodland on its southern boundary and this obscures a sand pit. Unfortunately for birdwatchers, this pit is just a deep quarry where the water is brown with sand suspension - a few pairs of Sand Martins may breed, but viewing is difficult and don't expect to see any birds on the water.

At times, particularly in winter or the heat of a summer's day, it can appear birdless and in windy or wet conditions the Dartford Warblers stay low and unobtrusive, the Wood Larks

stop singing and there is little left to see.

In mid-winter, the Commons themselves seem to hibernate but you may still be lucky and see a small flock of Siskins, a couple of Redpolls or even just a Kestrel to

brighten the gloom. There is the potential however, for an occasional Great Grey Shrike to arrive and over-winter, or perhaps a party of Crossbills may be around. Watch too for Fieldfares and Meadow Pipits at dusk as both species roost in this area.

Other nearby sites
Less than 5 miles: Woolbeding Common.
Less than 10 miles: Ambersham Common, Chapel Common,
Lavington Common, West Dean Woods.

101

Key points

- Allow 2 hours
- Expect 20-30 species
- SSSI, NNR and candidate SAC
- Open at all times
- Good small car park
- No toilets
- Small interpretation centre
- Some fairly steep downland slopes
- Access track can be a little muddy in winter but is being improved for wheelchair access
- Poor access by public transport
- Keep dogs under close control

Contacts

English Nature, Sussex & Surrey Team
01273 476595
sussex.surrey@english-nature.org.uk

KINGLEY VALE IS Europe's largest yew forest, set on the sunny, steep, south-facing slope of the South Downs. It is a wonderfully unique place in which to enjoy habitats and scenery, as well as a good range of common woodland and downland bird species.

Target birds *Breeding season* - Turtle Dove (25%).

Other likely bird species

All year	Marsh Tit	*Winter*
Scrub birds	Nuthatch	Thrushes
Woodland birds		
Farmland birds	*Passage*	*Occasional*
Buzzard	Hirundines	Hobby
Little Owl	Thrushes	Ring Ouzel

Background information and birding tips

KINGLEY VALE is a steep hollow bowl on the southern side of the chalk downs, north of Chichester. The yew trees that cloak it make the hillside appear dark, even in sunshine. The trees, considering their age, are a lot smaller than we first expected - this is not a forest of great soaring trunks, but a knotted tangle of gnarled boughs that cut out all light from the forest floor.

There are Tawny Owls nesting in the Yews which you may hear, especially if the young are vocal, but it is a needle-in-a-haystack job to see them. This was once the main Sussex site for Golden Pheasants but it now appears that they are no more.

The gentle and slightly muddy 15-minute walk up to the Vale from the car park is not great for birds, with Little Owls being about the most notable if elusive species in the old oaks and hedgerows. On reaching the bottom of the Vale, the 'woodland museum' in front of you - a fun little wooden interpretation hut - is worth a look and has nature trail pamphlets. At the time of writing, the access track is being upgraded for wheelchair use.

Which route you take is now your choice - a dark nature trail leads straight on through the yews, while other tracks climb up steeply around the edges of the vale, through downland scrub with the yews below. The latter route gives more opportunity to see passerines. There are Blackcaps, Chiffchaffs, Garden Warblers and Whitethroats in the breeding season. Tits (including Marsh) are there all year, with thrushes in autumn feeding on the yew and hawthorn berries. Ring Ouzels are perhaps the biggest prize here on autumn migration, but they are few and far between - only their tendency to make loud 'chacking' noises gives you a chance of seeing them.

The top of Kingley Vale (Bow Hill) is one of the highest points on the southern edge of the Downs. There are two tumuli here, the Devil's Humps, from where the views are fabulous. To the north stretch the wooded Downs, with great walks out into them and, to the south, the panorama extends to Pagham and

Access details

(4 miles NW of Chichester)

Approach from A286 2 miles N of Chichester, if coming from the N or E, or from B2178 if coming from W. From A286, turn L in Lavant Village opposite the church towards the hamlet of West Stoke. After 3 miles, pass the tiny church at South Stoke and 200 yards later, at a sharp L bend, turn R and immediately on the R is a simple neat car park marked 'West Stoke Car Park, Sussex Downs AONB' with enough space for 25 cars (SU824087). From B2178, turn L just before entering East Ashling. In 0.5 miles, at the first R bend, turn L and the car park is immediately on your R.

BY TRAIN: No direct access.
BY BUS: Difficult - limited No.54 service (Chichester-Petersfield) passes through West Stoke.

Chichester Harbours and, on a good day, right across the Solent to the Isle of Wight.

Some migrants may pass overhead here, especially in autumn, including hirundines and pipits in September and fnches later in the autumn. Any open area of downland grass attracts Green Woodpeckers, to feed on the ants, as well as Mistle Thrushes. The downland butterflies can also be abundant and listen for Linnets and Yellowhammers in the scrub.

Other nearby sites

Less than 10 miles: Chichester gravel pits, Chidham and Cobnor, Thorney Island, West Dean Woods.

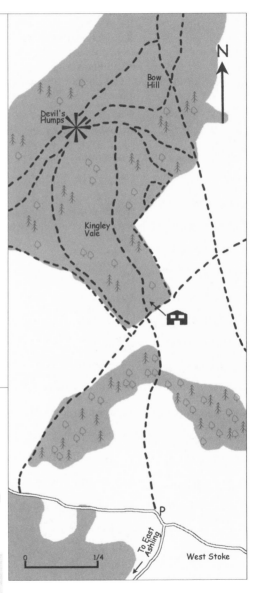

Key points

- Allow 1-plus hours
- Expect 15-20 species
- SSSI, and National Trust site
- Access open at all times
- Free car park - no other facilities
- Not suitable for wheelchairs
- Paths boggy in winter
- Keep strictly to paths and keep dogs on leads to protect ground-nesting birds
- Take care during felling operations
- High risk of fire at all seasons - take every precaution
- Dusk visit essential in summer

Contacts

National Trust,
West Sussex
Downs(West)
01730 816638

L AVINGTON COMMON is a small area of National Trust heathland - an island in a sea of pines. Its scale does not detract from its excellence for heathland birds - it still holds Nightjars, Dartford Warblers, Crossbills and Wood Larks with the first two relatively easy to see. What's more, in early 2003, work began to double its size.

Target birds *All year* - Dartford Warbler (70%), Crossbill (5-30%). *Breeding season* - Nightjar (at dusk, hear 90%, see 80%), Tree Pipit (80%), Woodcock (at dusk, 90%), Wood Lark (20%). *Winter* - Redpoll (20%).

Other likely bird species

All year	*Breeding season*	Siskin
Woodland birds	Sand Martin	
Stonechat	Whitethroat	*Occasional*
Marsh Tit		Buzzard
Linnet	*Winter*	Hobby
Reed Bunting	Meadow Pipit	Kestrel

Background information and birding tips

Y OUR POSSIBLE routes around Lavington Common are quite easy. A track leads from the car park across the centre of the heath, and then you can either circle the outside of the heath to the left through the pines, or go to the right, through the rhododendron jungle of

Merlin's Wood. Both routes lead back to the car park, which is small but well laid out with picnic tables and a map.

It is worth lingering on the track at the heath's heart. There is a little clump of pines half way, where we have had superlative views of Crossbills (the car park is another regular spot).

The heather on Lavington Common can make Dartford Warblers rather easier to spot. (John Davis)

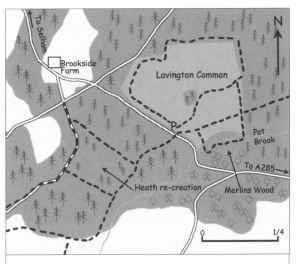

Open heathland is so close to the car park that it makes it an ideal spot for Nightjar watching too and we've even had a bird churring in the middle of the day here. Stonechats are common, and the heath is heather rather than gorse, which always seems to make Dartford Warbler-spotting easier.

It's quite a damp heath, so the tracks do get wet. A rather unexpected sight are the hirundines overhead in summer - many are likely to be Sand Martins, as their breeding site at Duncton sand pit is only half a mile away.

There aren't many trees of any great height actually on the heath, so the Wood Larks and Tree Pipits are around the edge of the heath as often as they are in its middle. The surrounding pine plantations are also the best place to pick-up the calls of Siskins in winter.

Kids will love winding their way through the tangled dark jungle of rhododendron in Merlin's Wood. The tinkling Pot Brook cuts through the wood here, and it all looks very lush and luxuriant. The 'rhodos' have enough native trees among them to attract a few tits, including Marsh, and Great Spotted Woodpecker.

The great news is that, across the road from the car park, the National Trust is opening up areas of pine wood that old photos from 1925 show were then pristine heathland. The bank of heather seed will hopefully still be

Access details

(2.5 miles SW of Petworth)

Turn W off A285 3 miles S of Petworth (and 1.5 miles N of Duncton) onto the minor road to Graffham and Selham. The National Trust car park is among the trees after 1 mile on R (SU947187).

BY TRAIN: No direct access.
BY BUS: Irregular 71 Midhurst-Graffham loop, or take No.99 Petworth-Chichester on A285

and alight at Heath End from where it is possible to walk through the woods to Lavington.

viable, and more Tree Pipits, Nightjars and Dartford Warblers should be the net result, hopefully very quickly.

Be aware that the site is on the circuit of car thieves, or at least those who smash vehicle windows. Here, as at all sites in the book, you are recommended not to leave any valuables in your car.

Other nearby sites

Less than 5 miles: Ambersham Common, Burton Mill Pond, Lord's Piece. Less than 10 miles: Iping & Stedham Commons, Amberley Wild Brooks, Pulborough Brooks.

Key points

- Allow 2-plus hours
- Expect 30-40 species
- Part SSSI
- Access at all times – please keep to public rights of way, and keep dogs under control around livestock
- Very limited parking and no other facilities
- River bank, where churned by livestock, can be a trial of mud in winter!
- Some stiles to climb
- Little chance of circular walk
- Not suitable for wheelchairs

BETWEEN LEWES and Newhaven, two high banks now bar the River Ouse from overflowing into the floodplain it once created. There are still plenty of birds to be seen here though, including waders, especially dozens of Common Sandpipers and Kingfishers, which turn up along the river. Small numbers of Bewick's Swans occur annually out on the Brooks in winter, when a wide range of raptors may also be seen.

Target birds *All year* – **Peregrine (60%)**. *Winter* – **Kingfisher (60%), Bewick's Swan (10%), Corn Bunting (10%), Common Sandpiper (5%).**

Other likely bird species

All year	Hirundines	Green Sandpiper
Waterbirds	Greenshank	
Gulls	Common Sandpiper	*Occasional*
Farmland birds	Stonechat	Bittern
Mute Swan		Hen Harrier
	Winter	Merlin
Passage	Little Egret	Dunlin
Inland waders	Snipe	

Background information and birding tips

ANYWHERE along this stretch of the River Ouse can turn up birds. Mute Swans, Black-headed Gulls and wary Cormorants are likely to be the most obvious, but it is amazing how many waders sneak along the banks. Redshanks can be seen at any season, but Common Sandpipers are the speciality. Late summer sees large numbers return, with loose flocks of a dozen not unusual. One or two may even stay to winter.

Other passage waders can include Ringed Plovers, Greenshanks and Dunlins in small numbers, with Green Sandpipers preferring the wet ditches. Little Egrets are a regular sight now, in late summer, while Little Grebes fish, despite the strong tides, from September to spring. This is the best time to see Kingfishers too, which can give great views.

Footpaths run all the way, some six miles or so, along both banks between Lewes and Newhaven. Elevated several feet above the flood plain, these banks are the obvious place from which to check the flat open Brooks as well as the river channel.

Out on the Brooks, grazed by sheep and ponies, the shortage of paths means the birds can be distant, especially on the mile-wide northern Brooks. Damp fields pull in reasonable flocks of Lapwings over winter, often with a few Golden Plovers, but the Snipe, which *are* out there, tuck themselves away.

In a wet spring, a few Shelducks may be out grazing but wildfowl numbers are generally low, apart from the resident herd of Mute Swans which can number 80 or more. It is these which pull in the few Bewick's Swans each winter, but

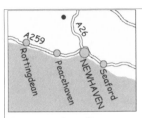

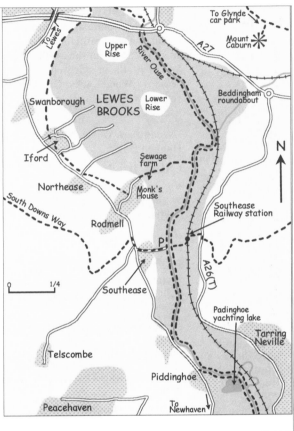

Access details

(1 to 5 miles SSE of Lewes)
Bounded by the Newhaven-
Lewes minor road (the
'Kingston Road') to W, and
A26 Newhaven-Beddingham
road to E. Access onto The
Brooks is problematical. The
best access is from very
limited verge-side parking E
of Southease. From the
Kingston Road, turn into
Southease past the church
and out onto the Brooks. Park
before the rickety wooden
bridge (TQ426053). Note the
level crossing just beyond the
bridge is for key-holders only
and there is no route through
to A26. Also the Monks House
car park at Rodmell is for
National Trust members only.

BY TRAIN: **0.25 mile walk**
from Southease station; 0.5
mile walk from Lewes station
(down Ham Lane past
amenity tip). BY BUS: No.123
Newhaven-Lewes travels
length of Kingston road.

they can be difficult to find if they are not near rights of way. The area east of Iford is often the best for them.

Any set-aside or stubble on The Brooks is attractive to finches and buntings, including Corn Buntings. By spring, the dominant passerine song however is that of Reed Warblers, with Sky Larks, Meadow Pipits and Reed Buntings joining in the chorus.

It is worth indulging in a spot of pylon watching. The reward may simply be a Kestrel, Crow or Cormorant, but Peregrines are just as likely at almost any time of year. The Brooks can also be good for other raptors with Merlins, Buzzards, Sparrowhawks and Hen Harriers coming across the Brooks, though in winter 2002-3 the long-staying Rough-legged Buzzard took all the attention!

Other nearby sites

Less than 5 miles: Castle Hill to Swanborough Hill.
Less than 10 miles: Newhaven Tide Mills; Arlington Reservoir; Brighton-Newhaven Cliffs; Cuckmere Haven; Ditchling Beacon to Ashcombe Bottom; Sheepcote Valley; Splash Point and Seaford Head

Key points

- Allow 1.5-plus hours

- Expect 15-25 species

- Privately-owned land with permissive access to public

- Access open at all times

- Good, if bumpy, car parks; no other facilities

- Wellies rarely needed on sandy paths

- Not suitable for wheelchairs

- Respect and keep distance from ponies - they are at work for wildlife!

- Keep strictly to paths and keep dogs under control

- Very difficult to reach by public transport

Contacts

Chittons
01903 882213

THIS SANDY heath, widely but mistakenly known as Coates Common, sits towards the eastern end of the string of good heathy bird sites in West Sussex. Though only a small site, without the heather/gorse necessary for Dartford Warblers, the area is well worth exploring for three big bird reasons - Wood Larks, Crossbills and Nightjars. All are as reliable here as almost anywhere in Sussex.

Target birds *All year* - Crossbill (50%). Breeding season - Wood Lark (75%), Nightjar (at dusk: hear 90%, see 70%), Hobby (25%).

Other likely bird species

All year	*Winter*	*Occasional*
Woodland birds	Siskin	Buzzard
Corvids		Tree Pipit
		Brambling
Breeding season		
Hirundines		

Background information and birding tips

BIRDERS KNOW this as Coates Common, but the real name - or rather names - for this site are Lord's Piece and Sutton Common (Coates Common is actually 0.5 mile east of here). A couple of hours here is plenty and it is ideal as a second venue after somewhere like Pulborough Brooks RSPB.

The site is a triangular block of private land, less than a mile in any direction, and is the last place in the UK where field crickets survive naturally. Full credit to the estate owners whose excellent management work makes this possible. Attractive Exmoor ponies graze the heathland grass short and scuff up bare bits of sand essential to the nocturnal crickets.

In spring, Wood Larks can be encountered any time from February onwards, one often singing engagingly from small

trees close to the car park (marked **(1)** on map). You can enhance your chances of seeing - and hearing - Wood Larks by visiting in early morning (before the dog walkers arrive) and on sunny warm days. Familiarity with their lilting calls is useful to help find them. In winter, it appears that many of them stay relatively close-by on stubble fields, but they are unobtrusive.

Crossbills can be seen in any month and, once again, knowing the call is invaluable. They are seen most regularly around the tall conifer plantation **(2)**, though the other pines dotted about the heath can be good, and we have also seen them in the larch plantation at **(3)**. We've had some cracking views.

Being a small area, the few pairs of Nightjars, that arrive back from Africa by the second week of May, are usually quite easy to hear, if not to see. Of all the heathland sites, this with its short dry grassland and lack of heather, might be the easiest to stray off the paths and in doing so disturb the nesting Nightjars and other key wildlife - please be careful.

As this is heathland, the number of bird species present is quite limited. There will probably be Mistle Thrushes and Green Woodpeckers out on the short turf and the odd winter Meadow Pipit in the wetter flushes, but any other birds, tend to be found in the woodland fringes.

Here there are some gnarled old oaks and so Nuthatches are common, as are Great Spotted Woodpeckers. Lesser Spotteds are only occasional, and Buzzards not as regular as might be imagined. Check out the pool **(4)** for a great range of dragonflies though.

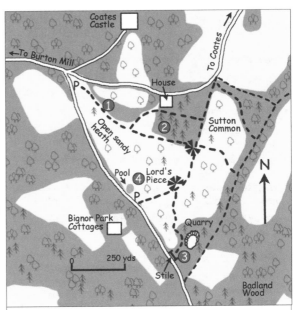

Access details

(4 miles WSW of Pulborough)

Coates Common lies S of Petworth off the minor road between the villages of Coates and Burton Mill. From A285, 3 miles S of Petworth, turn E on minor road to Burton Mill. After 2 miles, ignore cross-roads to Duncton/Byworth. 1 mile later, road forks, and car park sits between the fork.
From Arundel, head N on A284 to A29 then turn N on B2138 at Watersfield. After 2 miles, turn W on rather hidden minor road to Coates. Wind through

Coates village; car park is on L after 2 miles (SU999174)

BY TRAIN: No direct access.
BY BUS: Very difficult - No.99 'demand responsive' service from Petworth-Chichester gives only option.

Other nearby sites

Less than 5 miles: Burton Mill Pond, Amberley Wild Brooks, Lavington Common.
Less than 10 miles: RSPB Pulborough Brooks, Ambersham Common.

Key points

- Allow 3-plus hours

- Expect 20-30 species

- SSSI and NNR

- Access open at all times

- Good pay & display parking with toilets at Friston Forest

- Other facilities 1 mile away at Seven Sisters CP

- Allow time for extensive walking with moderate but lengthy ascents

- Some mud in winter

- Not suitable for wheelchairs

- Keep strictly to paths and keep dogs under control

- Risk of fire in all seasons

- Useful to take map

Contacts

English Nature, Sussex and Surrey Team
01273 476595
sussex.surrey@
english-nature.org.uk

L ULLINGTON HEATH, high in the Downs above the Cuckmere Valley, will be attractive to people who enjoy birdwatching as part of a long hike through glorious downland scenery. Expect the sound of Nightingales ringing out of the scrub, interesting flora underfoot and butterflies on the wing.

Target birds
Breeding season – Nightingale (hear 75%, see 20%); Turtle Dove (hear 60%, see 40%). *Winter* – Brambling (5% in Friston Forest).

Other likely bird species

All year	*Breeding season*	Thrushes
Scrub birds	Cuckoo	
Woodland birds	Garden Warbler	*Occasional*
Farmland birds		Hobby
	Winter	Redstart
	Gulls	

Background information and birding tips

L ULLINGTON HEATH is the best-preserved chalk heath in the UK, a very unusual habitat high on the Downs where a slightly acid soil over alkaline chalk means that a strange mix of plants grow together.

It is a place to visit on sunny spring and summer days, when you can enjoy a walk accompanied by butterflies and the songs of Nightingales in the scrub and Sky Larks above.

Actually getting to the Heath is quite a trek. The site is best accessed from one of two car parks, both of which require a walk past the frankly uninspiring beech monoculture of Friston Forest. Perhaps one positive memory we have of Friston Forest itself is of Wood Pigeons in November! Looking out over the vast forest canopy, it was studded with more than 2,000 dots, all pigeons, and all probably set to make the Channel crossing the next day.

The other potential highlight from Friston is Bramblings. At the car park on the Cuckmere side of Friston Forest, the beech trees are mature enough to produce beechmast, so check the winter Chaffinch flock, where Bramblings can be best picked up by their wheezy calls.

From the car park you can walk through the forest on a number of tracks, but it is much better to cut to the northern edge of the trees where a long grassy track climbs up Charleston Bottom towards the heath, with open farmland climbing to your left. The forest edge holds plenty of warblers and thrushes in spring and summer.

Climbing up into the heath reserve itself, Green Woodpeckers are likely on the short flower-rich turf. It is from within the scrub that you are likely to hear the Nightingales, and the bird community is rich with warblers, Yellowhammers, Whitethroats and finches. Grasshopper Warblers have been regularly recorded from here in the past, though not so much nowadays. Lullington Heath also once held a healthy Dartford Warbler population and, while they are absent today, with the current buoyant Sussex population they may well return.

The path climbs to the South Downs Way which runs along the top of the heath. Along to the left is Winchester Pond, a 19th Century dewpond. Well used by small birds such as Goldfinches and Yellowhammers and also dragonflies, it is a great spot for a picnic to watch the comings and goings, before heading back down the valley.

Alternative access to the heath is from the Forestry Commission car park on the Jevington road. From here, it is possible to cross some gallops (when the horses aren't charging about) and take the long, muddy walk through Friston Forest and onto the top of Lullington Heath.

It was over this part of the forest that we watched six immature Marsh Harriers circling above the canopy one memorable day This sight will probably not to be repeated but, with Montagu's Harriers once having bred here, it just shows what is possible.

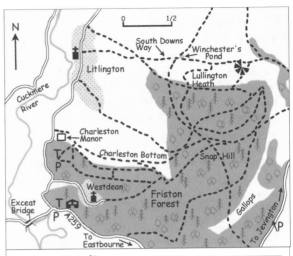

Access details
(5 miles WNW of Eastbourne)

From Eastbourne or Seaford, head for Seven Sisters Country Park (see Cuckmere Haven, p80). Here, turn N off A259 onto minor road towards Litlington and Westdean. Follow for 1 mile to car park on R in trees (TQ518002).

To reach here from A27, turn S on minor road through village of Wilmington 2 miles W of Polegate. Follow road through Litlington on; 1 mile S, parking is on L. Alternative parking on W side of road 1 mile S of Jevington on minor road

between A259 at East Dean and A22 at Polegate.

BY TRAIN: No direct access.
BY BUS: Various Cuckmere Community Bus services pass along Litlington road. Otherwise walk from Seven Sisters Visitor Centre at Exceat from No.712.

Other nearby sites
Less than 5 miles: Cuckmere Haven; Splash Point and Seaford Head; Beachy Head.
Less than 10 miles: Arlington Reservoir; Brighton-Newhaven Cliffs; Newhaven Tide Mills; Pevensey Levels

Key points

- Allow 1.5-plus hours
- Expect 25-35 species
- Parts are proposed LNR
- Public rights of way and beach open at all times
- Limited but adequate parking
- No other facilities on site
- Flat terrain but hard-going on shingle beach
- Wheelchair access possible to some parts of site
- Care needed at level crossing
- Get in early to beat the dog walkers

Contacts

For Ouse Estuary Project:
East Sussex County Council
01273 481614

MANY WOULD describe Newhaven Tidemills as 'wasteland', but wasteland often, as here, equals birding richness. The small tidal creek attracts waders and the open weedy ground is used by Sky Larks, finches and migrants. The Ouse Estuary Project should develop into a wonderful little reedbed reserve and Newhaven East Pier is perhaps the county's best site for seeing wintering Purple Sandpipers up close.

Target birds

All year – Peregrine (20%). *Winter* – Purple Sandpiper (60%), Black Redstart (30%), Mediterranean Gull (10%), Water Rail (10%), Short-eared Owl (5%).

Other likely bird species

All year		
Gulls	Shelduck	Dunlin
Farmland birds	Common Tern	Curlew
Cormorant	Sandwich Tern	Razorbill
Ringed Plover	Yellow Wagtail	Guillemot
Redshank	Whinchat	Rock Pipit
Stonechat		
	Breeding season	*Occasional*
Passage	Wheatear	Red-throated Diver
Seawatching species	Reed Warbler	Shag
Hirundines	Sedge Warbler	Bar-tailed Godwit
Warblers		Grey Plover
	Winter	Sanderling
	Little Egret	Serin

Background information and birding tips

EAST OF NEWHAVEN, the A259 coast road to Seaford runs along the back edge of what would once have been the estuary of the River Ouse. Long since reclaimed from the sea, the Newhaven side of the small floodplain is covered with industrial units, but enough remains undeveloped elsewhere to attract plenty of birds.

Parking next to the level crossing, check the arable fields either side in winter for Curlews and Lapwings. Cross the railway line carefully and follow the track through the crumbled ruins of the Tidemills (with the tamest Dunnocks we know) to the head of the tidal Mill Creek. There are almost always Redshanks amongst the shopping trolleys in the mud, a Little Egret now seems a permanent fixture, and there is the chance of Dunlins, Bar-tailed Godwits (on spring passage), Teal, Ringed Plovers etc.

The track leads out onto the shingle beach overlooking Seaford Bay. Turning right, the earth bank to your right hides a big 'wasteland' of teasels and thistles, ideal for breeding Linnets, Stonechats and Sky Larks, with flocks of Goldfinches throughout much of the year. Occasionally Wheatears breed too, and they are a constant presence on migration, sometimes dozens of them. Tawny Pipits have been recorded in September and Serins on several occasions.

The western end of the wasteland, by the industrial area, is a favoured spot for Black Redstarts in autumn and winter, while out on the shingle beach, the winter Greenfinch flock can reach 200, a good figure for Sussex.

The cross-Channel ferries to Dieppe dominate the harbour and there are few birds here, although Sandwich and Common Terns often linger in autumn and Rock Pipits are present in winter.

But it is the Purple Sandpipers which are the real prize. High tide is best – walk out along the quiet pier, looking over the left-hand side onto the concrete struts only a few feet below. The Sandpipers, up to a dozen, are usually out towards the end of the pier.

The area of floodplain back towards Sainsbury's, and requiring a walk back from the car down the lane and along the roadside, is getting a wonderful renovation for wildlife. The Ouse Estuary Project is restoring the wet grassland and creating a reedbed. The scrape for the reeds was dug in 2002, enticing a flush of waders, gulls etc. They will mostly go as the reeds develop, but we hope they will be replaced by Water Rails, wintering Bitterns and even Bearded Tits. A public footpath leads along the Parget Bank, giving good views over what is an exciting addition to birdwatching in the area.

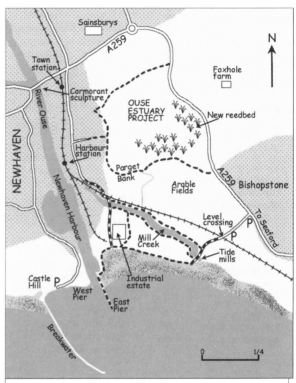

Access details

(1mile SE of Newhaven town centre)

One mile E of Newhaven Sainsbury's on the A259 to Eastbourne, turn R off the coast road at a pelican crossing onto an unsigned single-track lane. From Seaford in the opposite direction, the turning is on the L 0.25 mile after the turning on the R to Bishopstone. Go 300 yards down lane and park just before the level crossing where the track widens (TQ461003). Alternatively, there is a muddy car park just as you turn off the A259 (under a height restriction barrier). The latter is the best

parking, but 400-yard walk along the busy A259 to Parget Bank. Alternative access over railway footbridge at TQ452005, with limited roadside parking next to the sewage works.

BY TRAIN: **0.25 mile walk from Newhaven Town Station.**
BY BUS: **No.712 stops on the A259 at the end of the lane to the level crossing.**

113

Key points

- **Allow half an hour**
- **Expect 20-25 species**
- **Part of Dungeness and Pett Level SPA, plus SSSI status**
- **Viewing possible at all times, but no access to near edge of pit**
- **No facilities**
- **Roadside parking and watching - park carefully**
- **Wheelchair viewing marred by roadside fence**
- **No direct public transport links**
- **Telescope helpful**
- **Pit can get disturbed by windsurfing activities**
- **Morning recommended for light**

Contacts

English Nature, Sussex and Surrey Team
01273 476595
sussex.surrey@
english-nature.org.uk

JUST OUTSIDE RYE on the road to Camber is a rather unexceptional-looking roadside gravel pit. There is good reason for at least a ten-minute pull in here though, as winter after winter, it proves irresistible to Smew. Quite why is unclear, but numbers in excess of 20 can occur and males are regular.

Target birds Winter - Smew (80%), Goldeneye (60%).

Other likely bird species

All year	_Passage_	_Occasional_
Wildfowl	Hirundines	Whimbrel
Gulls	Common Sandpiper	Greenshank
Redshank	Common Tern	Spotted Redshank
Oystercatcher		Black Tern
Starling	_Winter_	Barn Owl
	Mistle Thrush	

Background information and birding tips

NORTHPOINT PIT is self-evident on your right-hand side as you drive from Rye on the road to Camber. It is only a few hundred yards in a straight line from Castle Water at Rye Harbour, on the other side of the river, despite being a five mile drive from there. Undoubtedly there is a bird interchange between the two sites.

Driving past, it is possible to spot a few Tufted

Ducks on the water, but although the pit appears quite modest, it is actually deceptively large and any wildfowl species out towards the far side, won't be apparent to the naked eye.

This is where the Smew tend to hang out and, even with binoculars, the stunning males can be amazingly inconspicuous if the surface of the water is rippled. The red-heads are far more obvious however, and

Northpoint Pit seems to be irresistible to Smew in winter.

are often a good guide to where the males may be.

The first Smew tend to arrive in November, with peak figures in January and February and the last birds often gone by March. At times there may be only a couple or so, or even, if the Rye Watersports Club have been out, none whatsoever. However, they are usually there.

Northpoint Pit is also good for Goldeneyes, which are not too easy to find in Sussex. Great Crested Grebes, Little Grebes, Tufted Ducks, Mallards and various gulls are also likely on the pit.

The near shoreline can hold a small wader roost, predominantly Redshanks. However, Spotted Redshanks have also been recorded here, Common Sandpipers are likely on passage and flights of Whimbrels sometimes drop-in in April and May.

It is also worth turning to look behind you over the sheep-grazed East Guldeford Levels. Lapwings are spread far and wide here in winter with inevitable roving Starling flocks. They can also be with Mistle Thrushes and the odd covey of Red-legged Partridges or flock of Golden Plovers.

A Mute Swan herd is usually just north of here on agricultural land and, though Bewick's or Whooper Swans are far from expected, it's worth having a check through the Mutes just in case.

Though you can't see it from the parking area, the River

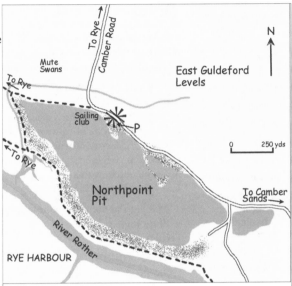

Access details

(1mile south east of Rye)

From Rye, follow A259 E. Turn right at East Guldeford towards Camber and Lydd, and Northpoint Pit is on R after 1 mile of S-bends. Park on the broad but potholed verge near the watersports club huts and watch from this side of the fence (TQ935201). Alternatively, walk from here to the public footpath at the north corner of the lake, which

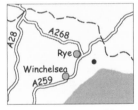

leads around the top and far side of the Pit.

BY TRAIN: 1 mile walk from Rye Station.
BY BUS: No service.

Rother is just over the far bank of the pit - a walk through to the river can be rewarding as waders such as Little Stints, Curlew Sandpipers and wintering

Spotted Redshanks can be found here. The riverside saltings between here and Rye also attract large numbers of roosting gulls and high tide wader roosts.

Other nearby sites

Less than 10 miles: Pett Level, Rye Harbour, Scotney Court.

115

Key points

- **Allow all day if possible**
- **Expect 50-80 species**
- **SPA, SSSI & WSCC/SWT reserve**
- **Access open at all times on rights of way**
- **Limited areas suitable for wheelchair access and viewing**
- **Visitor centre (free entry, open Tues, Thurs & Fri am, and 10am-4pm Sat & Sun, staffed by volunteers) with limited facilities but including toilets (open at all times)**
- **Main access from three free car parks.**

Contacts

Pagham Harbour LNR Visitor Centre
01243 641508
pagham.nr@
westsussex.gov.uk

PAGHAM IS probably the most famous birdwatching location in Sussex and rightly so. Indeed, it is difficult to have a bad day's birding here at any season. The word 'Harbour' conjures images of yachts, quays and people. Not so Pagham Harbour - this is a 'harbour' as birdwatchers would want it, a large tidal basin of channels, mudflats and saltmarsh reserved almost wholly for wildlife.

With a host of habitats crammed around the harbour, expect great views of upwards of 60 species in a day. There is a wonderful array of waders and wildfowl in all seasons, plenty of passerine migrants and a delectable list of rarities to its name, such as the UK's first Greater Sand Plover AND the UK's first Lesser Sand Plover!

And yet Pagham Harbour still feels delightfully low-key, with no huge car parks or overwhelming visitor facilities. Our verdict - brilliant!

Target birds

High numbers of common wintering wildfowl (including several hundred Pintails and up to 2500 Dark-bellied Brent Geese) and common passage and wintering waders (including up to 2000 Dunlins and 1000 Grey Plovers), plus:

All year – Peregrine (30%), Little Owl (20%).

Passage – Little Ringed Plover (40%), Hobby (20%), Marsh Harrier (10%), Osprey (5%),

Spring - Temminck's Stint (early-mid May 5%).

Autumn - Yellow-legged Gull (90%), Little Stint (50%), Curlew Sandpiper (50%), Wood Sandpiper (40%), Black Redstart (10%), Redstart (50%), Whinchat (60%), Pied Flycatcher (5%).

Breeding season – Little Tern (30% - doesn't breed), Turtle Dove (20%).

Winter – Black-tailed Godwit (95%), Slavonian Grebe (75%), Avocet (80%), Knot (80%), Bar-tailed Godwit (80%), Mediterranean Gull (80%), Spotted Redshank (60%), Goldeneye (40%), Whimbrel (40%), Red-throated Diver (30%), Eider (30%), Firecrest (30%), Smew (10%), Water Rail (10%), Glaucous Gull (10%), Kingfisher (10%), Dartford Warbler (10%), Scaup (5%), Great Northern Diver (5%).

Other likely bird species

All year
Waterbirds
Wildfowl
Coastal waders
Freshwater waders
Gulls
Woodland birds
Farmland birds
Garden birds
Little Egret
Shelduck
Stonechat

Passage
Hirundines
Warblers
Ruff
Greenshank

Grey Wagtail
Wheatear
Spotted Flycatcher
Siskin

Breeding season
Sandwich Tern
Common Tern

Winter
Wigeon
Gadwall
Shoveler
Red-breasted
Merganser
Golden Plover
Knot
Rock Pipit

Occasional
Gannet
White-fronted Goose
Pale-bellied Brent Goose
Garganey
Honey Buzzard
Merlin
Grey Partridge
Purple Sandpiper
Short-eared Owl
Wryneck
Water Pipit
Cetti's Warbler
Bearded Tit

Background information and birding tips

IT IS POSSIBLE to birdwatch from almost anywhere around Pagham Harbour's mile-wide sheltered bay, as public footpaths circle the seven miles or more of Harbour perimeter.

With so much to cover, fitting in everywhere in a day is difficult, especially as the North Wall/Pagham Spit area, although only a two and a half mile walk from the main visitor centre, is actually a ten mile drive. A sensible itinerary, therefore, is to either combine the Sidlesham Ferry and Church Norton areas, or alternatively concentrate on the North Wall area with perhaps a quick drop in at one of the other two sites. Indeed, the Ferry Pool at Sidlesham Ferry can be adequately checked in half an hour if pressed.

Sidlesham Ferry Area

The Visitor Centre is usually the first port of call. Low-key and with no refreshments, there is nevertheless a warm welcome, plenty of free info and the essential sightings board and book. There are also toilets, the only ones on the whole reserve.

Sidlesham Ferry Pool

From the Visitor Centre, most birders make a bee-line for the Ferry Pool. No wonder – it is one of the best magnets for rare waders in the UK. Baird's Sandpiper, Least Sandpiper, Wilson's Phalarope – you name it, it has occurred here.

The Pool can be accessed in two ways - by heading out of the car park entrance and left along the busy road, or by taking the broad reserve footpath. Going along the road has obvious dangers and also the sad trend for some motorists to play 'birder baiting' with frequent blasts of their horns.

The more sensible option is to take the track through the reserve, alongside scrub and shrubs used by tits, finches and passerine migrants. In less than 400 yards, you reach a hide overlooking the Ferry Pool, but most birders usually enjoy the wider views by standing either side of it.

Take time scanning over the Ferry Pool, even if at first glance it looks insignificant. Split from the tidal Harbour by a sluice, it hosts much more in the way of freshwater waders. In autumn, expect half a dozen or so Little Stints, Curlew Sandpipers, Green and Common Sandpipers, Ruffs and maybe an eclipse Garganey. It is also Sussex's best place to see a Wood Sandpiper (or three) at this time.

Continues overleaf

Key points

- Overflow car park at Sidlesham Ferry is locked at 5pm, but main car park remains open

- Three hides, but otherwise exposed

- Some paths can get muddy, some walking on shingle, but terrain flat

- Light best in morning at Ferry Pool

- Telescope useful throughout

Access details

(5 miles S of Chichester)

SIDLESHAM FERRY: Take B2145 from A27 Chichester by-pass S towards Selsey for 5 miles passing through long village of Sidlesham. Pagham LNR Visitor Centre is on L just beyond low-key garden centre selling paving-slabs. (SZ856966). Church Norton: Continue along B2145 from Sidlesham Ferry for a further 1.5 miles. As road swings R, turn L down narrow road signed to Church Norton. Car park is after 1mile at end of road (SZ871956).

PAGHAM SPIT: From the A27 Chichester by-pass, take the B2166 towards Bognor. After 2.5 miles, the B2166 turns left but carry straight on towards Pagham. Pass right through the village (past three pubs) to the Church farm Holiday Village. Just before the road swings right in front of the Holiday

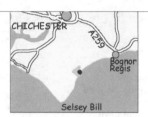

Village, turn left down Sea Lane (signed 'To the Sea'). Where this road reaches a T-junction, turn R down the narrow Harbour Road out to Pagham Spit (SZ882964), where sometimes there is a parking charge. There is alternative but limited roadside parking nearer to the North Wall at SZ880976.

BY TRAIN: No direct access.
BY BUS: No.51 Chichester-Selsey service is half-hourly, with hourly Sunday service. Stops directly outside Sidlesham Ferry reserve. No.60 Bognor-Chichester-Midhurst stops in Pagham village, allowing 0.5 mile walk to Pagham Spit or North Wall.

Temminck's Stints are spring annuals (try between May 5-12) and there is always a good selection of wildfowl too. Curlews and Lapwings, the latter breeding, are always likely. Snipe frequent the muddy stretches just to the right of the pool and note that the godwits here are usually Black-tailed, but not always.

The grass fields beyond have ever-present Stock Doves, with Turtle Doves and Yellow Wagtails in summer and, at migration time, any fence post can be topped with a Whinchat, Wheatear or Stonechat.

Ferry Pool is best viewed in the morning with the sun behind you - on a sunny afternoon, you'll be testing your silhouette skills!

Ferry Long Pool

Through the 'kissing gate', you are now at the head of the harbour. A good path runs immediately left following its west bank, but it isn't the best for birds. Instead cross the sluice (we call it 'The Dragon', on account of the sporadic unannounced 'roar' when it pumps water through). Look down the muddy channel from The Dragon - one or two Spotted Redshanks are incredibly reliable here in winter.

Now turn left down a choice of two tracks either side of the narrow reed-fringed Ferry Long Pool. The pool hosts winter Water Rails, breeding Reed Warblers and Reed Buntings, plus Coots, Mallards and Little Grebes. The harbour bank gives views over farmland, good for Curlews, raptors, Short-eared Owls,

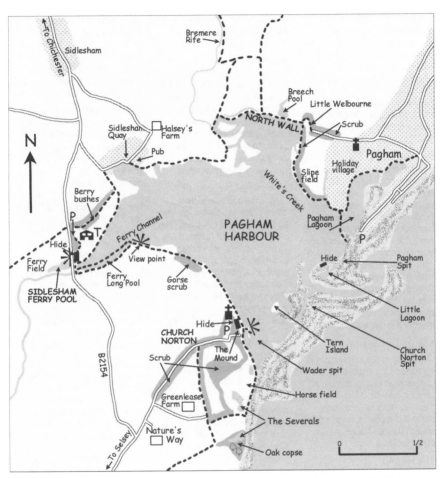

Meadow Pipits and Sky Larks, while the scrub close to the path attracts Linnets, Whitethroats, Whinchats and Stonechats.

Viewpoint

At the end of the Long Pool is a bench giving expansive views down the open Harbour. Massed in the tidal ferry channel should be plenty of winter Wigeon, along with handfuls of Redshanks, Grey Plovers, Curlews, Little Egrets and Dunlins, with a good chance of Pintails or Avocets (usually distant). The raised areas of saltmarsh above the channels are good for the odd wintering Whimbrel and we've seen a superb summer-plumaged Water Pipit here in spring. Panic in the Harbour is a good signal to check the skies above for usually a Peregrine or maybe a passage Marsh Harrier.

Gorse Scrub

From the southern end of the Long Pool, it is possible to continue down the Harbour bank the mile to Church Norton. The patches of gorse

Continues overleaf

alongside the path are reliable for Dartford Warblers in autumn, although seeing one is not so easy. It's a long walk, though, (and seemingly even longer back) and we find it more time-efficient, in a reserve where there is so much to see, to return to the Visitor Centre and then drive to Church Norton car park.

Berry Bushes

From the back of the Visitor Centre a track heads out north-eastwards, with restricted views over the least productive shore of the harbour. However, the hedges are thick with dense berry bushes, attracting migrants in spring and especially autumn. Lesser Whitethroats and Spotted Flycatchers are regular and it is a good place to look for Wrynecks or Barred Warblers in September.

Church Norton

Parking at Church Norton is restricted to less than 20 spaces next to the church. At times it may be difficult to find a space, but please always respect the places reserved for church users. There are no other facilities here.

The Mound

From the car park, head past the gate marked 'Pagham Harbour Local Nature Reserve' down the shady track. It is worth lingering to watch the bushes either side, especially around the Iron Age Mound on the left. The area seems irresistible for passage and wintering Firecrests, migrant Redstarts, Pied Flycatchers, warblers and even passing

Crossbills. The spring male Collared Flycatcher of 2002 shows the potential here.

Wader Spit

Where the track emerges on the edge of the Harbour mud, turn left fifty yards to a small shingle spit overlooking the open Harbour. The waders seem quite oblivious to people here, so the hide set back behind you is only really necessary in wet weather.

Whatever the state of the tide, whatever the season, there is almost always plenty to see here and birds are often close-to. Several hundred Grey Plovers coming into breeding plumage in spring is a fabulous sight. In a good Curlew Sandpiper and Little Stint year, they can be a dead-cert and ever-present, in all but mid-summer, are Ringed Plovers, Turnstones, Dunlins, Redshanks and probably a few Knots and Bar-tailed Godwits (though Pagham is surprisingly poor for the latter).

Further back is 'Tern Island', although unfortunately, terns being fickle things, no species now breed. Sandwich and Common Terns may still be around however, whilst squadrons of Cormorants and the larger gulls line up on the distant mud. Mediterranean Gulls are likely in winter.

Hide

What the hide does have in its favour is two-way viewing. From the back, it looks into a small paddock, where a fantastic range of autumn migrants have been found, especially warblers, but you'll

need patience. It is also possible to walk on from the hide and cut back to the car park through the churchyard, looking for Redstarts and other migrants, but please birdwatch respectfully in the graveyard.

'Horse Field' and Beach

From the Mound, the walk right takes you to the beach. *En route*, to your right, is a little marsh, good for either of the Redshanks. The fence beyond is reliable for Wheatears and Whinchats, and the horse field beyond that is used by Whimbrels in spring. But beware - the path-side mud to your left here is *very* soft and sticky.

The beach is perfect for either a summer picnic or winter seawatching. Pagham is too far round the corner from Selsey to enjoy good sea passage so attention is on the birds on the water instead.

The sea straight out in front of you has consistently been Slavonian Grebe heaven, usually reaching double figures in November, peaking in March (up to 70), and then swiftly departing. Numbers were reduced in the 2001/2 and 2002/3 winters, hopefully a short-term blip. You should also see plenty of Great Crested Grebes too, with Mergansers, Eiders and a fair chance of divers including Great Northern.

On the shingle of Church Norton spit, towards the harbour mouth, Ringed Plovers try to breed and the odd Twite or Snow Bunting may turn up in early winter. Both of the latter are now county rarities. In summer, terns, including a few Little, pass to and fro offshore, while at all seasons, check the shoreline for waders, as the low tide exposes a flat bed of shingle for feeding and roosting. Be aware, when scanning with your telescope, the Spit is used by naturists.

The Severals

The Severals are two brackish pools on the right when walking south along the beach. The first Several is reed-choked and there's not much water to see on the second either. Reed Warblers are inevitable in summer, and Cetti's Warblers may be heard at times but the scrub between the beach and the pools is more productive, excellent for drift migrants, with Wrynecks annual and Barred Warblers and Red-backed Shrikes possible.

Greenlease Farm

From The Severals, you can take a track through farmland back to Church Norton car park. To be honest, you are leaving quality and quantity behind, though we did see a small party of Bean Geese in this area in 2001. You will only add a few farmland and woodland birds to your day list though, including a good chance of Little Owl. If you like circular walks however, this is for you.

North wall area

Pagham Spit

A walk around the sparsely-vegetated shingle of the Spit itself takes only half an hour or so. Keep an eye out for migrant

Wheatears and Black Redstarts, as well as Linnets, Stonechats and Sky larks. The wet hollows in the shingle and the seaweedy tidal margins here are good for Rock Pipits throughout the winter, with Purple Sandpipers sometimes amoung the Turnstones.

It is worth looking into the Harbour from the spit for distant views of waders out on the mud but especially for Brent Geese, Red-breasted Mergansers and Goldeneyes using the deeper channels. The hide here is only open March-October to counter vandalism.

Pagham Lagoon

A short walk along the Harbour edge brings you to Pagham Lagoon. It doesn't look hugely promising, but don't overlook it. What you think may just be a few Tufted Ducks and Little Grebes will often prove to include a Smew, Scaup or Goosander. Mediterranean Gulls are regular in winter, and this is where the Bonaparte's Gull entertained in 2002 and the Sora in 1985.

White's Creek

Continuing north around the Harbour, the edge can be boggy and can flood at high tide, but the birds are worth it. Here, in White's Creek and on the mud beyond, gulls, waders

and wildfowl gather. In July, up to 300 Yellow-legged Gulls stand out, while the winter roost of Great Black-backs is huge, attracting annual Glaucous Gulls. This part of the Harbour, up to the North Wall, is the favoured area for Brent Geese and Golden Plovers, with Black-tailed Godwits often in three figures.

North Wall

A mile from Pagham Spit, you reach the North Wall at a little building called The Salthouse. Beyond is a damp paddock, used by Black-tailed Godwits, Brent Geese and Curlews.

From the top of the wall are views over the reed-fringed Breech Pool. It isn't large, but has reeds, open water and often some muddy margins. The birds here are seemingly oblivious to the stream of human silhouettes on the skyline and it attracts small numbers of a lot of species.

In winter there are dabbling duck including Gadwalls plus regular Water Rails. By March, Little Ringed Plovers arrive and maybe an Avocet or Greenshank. It is then as good as Ferry Pool for Temminck's Stints, while a dozen pairs of Reed Warblers take up territory. All of autumn's passage waders may drop in, so do give it a try – it is much underwatched.

Other nearby sites

Less than 5 miles: Selsey Bill and West Fields, Less than 10 miles, Chichester Gravel Pits, Chidham and Cobnor, East Head & West Wittering, Kingley Vale.

40 ***   PETT LEVEL & RYE BAY

Key points

- Allow 1-plus hours

- Expect 30 species from the beach; 50-80 inland

- Part of Dungeness and Pett Level SPA, SSSI. Pett Pools is a no access SWT reserve

- Open at all times on public rights of way and beach

- Free roadside parking under seawall

- Public toilets in Cliff End village

- Wheelchair access to seawall only at Winchelsea Beach and Smugglers PH

- Sheep are present, keep dogs on leads

- Telescope useful

Contacts

English Nature
01273 476595
sussex.surrey
@english-nature.org.uk

For Pett Pools:
Sussex Wildlife Trust
01273 492630

PETT LEVEL is a flat expanse of grazing land and ditches behind Rye Bay, backed by a wooded old cliff-line and with the sea kept out by a high seawall. The beach has confiding waders, while the bay has the best inshore flocks of grebes, divers and scoters in Sussex. Add to this the pools and reedbeds, farmland and woods and Pett Level can almost match Rye Harbour species for species!

Target birds *Spring passage*- Whimbrel (50%). *Breeding season* - Common, Sandwich and Little Terns offshore (80%). *Autumn passage* - Hobby (40%). *Winter* - Red-throated Diver, Great Crested Grebe and Common Scoter flock (75%), Velvet Scoter (10%), Water Rail (10%). Avocet Little gull.

Other likely bird species

All year	Brent Goose	Water Pipit
Waterbirds	Little Ringed Plover	Stonechat
Wildfowl	Yellow Wagtail	
Coastal waders	Wheatear	*Occasional*
Inland waders	Whinchat	Black-throated Diver
Gulls Little gull ✓	Avocet	Bittern
Woodland birds	*Breeding season*	Scaup
Farmland birds	Fulmar	Marsh Harrier
Peregrine	Cuckoo	Hen Harrier
	Lesser Whitethroat	Little Stint
Passage		Curlew Sandpiper
Hirundines	*Winter*	Kingfisher
Warblers	Wigeon	Bearded Tit
Gannet	Shoveler	Tree Sparrow
✓ Little Egret	Gadwall	Snow Bunting
	Golden Plover	

Background information and birding tips

FROM THE seawall just east of Pett, there is 360° birding. In winter, the sheltered sweep of Rye Bay can be stocked solid with Great Crested Grebes (up to 600), Red-throated Divers (up to 400) and Common Scoters (up to 500). Diligent searching can turn up Velvet Scoters, too. Alternatively, there could be barely anything on the sea - such is birdwatching! Sea conditions and state of the tide affect your success rate too - a calm sea on a rising tide is good, a windy day blowing straight from the cold Continent is unbearable.

On the beach, Turnstones tamely pick along the shingle and at low-tide, the slippery 'moorlog' (the remains of a prehistoric forest) is used by Oystercatchers, Curlews, Redshanks, Dunlins and Grey Plovers. In summer, terns fish close inshore, with Sandwich, Little and Common Terns from Rye Harbour all likely. The top of the seawall, especially where there are a few weedy patches, can hold a variety of migrants and, if you are really lucky, the odd winter Snow Bunting, now a major rarity in Sussex.

Turning inland, scan Pett Pools from the seawall as access around the pools is not permitted. The seawall is a perfect vantage point, adequate enough to see most birds, though it may be a while before we see a repeat of the Squacco Heron of 2000. Alongside the common wildfowl, in winter the duck tally increases with fair numbers of Shovelers, Teal and smaller numbers of Gadwalls, with maybe 200 or so Wigeon grazing the margins.

The water levels used to be dropped deliberately in autumn, attracting an exciting wader passage. With Little and Great Crested Grebes and Tufted Ducks now breeding, this practice has been stopped and the water levels remain high throughout.

If you fancy a walk inland, try the path from Pett up the ruler-straight Royal Military Canal. Flocks of Curlew on the Levels are joined by Whimbrels in spring. It's also worth checking through any goose flock in winter - White-fronts and Pink-feet are sometimes drawn in by the Canadas and Greylags.

Where the canal bends right, a couple of slender footbridges lead into the Pannel Valley where a local landowner has turned some farmland back to reedy marsh, with a small hide overlooking a scrape. The valley has a mouth-watering list of passerine rarities but this is thanks to a sterling bird-ringing

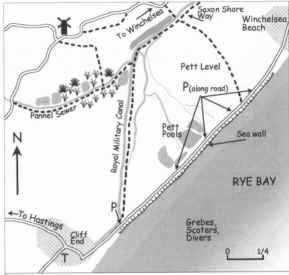

Access details

(6 miles ENE of Hastings)

Pett Level is accessed via a minor road along the seawall between Pett village and Winchelsea. From Rye, travel W towards Winchelsea on A259, turn L after 2 miles to Winchelsea Beach. Pass through this seaside village and out on the straight road under the seawall, stopping on the roadside (either side) where you see Pett Pools to your R after 1mile. From Hastings on A259 drive through Ore, turning R to Pett where you see the signs. Pett

effort in the reeds and not what you should expect to see. Rather, the list reveals what is waiting to be found out there in coastal Sussex.

Other nearby sites

Less than 5 miles: Hastings Country Park.
Less than 10 miles: Northpoint Pit, Rye Harbour.

Pools are on the L after 0.5 mile (TQ900144). Access to the seawall is up flights of concrete steps or steep access slopes.

BY TRAIN: Two mile walk from Winchelsea Station.
BY BUS: Regular No.344 Northiam-Rye-Hastings service drops at Pett Level.

A good circular walk is possible by following the back of Pett Level along the old wooded cliff there and back out to the coast road.

Key points

- Allow 2-plus hours

- Expect 25-35 species

- Ramsar site and SSSI, with NNR on Pevensey Bridge Level

- Public rights of way open at all times - please keep to them

- No facilities; even parking very difficult

- Public footpaths can be muddy and poorly signed

- Not suitable for wheelchairs

- This is sheep-rearing country - pay extra attention to the Country Code, close gates, and keep dogs on leads

- Telescope and map helpful in big landscape

Contacts

English Nature, Sussex and Surrey Team
01273 476595
sussex.surrey@english-nature.org.uk

PEVENSEY LEVELS are a whopping 14 square miles of flat grazing marsh dissected by reed-lined ditches. With wildlife-minded farmers 'rewetting' some of the land, numbers of wetland birds, such as winter wildfowl and breeding waders, are now beginning to return to healthy numbers.

Target birds *All year* - Peregrine (30%, higher in winter). *Passage* - Hobby (30%), Whimbrel (30%). *Winter* - Short-eared Owl (30%), Green Sandpiper (25%), Kingfisher (25%), Hen Harrier (5%).

Other likely bird species

All year	Yellow Wagtail	*Winter*
Waterbirds	Lesser Whitethroat	Thrushes
Wildfowl		Golden Plover
Farmland birds	*Passage*	Snipe
Shelduck	Hirundines	Stonechat
Lapwing	Little Egret	
	Greenshank	*Occasional*
Breeding season	Wigeon	Garganey
Cuckoo		Black-tailed Godwit

Background information and birding tips

ONCE A TIDAL BAY, the Pevensey Levels have long been reclaimed from the sea for agriculture. For birds it was no disaster, as the land remained extremely wet and prone to flooding. As recently as 1976, up to 27 pairs of Snipe and 29 of Redshanks were present.

From the 1980s onwards, better pump drainage and more intensive grazing spelt problems for wetland birds. Water became confined to the miles of ditches, and today many parts of the levels are bone dry even in winter.

However there is optimism! 'Rewetting supplements' available under Government schemes mean that, under the guiding hands of inspired farmers, water is returning to parts of the Levels. The best areas are:

Horse Eye Level
One mile north on the minor road from Rickney, a little pull-in on the left overlooks some wet rushy pasture, attracting passage waders, plus Lapwings, Shelducks and Redshanks in summer **(1)**.

Half a mile further on, just before the road bends right over a little bridge, a track leads out onto the Levels with Horse Eye Farm to your right **(2)**. A walk out here should produce flocks of Wigeon and Teal in winter, plus Golden Plovers among the Lapwings, Snipe and occasional Green Sandpipers in the ditches.

We've seen Little Egrets, several species of passage waders and Garganeys here. The Level has even attracted Great White Egret and Marsh Sandpiper.

Hankham Level
Approached either from Rickney or

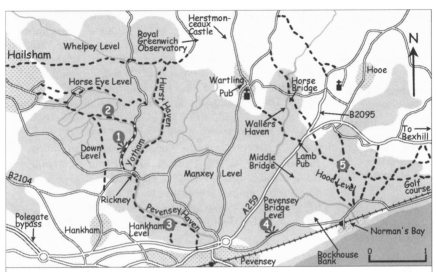

Access details

(6 miles N and NE of Eastbourne)

Pevensey Levels is crossed by A259 between Pevensey and Bexhill, and circumscribed by the B2104, A271 and B2095. The roundabout next to the Esso garage on the A259 just NE of Pevensey is a good central starting place (TQ651051). From here:

For Pevensey Bridge Level take minor road SE towards Norman's Bay. Occasional verge parking possible after 1 to 2 miles (eg TQ664053)

For Hooe Level, continue on along this road for another mile over level crossing. It is then possible to park on the shingle beach (TQ701062) and carefully walk back up road and out onto the Level.

For Horse Eye Level, turn N towards Wartling, but immediately turn L on narrow road. After 2 miles, pass through Rickney hamlet, and take next R. Horse Eye Level on L after 0.5 mile (TQ624075). Parking very difficult, please use extreme care and consideration.

BY TRAIN: 1 mile walk from Pevensey Station onto Hankham Level, or 1 mile walk from Norman's Bay Station or Cooden Station onto Hooe Level.

BY BUS: No.19 Eastbourne-Battle stops at Pevensey Castle - less than hourly.

---

from Pevensey along the river's south bank, the land between Pevensey Haven and the A259 **(3)** is good for Redshanks, Shelducks and Yellow Wagtails in the breeding season and winter wildfowl and Snipe.

Pevensey Bridge Level
Some pull-ins along the minor road between the A259 roundabout at Pevensey and Norman's Bay give adequate views north over this NNR **(4)**, where good flocks of Wigeon, Lapwings, Golden Plovers and Dunlins can gather.

Hooe Level
Extensive footpaths lead out and around Hooe Level and the reed-rich edge of the Cooden Golf Course. Short-eared Owls and Hen Harriers are recorded regularly from here in winter **(5)**.

Across all the Levels, expect clamorous flocks of Redwings and Fieldfares in the tall hawthorn hedges along the lanes and, if Pevensey Levels had a mascot, it would be the Reed Warbler, as every few metres of ditch seems to have a pair.

Key points

- Allow 1-plus hours at any of the sites

- Expect 25-40 species

- Reservoirs are owned by South East Water; Ashes Wood and Footland Wood are Forestry Commission sites; Darwell Wood is SSSI

- Public footpaths open at all times. Some of the permissive woodland rides may be closed during forestry operations

- Some parking at some sites, no other facilities

- Mud *very* likely in winter, some minor gradients

- Not suitable for wheelchairs

- Some of these sites difficult by public transport

O N A MAP, the sizeable reservoirs at Powdermill and Darwell look promising, but at neither site does public access extend to the water's edge. In the end it is the Wealden woodland birdwatching in the area, either around the reservoirs or at places such as Ashes Wood, Footland Wood and Battle Great Wood, that offers the most reward, with Willow Tits, Nightingales, Tree Pipits and Nightjars possible.

Key to bird areas	A-Ashes Wood, B-Battle Great Wood, D-Darwell Wood, F-Footland Wood, P-Powdermill Reservoir

Target birds *All year* – Woodcock (80% when roding, 10% in winter), Willow Tit (10%, especially at A), Mandarin (10%, especially at B, P and D), Crossbill (5-30%). *Breeding season* – Nightingale (hear 80%, see 10% at A), Tree Pipit (60%), Hobby (50%), Turtle Dove (30%), Nightjar (20%, especially at B), Hobby (10%). *Winter* – Redpoll (50%).

Other likely bird species

All year	Moorhen (P)	Siskin
Woodland birds	Grey Wagtail (A,D,P)	
Nuthatch	Marsh Tit	*Occasional*
Great Crested Grebe (P)	*Winter*	Lesser Spotted Woodpecker
Tufted Duck (P)	Gadwall (P)	Hawfinch (D,P,F)
Coot (P)	Teal (P)	Brambling

Background information and birding tips

L ITTLE VISITED, **Ashes Wood** near Netherfield is a gem. A narrow and easy wood to work, head straight down the hill, check out the old mill pond just to the left at the bottom of the hill, and work your way back up the wood.

There is a glorious mix of woodland here – pine, larch, hazel and birch, mature oak and beech. It is probably as good as any wood now in Sussex to try to find Willow Tits (there are Marsh Tits too, mind you), Nightingales sing deep in the dense young areas, Siskins and Redpolls are regular in winter and it is even open enough in places for Yellowhammers.

Some people like **Footland Wood** near Vinehall Street.

Certainly the parking is the best of any of these sites and, open glades near the car park and in Vinehall Forest on the opposite side of the road, can hold Tree Pipits and Nightjars.

Battle Great Wood is a much larger block of woodland with probably more Nightjars here than in other woods in the area, plus the possibility of Tree Pipits.

Any waders or wildfowl at **Darwell Reservoir** are impossible to see as public footpaths steer well clear of the water and the margins are flanked by thick stands of willows. So concentrate on the woodland birds, which can actually be quite good. Starting from Cackle Street, a public footpath leads off north along quite a wide track. The

Access details

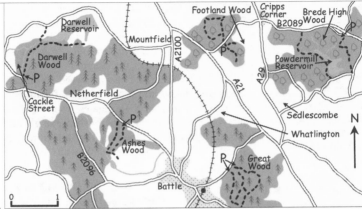

DARWELL WOOD: (9 miles NW of Hastings). Via the Battle-Heathfield B2096, turn N at Darwell Hole. Park at wide entrance to Darwell Wood in Cackle Street (TQ 695195). *POWDERMILL RESERVOIR:* (6.5 miles N of Hastings). From B2089 Cripp's Corner to Broad Oak road, park at TQ803206 (entrance to Brede High Wood) or vergeside at TQ790208. Parking near Powdermill Reservoir dam is difficult and footpath up the western side of the reservoir hard to find *ASHES WOOD:* (7 miles NW of Hastings). From Battle, turn W off the A2100 on B2096 towards Netherfield. After 1mile, there is a wide entrance marked 'Ashes Wood, Forestry Commission' on L (TQ729178). If you reach entrance to Netherfield Place

(hotel), you have gone 100 yards too far. *FOOTLAND WOOD:* (7 miles NNW of Hastings). Parking is well signed on B2089, 200 yards E off A21 towards Cripps Corner (TQ763203) *BATTLE GREAT WOOD:* (5 miles NW of Hastings). Parking on Marley Lane, which heads E out of Battle. Drive for 1mile from Battle, parking is on R at TQ765164.

BY TRAIN: From Battle station, 0.5 mile of pavement walking takes you into Battle Great Wood.

BY BUS: Plenty of bus services to Battle from Hastings. The 355 Heathfield-Battle service, less than hourly, passes through Cackle Street and Netherfield.

woodland is mixed, with some towering conifers to your right and wet young woodland to your left. Marsh Tits, Coal Tits, Goldcrests and winter Siskins are all likely.

The signed footpath leads through to a covered conveyor belt from Netherfield mines, which is a good landmark. The dark woods opposite here, running south of the reservoir, are very good for Marsh Tits. Retracing your steps, the woodland slopes above Cackle Street lead to the higher ground of Darwell Hill.

Clearings here attract small numbers of Tree Pipits, Turtle Doves, Yellowhammers, plus Woodcocks and even Nightjars at dusk, though night visits are far easier elsewhere.

At **Powdermill Reservoir**, deep in a shady wooded valley, there are at least some limited views of the water birds from between the branches and trunks. Great Crested Grebes, Gadwalls and Teals are regular. Some determined effort by a very few local observers however, has turned up mouthwatering

species in the wood, such as Crossbills, Willow Tits, Golden Pheasants, Hawfinches, Lesser Spotted Woodpeckers and Mandarins, plus plenty of Siskins and Redpolls. Not forgetting the small flock of three Red-footed Falcons in 1992!

The footpath down through Brede High Wood can be good too. All the footpaths shown on the map are worth exploration, and the woods include some good mature hornbeams (listen for those tell-tale Hawfinch calls) and are florally rich, too.

127

Key points

- Allow 3-plus hours

- Expect 40-60 species

- Part of Arun Valley SPA, Ramsar site, SSSI and RSPB reserve

- Free entry to visitor centre & shop (open 10am-5pm), & tea-room (closes slightly earlier)

- Reserve open at all times

- Extensive free parking

- Entrance fee to reserve (free for RSPB members)

- Toilets including disabled

- Motorised scooters available for disabled, giving access to almost all of reserve

Contacts

RSPB Pulborough Brooks
01798 875851

WITHIN ten years of RSPB management, Pulborough has become internationally-important for wintering wildfowl and is now the Society's flagship reserve in the South East. As it is almost exactly ten miles from the sea, birdwatching here lacks the drama of the coast (hence our lowly four star rating). But with breeding and passage waders, and hedgerow, woodland and farmland birds in abundance, including Nightingales, you can see up to 60 species in a visit. If you enjoy birdwatching with fine views, pleasant walks and all the facilities (including home-made cakes!), Pulborough will be the five-star site you've been looking for.

Target birds
All year – Little Owl (40%), Peregrine (30%). *Passage* – Little Ringed Plover (40%), Garganey (spring – 5%), Wood Sandpiper (autumn - 5%), Short-eared Owl (late autumn – 5%). *Breeding season* – Nightingale (hear 90%, see 40%), Hobby (60%). *Winter* – Large flocks of wildfowl (100%), Ruff (50%), Bewick's Swan (10%), Merlin (10%), Lesser Spotted Woodpecker (5%).

Other likely bird species

All year	*Passage*	*Winter*
Waterbirds	Shelduck	Gulls
Wildfowl	Common Sandpiper	Thrushes
Woodland birds	Green Sandpiper	Wigeon
Farmland birds	Greenshank	Pintail
Little Egret	Wheatear	Pochard
Greylag Goose	Spotted Flycatcher	Snipe
Shoveler		Dunlin
Redshank	*Breeding season*	Stonechat
Lapwing	Hirundines	
Marsh Tit	Yellow Wagtail	*Occasional*
Nuthatch	Garden Warbler	White-fronted Goose
Treecreeper		Mandarin

Background information and birding tips

HOW LUCKY we are to have places like Pulborough Brooks! Here birdwatching isn't something that has to slot in alongside other human activities. It's what the place is geared up for, and everything is laid on to make the activity all the more easy and enjoyable.

Having parked (which may be in the overflow car park at weekends), you'll be birdwatching even before you get in the Visitor Centre. The feeders in the courtyard garden entice regular Marsh Tits, Great Spotted Woodpeckers and Nuthatches, giving superb views. Bramblings occur most winters and

even Lesser Spotted Woodpeckers have come onto the nuts. The sightings board is here too, with several days' sightings on view.

Visitors are funnelled through the Visitor Centre, which is a converted barn. (When it is closed, you can still access the reserve – free of course to RSPB members and an honesty box is there if you're not.)

We know we're biased, but we think the Visitor Centre houses the best tea-room of any RSPB reserve (no need to bring a packed lunch here). There is a well stocked shop and warm toilets that *feel* clean.

It's often really busy in the shop and tea-room, but don't be put off. The reserve is large enough to accommodate plenty of people, and many come just for the cakes or to buy their birdseed or a new pair of bins.

You can check out those new optics through the floor-to-ceiling window – the views are fabulous and staff can often point out the resident pair of Little Owls in a distant oak tree.

Having shown your membership card or paid your reserve entrance fee, the first part of the walk takes you along the top of a large field **(1)** that is being managed experimentally for farmland birds.

Sown in spring, the crop is left as stubble in winter and, though many of the small birds are likely to be bedded down, at intervals flocks of

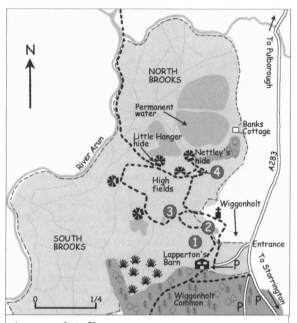

Access details

(1.5 miles SE of Pulborough)

Easy to find on A283 half-way between Pulborough and Storrington. There is a big RSPB sign at the entrance (and an even bigger tea shop sign). Turn in, and the car park and visitor centre is 200-yards up the drive (TQ059163).

BY TRAIN: Two mile walk from Pulborough station – turn L out of station, walk ? mile along A283 to Barn House Lane on R, and from here a

public footpath leads across the valley to the reserve.
BY BUS: No.100 Henfield-Pulborough passes reserve entrance.

Other nearby sites

Less than 5 miles: Amberley Wild Brooks.
Less than 10 miles: Lord's Piece, Burton Mill Pond, WWT Arundel, Swanbourne Lake, Cissbury Ring to Chanctonbury Ring, Lavington Common.

Continues overleaf

Key points

- **Full programme of activities and guided walks**
- **Four large hides, plus visitor centre with picture window**
- **Sightings board and book**
- **Binoculars for hire**
- **Going can get a little muddy at times, but generally good**
- **Occasionally river bursts its banks making some hides inaccessible**
- **Telescope helpful – the wildfowl can be fairly distant**
- **No dogs on nature trail**
- **Visitor centre and tea shop can be busy**

Greenfinches and Goldfinches fly up, often with Yellowhammers and Sky Larks in tow and Wood Larks and Corn Buntings have also been found here.

The track turns down the far side of the field, the new hedges ideal for nesting Yellowhammers, Whitethroats and Dunnocks (2). The older hedge to your right may have tits, warblers and finches, and Coal Tits and Goldcrests call from the small conifer plantation half-way down on the right.

The track leads to a shady pond, in between some mature oaks, from where a T-junction marks the start of a circular trail (3). Occasionally you will require wellingtons from this point on. Piping calls reveal Nuthatches here, Blackcaps sing in spring, and Spotted Flycatchers turn up on passage.

This is one of the prime spots for Lesser Spotted Woodpeckers too. There are almost as many records of Lesser Spots at Pulborough each year than for the rest of the county combined, in part testimony to the amount of coverage Pulborough gets.

At the T-junction, we usually turn right, eager to get to Nettley's Hide, the best on the reserve, though prone to occasional dramatic flooding!

On the way, listen for summering Garden Warblers, which usually sing from scrub near the double gates. You can detour right, if you want, up the public footpath towards the church and listen for Nightingales in the scrub. Return back to the double gates once you've had your fill.

Head on through 'Green Lane', the shady walkway surrounded by overgrown hedges and, at the next junction in the track, turn half-right past dense scrub and to the top of the steps down to Nettley's. Pause here though for Nightingales (4).

Nettley's Hide overlooks the North Brooks (the 'Brooks' being the wet grassland of the floodpain for which the reserve is so important). Water levels are kept high and the reserve's main area of open flood is here, which has a dramatically different surface area in winter compared with hot summer days.

In winter, the numbers and variety of wildfowl can be impressive – a thousand or more each of Teal and Wigeon, several hundred Pintails, a hundred Shovelers, all looking immaculate. They are spread over a large area, so don't expect them to be dabbling right in front of the hide – a telescope can help to sift through the more distant birds.

At all times of year there are likely to be waders of some sort. In winter, Lapwings will predominate, but check for Redshanks, Snipe, Ruff, Dunlins and Black-tailed Godwits. During spring and especially autumn passage, it would be unusual not to see a choice of Green, Common or Wood Sandpipers, Greenshanks, or even Grey Plovers.

It's a good place too for Garganeys – on a good spring day, an influx of several pairs may be present. Rarities recorded at Pulborough are often seen from Nettley's Hide. In recent years these have included American Wigeon, Green-winged Teals, and Pectoral Sandpipers.

Climb back up the steps from Nettley's Hide and head right for

Early morning or late afternoon are the best times to see Bewick's Swans at Pulborough. (John Davis)

another chance to hear Nightingales. Soon after they arrive in mid-April, you may well see them singing out in the open and yet a few weeks later they seem to sing only from cover. A little while after that and you wouldn't know they were there.

Soon you will reach The Hanger viewpoint, affording open elevated views towards Pulborough village over the same North Brooks seen from Nettley's. In the foreground, dense bushes hold thrushes in winter, warblers in the breeding season and yet more Nightingales.

Over-wintering Bewick's Swans can sometimes be present (they often use the open water to roost, so an early or late visit helps), and you may find Golden Plovers among the Lapwings.

At the next hide, called Little Hanger, next to a splendid oak that attracts Treecreepers and woodpeckers, the brooks are narrower than at Nettley's and bird numbers are much reduced. The track then chicanes through a hedge and around one of the grazing fields through to Winpenny Hide and the final West Mead Hide, both overlooking the South Brooks.

Both hides can, in drier weather, offer a waterless view, though with the RSPB having only acquired much of the South Brooks in 2002, bird populations are still developing.

They are, nevertheless, good hides from which to glimpse a Kingfisher perched on a ditch-side fence post, and expect yet more breeding waders. Often this area is good for geese flocks in winter.

The open fields beyond can produce Hen Harriers and perhaps Short-eared Owls and the vista is a good one to look for Hobbies in summer. The hedgerows along the track as you complete the circuit can turn up Whitethroats and other warblers, with perhaps a Redstart, Spotted Flycatcher or Whinchat at migration time.

It's then back to the starting point of the circular trail and time to head back up to the visitor centre and perhaps one of those coffees and calorie-soaked cakes!

Key points

- **Allow 4-plus hours**
- **Expect 50-80 species**
- **Part of Dungeness and Pett Level SPA, plus SSSI & LNR status**
- **Managed by East Sussex County Council on land owned by Environment Agency, SWT and private landowners**
- **Access free**
- **Reserve open at all times**
- **Good wheelchair access to parts of the reserve**
- **Excellent large free car park but with height barrier**

Contacts

Rye Harbour Nature Reserve
2 Watch Cottages, Nook Beach, Winchelsea, E. Sussex, TN36 4LU

Sussex Wildlife Trust
01273 492630

RYE HARBOUR ranks alongside Pagham Harbour as the top birdwatching site in Sussex, with excellent breeding tern and gull colonies, the best breeding concentrations of Ringed Plover and Wheatear in the county and almost guaranteed views of Bitterns and Smew in winter. It has such a range of habitats, that a day list to match or exceed that at Pagham is quite possible.

Target birds

All year –Barn Owl (10%).

Passage – Garganey (15%), Marsh Harrier (5%), Hobby (30%).

Spring – Mediterranean Gull (80 %), Whimbrel (50%), Little Ringed Plover (20%), Avocet (5%).

Autumn - Bearded Tit (20%), Little Stint (20%), Curlew Sandpiper (20%), Firecrest (10%), Black Redstart (10%).

Breeding season –Little Tern (99%), Sandwich Tern (99%), Turtle Dove (85%), Wheatear (80%), Corn Bunting (10%).

Winter – Bittern (80%), Smew (80%), Water Rail (hear 75%, see 20%), Kingfisher (50%), Goldeneye (60%), Red-throated Diver (30%), Eider (20%), Cetti's Warbler (hear 20, see 5%), Merlin (15%), Hen Harrier (10%), Spotted Redshank (5%).

Other likely bird species

All year	Bar-tailed Godwit	✓Turnstone
Waterbirds	Knot	Rock Pipit
Wildfowl	Greenshank	Stonechat
Coastal waders	Arctic Skua	
Gulls	Ruff	*Occasional*
Farmland birds	Whimbrel	Black-necked Grebe
Garden birds		Bewick's Swan
Little Egret	*Breeding season*	White-fronted Goose
Shelduck	Hirundines	Pintail
Gadwall	✓Common Tern	Scaup
Shoveler	Cuckoo	Goosander
Common Scoter	✓Yellow Wagtail	Peregrine
	✓Wheatear	Jack Snipe
Passage		Wood Sandpiper
Warblers	*Winter*	Arctic Skua
Brent Goose	Wigeon	Black Tern
Green Sandpiper	Pochard	Roseate tern
Common Sandpiper	Golden Plover	Redstart
Black-tailed Godwit	Sanderling	Tree Sparrow

Background information and birding tips

RYE HARBOUR is a large triangle of bird-rich land between the mouth of the River Rother, Winchelsea Beach and Rye. In the last few centuries, storms have filled what was once a tidal bay, with shallow ridges of shingle. Those ridges furthest inland are now well-vegetated and cultivated and only the newest ones at the sea's edge are still bare.

The habitat shares many of the features of its more famous 'neighbour', Dungeness (from Rye beach you can see Dunge's nuclear power station on a clear day). The shingle has special plant and insect communities, while the natural wet depressions and especially the man-made gravel pits attract much bird wealth.

Birdwatching at Rye Harbour is great at any time of year, but most visits will entail a long walk (usually two to four hours), so it's one of those sites where we come prepared with lunchbox and flask. Bear in mind also that there are no toilets on the reserve itself - so the ones by the car park are most welcome! This site is very exposed to the elements – out come the warm and weatherproof clothing in winter, and the Factor 25 suncream in summer.

The site is so large, we've divided it into sections:

Car park to river mouth

Before setting off, the information kiosk in the car park is worth a look – it is unmanned but has displays and information about the history, natural and otherwise, of the harbour. It's then hard to resist heading straight for the sea.

Take the flat metalled track from the car park entrance – ideal for wheelchair users - with the Martello Tower over to your right. More often than not, Blackbirds, Mistle and Song Thrushes use the grassy lawn in front of the Tower, and the tall trees are sometimes a pre-roost site for Corn Buntings. This 'lawn' ends at a ditch, good for Reed Warblers in spring and summer.

To your left is a thin strip of saltmarsh beyond which the canalised River Rother runs unseen to the sea. Redshanks, Reed Buntings and gulls can be seen here, especially in winter, with an intriguing switch between summer Meadow Pipits and winter Rock Pipits.

In 300 yards you reach Lime Kiln Cottage, the reserve's Information Centre, where there are volunteers to welcome you and give information, plus sell you publications and other merchandise. There are no facilities here but there is the all-important sightings board.

Just beyond Lime Kiln Cottage on the right is the wader scrape overlooked by a hide suitable for wheelchair users. Don't expect the scrape to be filled with birds but, among the breeding Lapwings, Ringed Plovers and Redshanks we have seen Kentish Plovers and Avocets, so you'd be wise to take a look.

Corn Buntings sometimes top the line of fence posts to the right of the scrape in summer and you might see a Cuckoo. Behind the scrape is an expanse of shingle known as the Flat Beach where larger numbers of waders, Lapwings and Golden Plovers in particular, but a regular spot for Spotted Redshanks too - are possible though distant.

Telescopes are a must, especially if you want to find something like 2003's Pacific Golden Plover out there. It's the kind of landscape where a bird of prey – Merlin or Hobby, say – can dash through during the relevant season.

Further on, check the saltmarsh and river banks to the left for Ringed Plovers and Turnstones – until the mid-20th Century, it was the last UK breeding site of Kentish Plovers. Ringed Plovers still breed here and their chicks scurry like clockwork toys over the shingle in summer.

This is also a likely area for Wheatears around the pill-boxes – Rye Harbour remains

Other nearby sites

Less than 10 miles: Hastings Country Park, Northpoint Pit, Pett Level, Scotney Court.

Continues overleaf

Key points

- **Toilets, shop and pub close by in Rye Harbour village but no toilets out on reserve**
- **Small information centre**
- **Four good hides on the reserve**
- **A lot of walking involved, but on flat terrain**
- **Castle Water side of the reserve can get muddy**
- **Very exposed to the elements**
- **Telescope essential to get the most out of the reserve**

the Sussex breeding outpost for them.

At the end of the track, we often scan the sea, getting what shelter we can, from the wind, behind the wooden panels at the river mouth. In winter there is a chance of distant grebes and divers as well as Eiders. Common Scoter and Brent Goose flocks pass by in spring, though the number of birds on the sea pales in comparison to further along the bay at Pett. It takes a perfect south-easterly to bring any of spring's sea passage close to shore, so setting up shop for a good seawatch is not hugely productive.

At all seasons, it is as well to check the shoreline for Oystercatchers, Curlews, Grey Plovers, Dunlins plus occasional Knots and Bar-tailed Godwits. Several thousand Common Gulls roost here at dusk in late winter. Across the river to your left, but quite inaccessible without a ten-mile trip round through Rye, are the golden sands of Camber, loved by Sanderlings.

River mouth to Ternery Pool

To reach Ternery Pool, head west. Rather than struggle along the shingle, we head back to the Tarmac path. Much of the area inland of the path and a big rectangular section of the shingle at the top of the beach, is cordoned off with electric fences, inside which the Little Terns breed.

In summer, they fly noisily between Beach Reserve and the sea, right over your heads. Numbers however, seem to be very much on the wane, with perhaps just 12 pairs in 2003.

The shingle also attracts Meadow Pipits, Linnets, Greenfinches or maybe, just maybe, a Snow Bunting in winter.

A track leads to Parkes Hide on the north-east side of Ternery Pool. Viewing can be difficult on sunny afternoons, so arrive early to check this long narrow gravel pit. Little Grebes and Tufted Ducks swim close to the hide, but it is the noise of Black-headed Gull colony which overwhelms in summer. We've enjoyed wonderful views of Water Rails here too, trotting unconcerned directly in front, and this can be the best hide from which to find passage Mediterranean Gulls in among the Black-headeds.

When entering and leaving the hide, make sure you look back towards Camber as this is the best point to view 'The Quarry', a wet shingle area at this far side of Flat Beach. It attracts a good variety of waders and, if you arrive at dusk or dawn in early May, several hundred Whimbrels traditionally roost here.

The Crittall Hide on the south-east side is often more rewarding though. Common Terns nest sparingly among Black-headed Gulls in front, while the Sandwich Terns tend to cluster on an island to the right of the hide. The tern roost in late April and early May is especially noisy and impressive.

Ternery Pool attracts an impressive range of ducks and waders, given its relatively small size. Often none of the species are in sizeable numbers, so it is always quite impressive to tot up just how many different species are present. What may be only 50 or so ducks may include Mallard, Shoveler, Wigeon, Teal, Gadwall, Tufted Duck, Pochard and maybe a Pintail.

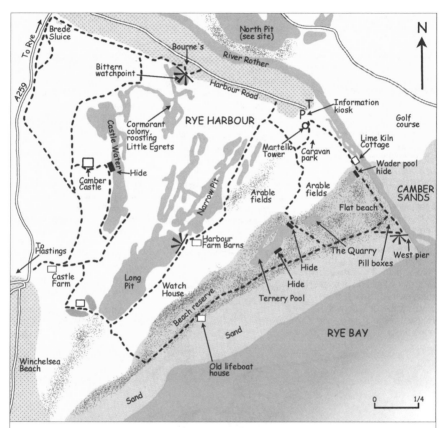

Access details

(1.5 miles SE of Rye)

From Rye head S on A259, then take minor road to Rye Harbour village, clearly signed with brown Nature Reserve sign on L. Just beyond the village, the road bends right to huge car park (with height restriction barrier) – TQ941189.

Bittern Viewpoint is accessed via an inconspicuous footpath entrance on R of road down to Rye Harbour just after a haulage company called Bournes (look for lorries) – TQ932193. It is possible to walk the 0.5 mile along the roadside from main car park, or there is limited roadside parking on the verge near the footpath entrance.

BY TRAIN: 2 mile walk from Rye station.
BY BUS: No.325 from Rye rail station takes less than 8 minutes out to Rye Harbour (no Sunday service).

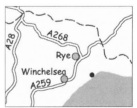

Continues overleaf

Waders include a regular Oystercatcher roost plus autumn visitors like Green, Common and Wood Sandpipers, Ruff, Greenshanks, Little Stints and Curlew Sandpipers alongside the usual Redshanks, Lapwings, Ringed Plovers and Dunlins.

Occasionally Ternery Pool produces great views of raptors - a dashing Peregrine or Hobby, or a quartering Marsh or Hen Harrier, while recent rarities have included a Semipalmated Sandpiper (three times!) and Gull-billed Terns, with Roseate Terns annual.

Ternery Pool to Long Pit
Heading west along the Tarmac path, it's worth popping over the shingle ridge to check the beach and sea. If it is blustery, the Old Lifeboat House gives an opportunity to set your scope up in a bit of shelter.

From here, it's a long slog to reach the right-turn which marks the half-way point! The path inland runs along the top of a dyke through ex-arable fields to Long Pit.

You may see Grey Partridges if you're very lucky, though Whitethroats, Sedge Warblers, Sky Larks and Yellow Wagtails are more frequent. We once watched a Barn Owl hunting here on a sunny morning in May, and have seen Kingfishers in the ditches in winter.

Long Pit to Rye Harbour Road
The fittingly long views at Long Pit from the corner gate are made easier with a scope - Great Crested Grebes, Tufted Ducks, Pochards and, usually, Goldeneyes often seem to favour somewhere near the far bank. We've seen both Black-necked and Red-necked Grebes as well as Smew here, and it's a shame the Ferruginous Duck didn't keep coming back after spending a couple of winters in the area.

The footpath continuing north inland alongside Long Pit heads towards what looks like a little copse. Much of it is someone's garden, so be careful not to trespass. With so few trees anywhere on the actual reserve, you can add a few more woodland species to your day list here, including, who knows, a Firecrest or even a Yellow-browed Warbler.

It is possible to walk through to Camber Castle here, but that makes for one *very* long walk. From Long Pit, we tend to head along its eastern side (the pit hidden from view by a tall

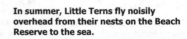

In summer, Little Terns fly noisily overhead from their nests on the Beach Reserve to the sea.

fenced bank) back towards Rye Harbour.

As you get towards the Harbour Farm Barns, you can get good reverse views over Long Pit. The barns themselves attract big congregations of Collared Doves, but look out too for Turtle Doves on the wires in summer, which are very reliable. Cuckoos are also frequent here.

Narrow Pit to your left has Great Crested Grebes, and there are a couple of even smaller pools rather hidden to your right, but please keep to the paths. The bramble and gorse scrub around these pools turns up skulking Dartford Warblers each autumn and further on, as you approach the village, Black Redstarts are possible in October on the waste ground on the left.

Castle Water, Camber Castle and Castle Farm

The Castle Water section of the reserve, huge as it is, remained little visited until Bitterns started performing in the late 1990's. Now it gets much more of the attention it deserves, but it is still underwatched compared to the beach side of the reserve.

From November through to March, birdwatchers now gather at the little worn mound half an hour or so before sunset. In front is part of Castle Water gravel pit, as complex a

shaped pool as you could imagine. Right in front of the viewpoint are reedbeds beyond which is a block of willows in the water where the Cormorants now breed in profusion.

As dusk approaches, Little Egrets drop in from high in the sky, a Kingfisher may scoot past and Water Rails call from the reeds. Then Bitterns do their short relocation flights to the roost spot. You will be unlucky if you don't see one as you may be blessed and get five or six, the last ones arriving when it's almost dark. And so often the action is set against great sunsets. But boy, it can get cold here!

To reach the viewpoint, follow the 'Access details' to get to the Bournes lorry park. Then simply follow the footpath from the road for about 50-yards and look for the white posts. In autumn, it's a good vantage point to see Bearded Tits and hear Cetti's Warblers and fair numbers of Pied and Yellow Wagtails can come in to roost.

There is a fine long walk around Castle Water. From the Bittern watchpoint, a footpath leads north, then turns left along a fenceline to the water's edge. Walking on around the lake, you will come to a hide in the bushes not far from Camber Castle, the remains of a coastal

fortification built by order of Henry VIII.

Castle Water holds breeding Black-headed Gulls and Common Terns. In mid-winter, it can be great for Smew, including regular males, with Red-throated Divers (sometimes oiled), or a rarer grebe alongside hundreds of Wigeon, Coots and other waterbirds.

It can be good at passage time too, with double-figure numbers of Green Sandpipers, half a dozen other wader species quite possible, and the occasional Jack Snipe. Best wader spot in late summer is the muddy shelf that juts out opposite the hide, while in winter it is quite possible to have Bitterns right in front of you here. Rarities have included Glossy Ibis and Great Reed Warbler.

The habitat around Castle Water, the castle itself and Castle Farm is largely open sheep pasture and scrub. Once-common Tree Sparrows are now very difficult to find, but Barn Owls are more reliable. Impressive flocks of Lapwings and Golden Plovers feed on the meadows north of Castle Water during the winter months.

It is possible to loop around Long Pit and back along Narrow Pits or alternatively, you can now retrace your steps back to the car.

Key points

- Allow 0.5-plus hour

- Expect 20-30 species

- Private site viewable only from roadside

- No designated parking - pull in with extreme care off busy road onto uneven verge

- Wheelchair users can view from car

- No facilities; nearest in Camber

- Very difficult by public transport

- Do NOT park or drive along lane to Scotney Court Farm

- Telescope will help get best out of site

- Combine with trip to Rye or over Kent border to Dungeness

STRADDLING the county border with Kent, Scotney Court is the premier site in Sussex for White-fronted Geese, with a chance of genuine Pink-feet or Beans among them. Just as exciting is this gravel pit's track-record for drawing-in divers, rarer grebes and Scaup. Scotney's only downside is that watching is restricted to the roadside.

Target birds *Passage (spring)* - Bar-tailed Godwit
(spring - 25%), Whimbrel (spring - 20%). *Winter* - White-fronted Goose (90%), diver or rarer grebe of any species (75%), Scaup (40%), Smew (20%), Hen Harrier (20%), Little Stint (10%), Short-eared Owl (5%).

Other likely bird species

All year	Stock Dove	*Occasional*
Wildfowl	Wood Pigeon	Bewick's Swan
Gulls	Meadow Pipit	Bean Goose
Corvids	Pied Wagtail	Pink-footed Goose
Great Crested Grebe		Whooper Swan
Cormorant	*Passage*	Pintail
Greylag Goose	Hirundines	Goldeneye
Shelduck	Ringed Plover	Marsh Harrier
Kestrel	Dunlin	Hobby
Coot	Greenshank	Avocet
Lapwing	Turnstone	Knot
Redshank	Yellow Wagtail	Barn Owl
	White Wagtail	

Background information and birding tips

IT IS RARE to see Scotney Court gravelpit looking anything less than half-full of birds. Most are Coots, but concerted scanning pays off! Gadwall, Teal, Pintails and, perhaps surprisingly, Goldeneyes are scarce, but all can turn up among plenty of Tufted Ducks, Pochards and Mallards. Wigeon numbers can exceed 1,000, but the key duck is Scaup. Though not guaranteed, in a good winter several or even several dozen can stick around for weeks.

The flat open landscape beyond the pit is Walland Marsh, and from there come big flocks of Golden Plovers and Lapwings to roost on Scotney's far bank **(1)**. Presumably Walland is where the big geese flocks feed too, before coming to the safety of the pit to rest. Loads of Greylag and Canada Geese are joined in mid-winter by a few hundred White-fronts. Very reliable, they frequent the far bank of Scotney and the peninsula half-way along the nearside **(2)**. Views are good to very good. To find a Bean or a Pink-foot among them after a cold snap is not unusual either.

Some waders moving up the Channel in spring drop in here, such as Bar-tailed Godwits in stunning breeding plumage. The surface pools on the grass at the eastern end of the pit are favoured **(3)**. (Avid

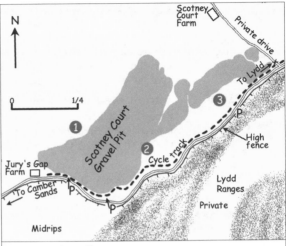

county listers be warned - this is actually in Kent!) This patch is good for Dunlins and Ringed Plovers, and the list of waders each year for the pit is fantastic including Greenshanks, Spotted Redshanks, Knot, and regular winter reports of Little Stints.

Being only a mile from Rye Bay, Scotney also attracts storm-blown or semi-oiled divers and grebes, often for long stays. To have all three divers or all five grebes present simultaneously has happened more than once.

As well as a water full of birds, in spring and summer the skies can be full of hirundines, especially Swifts, if conditions are right and Little Gulls and Black Terns can also be expected, May being a good month.

Passerines are rather impoverished here, though, due more to lack of cover than the fairly regular Hen Harriers and Short-eared Owls! Nevertheless, Tree Sparrows and Corn Buntings are both in the area.

Scotney's only problem is that the site isn't great for people. The only views are from the Camber to Lydd road along the south eastern side of the pit, where parking is limited to a few rough bits of roadside verge, with cars whizzing past you. Scotney thus tends to be a 30-minute stop-over for birders, rather than a fulfilling half-day's birding.

Access details

(6 miles E of Rye)

Head from Rye on A2359 E, and after a mile, take minor road to Camber. Two miles beyond Camber, the road passes along the shore of Scotney Court gravelpit. Parking is your choice of various deeply-rutted grassy verges at various points along the pit. Indicate well in advance as following drivers will be moving quickly.

There is a good pedestrian and cycle path, constructed in 2001/2, which runs right along the pit between the road and the water's edge, but the path is fenced and access to it only

possible at the Scotney Court Farm entrance (please never park here) or 200 yards W of the end of the pit.

BY TRAIN: No direct access.
BY BUS: No.711 hourly Hastings-Rye-Dover stops at Jury's Gap, giving 1mile walk to Scotney Court.

Other nearby sites

Less than 10 miles: Northpoint Pit, Rye Harbour

Key points

- Allow 1-plus hours (plus seawatching time)

- Expect 10-20 species (excluding seawatching species)

- Selsey West Fields is part SSSI

- Both sites open at all times on beach and rights of way

- Parking at both sites

- No other facilities directly on site, but all facilities easy to find in Selsey

- Some walking over shingle necessary

- Wheelchair users can view from car

- Good public transport links down to Bill

- Early morning best for migrants at Bill; late afternoon best for owls at West Fields

SELSEY BILL is primarily a great seawatching location (see p25), but its position, jutting into the Channel, means it is well-located for falls of migrant passerines. Serins are regular, with several records most springs. The rough wet grassland of Selsey West Fields, just up the coast, is a great spot for winter raptors such as Short-eared Owls.

Target birds Aside from seawatching, look for *All year* - Peregrine (20%). *Passage* - Black Redstart (10%), Marsh Harrier (5%), Serin (5%). *Winter* - Mediterranean Gull (60%), Short-eared Owl (50%), Barn Owl (30%), Merlin (10%).

Other likely bird species

All year	Hirundines	*Winter*
Gulls	Warblers	Brent Goose
Garden birds	Green Sandpiper	Teal
Grey Heron	Common Sandpiper	Golden Plover
Shelduck	Yellow Wagtail	Rock Pipit
Mallard	Wheatear	Goldfinch
Lapwing	Whinchat	
Stonechat	Stonechat	*Occasional*
Linnet	Redstart	Little Egret
Sky Lark		Hen Harrier
Meadow Pipit	*Breeding season*	Montagu's Harrier
Yellowhammer	Redshank	Ruff
Reed Bunting	Sedge Warbler	Firecrest
	Reed Warbler	Ring Ouzel
Passage	Whitethroat	Snow Bunting
Seawatching species		

Background information and birding tips

MOST BIRDWATCHERS go to Selsey Bill to look for seabirds so check the Seawatching section (p25) to see what will be on offer. Having done your bum-numbing, early-morning seawatching stint, 'on the wall,' though, it is not just a case of packing up and leaving, because while you've been busy looking seaward, passerines may have been dropping into the bushes nearby, or even onto the beach. A delectable list of scarce birds have come in over seawatchers' heads over the

years, such as Stone-Curlew, Golden Oriole and even Hawfinch!

There are some large gardens butting onto the beach with plenty of tamarisk to attract flitting Chiffchaffs and Willow Warblers. Other species include regular Common and Black Redstarts, plus the now-regular (though often short staying) Serins. The beach itself is good for Wheatears, though they are often disturbed by dog-walkers. In autumn, the passage of thousands of hirundines, so typical of the south coast, is normal.

Selsey West Fields

On the west side of the Selsey peninsula, the shingle seawall curves relentlessly around Bracklesham Bay towards the Witterings. A huge caravan site is immediately northwest of Selsey, but beyond that, behind the seawall, open treeless fields extend across towards the back of Sidlesham Ferry in the distance.

The area of rank grassland just behind the seawall is sliced through with deep ditches. This is known as the Selsey West Fields and it is a useful additional site to tack on to your visit to Selsey.

The best viewing is from the shingle seawall. A public footpath also leads part-way out along the top of a dyke around the main area of rough grassland. The arable land beyond is much less productive, though there are some rich areas of set-aside most years.

Ever-present birds of the grassland are Meadow Pipits and Sky Larks, parachuting everywhere in spring. Reed Buntings frequent the ditches, and a variety of wildfowl and waders have turned up on wetter areas, with Shelducks the most likely species to be seen. This site has breeding Lapwings, Stonechats and Corn Buntings.

Prize targets however are birds of prey. The grassland is used regularly in winter by Short-eared Owls and Merlins, with Marsh Harriers regular on spring and autumn passage,

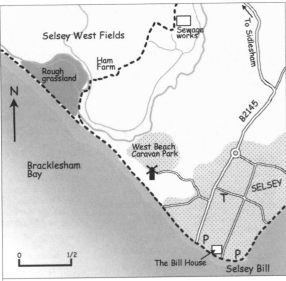

Access details

(8 miles S of Chichester)

SELSEY BILL: From Chichester travel into Selsey village on B2145, turning L at what is now the second roundabout, signed to 'East Beach'. Pass imposing Catholic church and follow road as it bears R. Ignore L-turn to East Beach past the Fisherman's Joy pub, but continue straight on. Park where the road ends with a playing field to your L, the Bill House to your R, and the sea ahead (SZ855921)

SELSEY WEST FIELDS: In Selsey, turn R in 'town' centre down West St, signed 'West Beach Caravan Park'. At next T-junction, turn R along Crablands, and this leads to

the caravan park (with a windmill at its entrance). The road into the park is not public, but access is tolerated allowing some parking against the beach, but don't get locked in! Access West Fields by walking along the shingle seawall.

BY TRAIN: No direct access.
BY BUS: Regular service from Chichester (No.51) including hourly Sunday service.

and Barn Owl possible year-round. Montagu's Harriers have turned up (and stayed) in the autumns of both 2001 and 2002. Autumn has also

been a good season for rarities in this area, with Buff-breasted Sandpiper and Lesser Grey Shrike among the most notable.

Key points

- Allow 1.5-plus hours
- Expect 20-30 species
- No designation – future use of valley hangs in balance
- Open at all times
- Café/toilets in valley by sports fields; all other amenities in Brighton Marina
- Some steep gradients
- Not suitable for wheelchairs
- Excellent bus links
- Early morning best for birds
- Site heavily used by dog walkers
- Ex-landfill site, so beware of rubbish sticking out of the ground
- Good numbers of butterflies

Contacts

Brighton & Hove Countryside Service
01273 292140

SITUATED against Brighton's urban east fringe, Sheepcote Valley is the kind of 'wasteland' birds love, a warm south-facing valley thick with scrub, great for migrants and with an enviable list of rarities to its name. We did say 'urban fringe', though!

Target birds *Passage – mainly autumn*: Tree Pipit (30%), Redstart (20%), Whinchat (60%), Ring Ouzel (10%), Firecrest (10%), Grasshopper Warbler (5%). *Breeding season* – Corn Bunting (Roedean Bottom - 50%).

Other likely bird species

All year	Warblers	*Occasional*
Gulls	Thrushes	Hobby
Scrub birds	Grey Wagtail	Peregrine
Garden birds	Wheatear	Short-eared Owl
Stonechat	Sedge warbler	Wryneck
	Reed Warbler	Dartford Warbler
Passage		
Hirundines	*Winter*	
	Meadow Pipit	

Background information and birding tips

SHEEPCOTE VALLEY is a mish-mash of habitats and public uses. Brighton Racecourse loops round the top, a golf course abuts its eastern ridge, and there are football pitches, a college, a BMX track (sometimes taken over by travellers) and a Caravan Club site in the valley itself. But alongside all of this is wild scrubby habitat which, being so close to the sea, attracts migrants in excellent numbers.

We prefer to start at the top of the valley. From the car park at the edge of Woodingdean with its long views down to the sea, a path crosses the racecourse and drops down into a big flat arena (1). Wheatears, on passage, are usually seen here. The centre of this amphitheatre is thick with umbellifers and balsam. Stonechats and Whitethroats

breed and they are joined on passage by Whinchats, with Reed and Grasshopper Warblers possible. The top of the valley is good too for migrants passing overhead - Tree Pipits, Yellow Wagtails etc.

Descending the valley, each tier is separated from the next by scrubby banks, ideal for any of the woodland warblers on passage. The second tier down (2) is a long thin grassy strip stretching from side to side across the valley, and the third tier includes an isolated little field (3), where we've seen Wheatears and Whinchats galore, popping up and down from the fence posts. Valley counts of 20 Wheatears and a dozen Whinchats are quite common.

Below the field is a big impenetrable bank of tall shrubs down to the caravan site (4). To carry on down, you'll need to get onto the grassland to the east side of the valley, where a berry-rich hedge leads down towards the

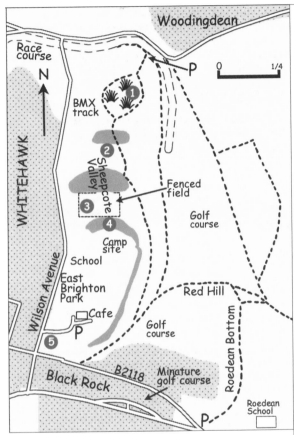

Access details

(2 miles E of Brighton city centre)

Sheepcote Valley,directly inland of Brighton Marina, is bounded by B2118 Roedean Road to S, Wilson Ave to the W and Warren Road (Brighton-Woodingdean) to the N.

Parking for c.10 cars at top of valley is on S-side of Warren Road, 0.25 mile W of Woodingdean Cemetery (TQ344055, under height-restriction barrier). Walk across racecourse into valley.

For parking in centre of valley, turn E at bottom of Wilson Ave just before traffic lights with B2118 Roedean Road. Parking by café after 0.25 mile (TQ339037).

For Roedean parking, car park where B2118 meets A259 coast road near Roedean school (TQ346031).

BY BUS: Very good coast road services (eg 712, 14, 27) from Brighton station stop on A259 S of the valley. No.21 route goes via Wilson Avenue. No.2 and No.22 pass along top of valley to Woodingdean.

valley-bottom football and cricket pitches.

Blackcaps and other warblers are the commonest migrants in the bushes, but Wrynecks and Pied Flycatchers are possible in August and September, Ring Ouzels and Firecrests in October and the chance of Pallas's Warbler at the tail-end of the season.

Good numbers of migrants are even found around the

cricket pitch (**5**). Indeed, anywhere in the valley can be productive – a Hume's Warbler hung out in the children's play area near the tennis courts!

It is also possible to park next to Roedean School and walk up into Sheepcote. The farmland in Roedean Bottom can be excellent for all the chats and this is also the prime spot for a pair or two of Corn Buntings.

Early morning is definitely Sheepcote's most rewarding time - you may avoid some of the dogs too. But development threatens Sheepcote far more than dogs. Let's hope the site is still intact when this book is revised.

143

Key points

- Allow 1-plus hours, more if combining the different areas

- Expect 10-15 species (more if seawatching)

- Widewater is LNR

- Public rights of way and beach open at all times

- Toilets at Shoreham Fort, Widewater and by Carrot's Café

- Good to moderate parking at all sites

- Walking generally on good paths, some accessible for wheelchairs

- All sites much used by public

THIS COMBINATION of sites offers several birding possibilities. Try Southwick Canal for winter divers, Black Redstarts and breeding Peregrines; the entrance to Shoreham Harbour for Purple Sandpipers; and Widewater, a slender brackish lagoon, for waders and Little Egrets. All are worth checking if you are passing and the area can also be used as a seawatching site (p25).

Target birds *All year* - Peregrine (50%, more at Southwick). *Winter* – Purple Sandpiper (50%), Black Redstart (30%), Shag (30%).

Other likely bird species

All year	Stonechat	Shelduck
Gulls	Pied Wagtail	Pochard
Cormorant	Dunnock	Sanderling
Little Egret		Rock Pipit
Mallard	*Passage*	
Greenfinch	Seabirds	*Occasional*
Goldfinch	Hirundines	Divers
Starling	Wheatear	Eider
House Sparrow		
Crow	*Winter*	
Jackdaw	Coastal waders	
	Great Crested Grebe	

Background information and birding tips

THE TWO-MILE long Southwick Canal is a narrow, active industrial harbour so it's not that attractive! The only crossing point on foot is at the western end by taking the well-signed public footpath that crosses the main A259 at a pedestrian crossing towards Carrot's Café, 400 yards west of the power station chimney (you can't miss the chimney, nor the Peregrine nest box high on its southern side).

The footpath shepherds you across a complex series of locks, with limited views into the Harbour basin, where Cormorants and Little Grebes are sometimes joined in winter by the occasional diver or stranded wind-blown seabird. It also hosts a big gull roost, with regular 'white-winged' gulls, especially Mediterranean. It's also as good a place as any, after a big blow, for a Grey Phalarope, rare skua or Sabine's Gull.

On reaching the shore, a walk right will take you past a timber yard, favoured by Black Redstarts in late autumn, to the eastern breakwater where Purple Sandpipers are possible, indeed check all the groynes for them. Auks and Red-breasted Mergansers are often offshore.

Far easier to reach, and with a better chance of Purple Sandpipers, is to park in Forthaven and climb over the shingle to the western breakwater. Rock Pipits are frequent here in winter, flitting about and keeping their distance from the fishermen. Inside the breakwater is a

Contacts

For Widewater:
Friends of Widewater Lagoon

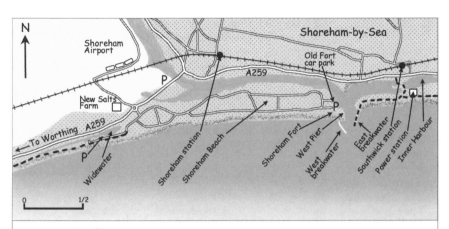

Access details

(4 to 7 miles W of Brighton)

The western harbour arm and Widewater accessed from Shoreham Beach. From A259 roundabout just W of Norfolk Bridge at Shoreham, turn S into residential area called Shoreham Beach. Take first right and follow signs to Widewater Lagoon – there is a height restriction barrier, about 6' 6" (TQ203032).

For western harbour arm, drive through Shoreham Beach until a 'P' parking sign directs

down street called Forthaven and Old Fort Car Park TQ232046. (Pay & Display April- Sept, free at other times).

For inner harbour, from A259 coast road between Hove and Portslade, turn S onto Basin Road South just W of Hove Lagoon (seafront pool used by windsurfers). Drive 1? miles to parking at TQ245047.

BY TRAIN: 0.25 mile walk from Southwick Station across harbour locks to Inner Harbour, 1.25 mile walk from

Shoreham station to Widewater/ Shoreham Fort.
BY BUS: No.19 hourly service Holmbush-Shoreham Beach. Alternatively, Nos.700 & 702 services from Brighton pass all the way along A259 coast road.

little shingle beach and, if the three or four Purple Sandpipers aren't here with Turnstones, they may well be on the Western Pier next to the beach. It sounds far grander than it is – it's just a few metres long, really rickety, and the Purple Sandpipers and Turnstones often spend high-tide on its dilapidated wooded end.

Shags are possible inside the harbour entrance and this is your easiest spot from which to seawatch. Check the Old Fort for Black Redstarts, too.

From here to Widewater stretches a long shingle beach with houses running all along the back of it. Waders from the Adur Estuary often pass over the houses at high tide to roost on the beach and run the gauntlet of the dogs being exercised. The upper beach here has some shingle plants that attract Wheatears on passage and Greenfinches with a few Goldfinches in winter

Widewater Lagoon LNR is about 0.5 mile long, a

brackish lagoon with beach huts and the thin shingle beach on one side and houses the other. You can expect to see Mallards and Redshanks here, while one or two Little Egrets are present almost year-round. A small Pochard flock installs itself each winter. A pair or two of Shelducks are often present, Ringed Plovers even try to nest, while Sanderlings sometimes step uneasily along the shingle beach. The little bit of scrub is good for Stonechats, and Wheatears scoot up and down on arrival in spring.

Key points

- Allow 2-plus hours
- Expect 15-30 species, more if seawatching
- SSSI; Seaford Head is LNR managed by SDCB
- Public footpaths and promenade open at all times
- Good free parking; toilets on sea front
- All other facilities in nearby Seaford
- Steep path up Seaford Head
- Excellent access to Kittiwakes/ seawatching for wheelchair-users
- Good public transport links
- The sheer and unfenced cliff edge is VERY dangerous – take great care
- Telescope useful for seawatching/ Kittiwakes, but not essential

THIS SITE IS principally a seawatching site (see p25), but it also has one of southern England's very few (and probably the most viewable) Kittiwake colonies and there are regular Peregrines and passerine migrants too. With some absolutely stunning coastal views (including the most famous panorama in Sussex, the Seven Sisters), take your camera as well as your bins!

Target birds Seawatching birds, plus - *All year* – Rock Pipit (80%); Peregrine (20%). *Breeding season* – Kittiwake (100%).

Other likely bird species

All year	*Passage*	*Breeding season*
Gulls	Hirundines	Fulmar
Farmland birds	Warblers	
Garden birds	Yellow Wagtail	*Occasional*
Cormorant	Wheatear	Black Redstart
Oystercatcher	Redstart	Spotted Flycatcher
Stonechat		

Background information and birding tips

AT THE EAST END of Seaford's shingle beach and genteel promenade, the white chalk cliffs of Seaford Head rise up impressively. Where the road finishes, the promenade continues 50-yards underneath the first little chalk bluff to a set of railings. It is from here that the Kittiwake colony of around 700 pairs can be seen (and heard) on the nearest and lowest section of cliff – Splash Point. Only with binoculars do you start to realise how many white birds there are against the white cliff; with a telescope, you get to see right into the nests.

The birds return to the ledges on and off from the middle of February. Even by May there is still fevered nest building, with adults sometimes flighting over in an endless stream onto the grassy areas behind the road, if there is some muddy grass there

that they can scrounge. Alongside them nest a couple of pairs of Fulmars and usually a pair of Rock Pipits. The first young Kittiwakes fledge by about July 20 and the cliffs are then deserted by late August.

The walk up to Seaford Head along the side of the golf course is steep. The views from the top are stunning and the views straight down the vertical cliff face are petrifying. All the while, watch out for Peregrines, often on one of the inaccessible ledges on the cliff or flying-by at sea. The cliff edge, though, is unfenced, sheer and deceptive – *do take the utmost care*.

On the top of the Head, the path leads down a shallow sloping gully to a 'crossroads'. This is in the Local Nature Reserve, where Wheatears are a constant presence here, during passage, on the rabbit-grazed turf. A set of steps descends onto the rocky beach below, where Oystercatchers are present year round, often with Whimbrels on spring passage. More Rock Pipits are also likely. Straight ahead leads through to the cottages at Cuckmere Haven and that Seven Sisters chocolate-box view.

Up to the left is Hope Gap, a scrub-filled sheltered valley, perfect for migrants. That's not to say it is perfect for birdwatching, as the bushes are thick and tall, and it takes an early morning visit to get the most out of the valley. Nevertheless, birds such as Ring Ouzels may well be annual.

The track up Hope Gap leads to the South Hill Barn car park, popular with dog walkers. The fields up here were once notable for their winter Sky Lark flock, but now just a few are likely, although again Wheatears are commonplace on migration. If the fields are ploughed, Dotterel are possible.

From here you can follow a footpath back east to Seaford, across the golf course, checking the gorse scrub for Stonechats, passage Whinchats, Whitethroats etc. However, we usually can't resist the temptation to return on the same route just for the views and the sound – and smell – of the Kittiwakes.

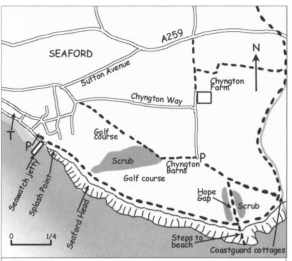

Access details

(7 miles W of Eastbourne)

For Splash Point, turn S off A259 in Seaford at the roundabout by the station and drive down Dane Road past Safeways to the seafront. Turn L along the promenade, past the Martello Tower Museum and toilet block. The road begins to deteriorate and ends just before the monolith of Seaford Head in front of you. Free parking along the roadsides here, with disabled parking at the far end. TV487983.

Parking at South Hill Barn is difficult to find. 0.25 mile E of Seaford town centre, turn S down Southdown Road

(signed Seaford Pool). Cross Sutton Avenue, and take the 2nd L into Chyngton Road. Follow to end, where turn R up single-width track 0.25 mile up to car park by barn. TV504980.

BY TRAIN: **0.75 mile walk from Seaford station to Splash Point. Bus: No.712 Eastbourne-Brighton service stops in Seaford.**

Contacts

Sussex Downs Conservation Board (Eastern Area Office)
01323 871095
east@southdowns-aonb.gov.uk

Other nearby sites

Less than 5 miles: Newhaven Tide Mills; Cuckmere Haven; Lullington Heath
Less than 10 miles: Brighton-Newhaven Cliffs; Lewes Brooks; Arlington Reservoir

Key points

- Allow 2.5-plus hours
- Expect 15-25 species
- Part SSSI; Forestry Commission site, with heath managed by West Sussex County Council
- Public rights of way and forest paths open at all times
- Small car park; no other facilities
- Going can get very muddy in places; unsuitable for wheelchairs
- Very difficult by public transport
- Best to take a map - the paths can be disorientating

Contacts

Buchan Park
Countryside Centre
01293 542088
01293 542120
buchan.park@
westsussex.gov.uk

THIS SITE is unlikely to repeat its 1902-3 feat when three White-tailed Eagles wintered here, but it gives you some idea of the expanse of habitat that is only a couple of miles to the east of Horsham. The area provides some varied and long woodland walks with most of the staple woodland species.

Target birds *Breeding Season* - Redstart (10%), Wood Lark (10%). *Winter* - Redpoll 30%).

Other likely bird species

All year	*Winter*	
Woodland birds	Siskin	Nightjar
Marsh Tit		Tree Pipit
Nuthatch	*Occasional*	Crossbill
Treecreeper	Mandarin	

Background information and birding tips

ALONGSIDE the White-tailed Eagles, St Leonards Forest's other claim to bird fame was that it was the first Sussex breeding site for Mandarins, as recently as 1971. A few pairs are still thought to be present, and the area remains ideal, with the wooded landscape dotted with pools. Most of these date from the time when iron ore was smelted in the forests. Few of these pools are readily accessible, however, so the text here is entirely for the woodland birds that can be found within the Forest.

Starting from the Roosthole car park, a wide track leads north-east. This and many other tracks in the Forest do get churned and stodgy in winter, and even with walking boots, time can be spent picking your route between the mud.

The woodland along this first stretch is pleasantly mixed. Yes, there are some stands of conifers, with their guaranteed bird list of two - Coal Tits and Goldcrests. But there are a few old oaks and beech, plus plenty of younger birch trees. There is little in the way of ground cover, but there are good scallops cut alongside the path, which open up the wood. Numerous Great and Blue Tits are joined by Blackcaps and Chiffchaffs in summer.

This track emerges at a very long, wide and dead-straight ride leading north and lined with pines. This is intriguingly called Mick Mills Race (Mick Mills had a race with a dragon here and won, apparently!) and is part of the High Weald Landscape Trail. There is an airiness to the wood here - the plantations are open enough for bracken to grow beneath them. The ride edges are effectively linear heaths, complete with heather, and kept open by West Sussex County Council and volunteer groups.

If you don't like the ruler-straightness of the ride, a winding path 50 yards to your right follows pretty much the same course and leads through some heathy woodland glades. It is possible a pair or two of Tree Pipits cling on here, as do a similar number of Nightjars, though looking for the latter condemns you to a long walk back in the pitch dark.

In total, some 50 acres of heath are maintained here, and although none of the blocks are quite big enough for Dartford Warblers or Stonechats, there are already a few Wood Larks with the potential for more when the conifer blocks are felled.

Though the pool next to Forest Grange school looks promising on the map, it is actually a fishing lake with signs which leave you in no doubt that you are not welcome! Content yourself instead with the woodland and its birds, including regular Siskins in winter, often in quite large flocks. Redpolls occur fairly frequently too - we've had wonderful views of both species drinking together at a muddy puddle.

Marsh Tits are quite common and we've found that the circular route down the west side of the wood, along the ghyll, is a good way to finish the walk, with the chance of Redstart in spring. This brings you back to the car park.

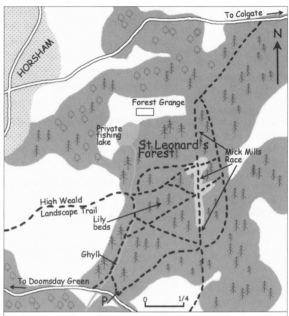

Access details

(2 miles ESE of Horsham)

From A23 just S of Crawley, turn off at Handcross junction onto B2110 towards Horsham. Once out of the village of Handcross, continue for just more than a mile and turn R at a crossroads, signed to Bucks Head. This road is very narrow follow for 2.5 miles past two obvious pools on the R-side and the Mannings Heath golf club on L. As road starts to descend into a wood, the Forestry Commission 'Roosthole' car park is on R (TQ207298).

Alternatively, from Horsham on A281, turn L through

Mannings Heath, emerging after 1mile at a T-junction, with the car park 0.5 mile down hill to your L.

BY TRAIN: 1.25 mile walk from Faygate station.
BY BUS: Very difficult - No.52 Horsham-Colgate circuit (at top end of Forest) travels three times a week!

Other nearby sites

Less than 5 miles: Warnham Mill Pond.
Less than 10 miles: Buchan Country

Key points

- Allow 2-plus hours

- Expect 15-30 species

- Mainly private farmland with rights of way; Lancing Ring is LNR; Steep Down is SNCI – both are managed by SDCB

- Public rights of way and Lancing Ring open at all times

- Reasonable free parking; no other facilities (Nearest ones in Lancing/ Steyning)

- Some moderate slopes to climb

- A little muddy underfoot in winter

- Not suitable for wheelchairs

- Very early morning definitely preferable

Contacts

For Lancing Ring and Steep Down:
Sussex Downs Conservation Board
01273 625242

WELL KNOWN to birders for turning up Quails on a regular basis, especially in late summer, this part of the Downs is also rich in other nationally-declining farmland birds such as Yellowhammers and Sky Larks, with a few Grey Partridges and especially Corn Buntings. Lancing Ring is a good place for observing diurnal migration on autumn mornings.

Target birds
All year – Corn Bunting (20%, rising to 90% in midsummer), Grey Partridge (hear 30%, though up to 80% on spring evenings, see 5%). *Passage – (autumn)* Tree Pipit (passing overhead 25%). *Breeding season* – Quail (hear 30%).

Other likely bird species

All year	*Passage*	Spotted Flycatcher
Farmland birds	Hirundines	*Winter*
Red-legged Partridge	Warblers	Thrushes
	Wheatear	
Stonechat	Whinchat	*Occasional*
	Redstart	Pied Flycatcher

Background information and birding tips

BIRDS ON OFFER here are downland/farmland birds plus passerine migrants. If it is the former you're after, the best starting point is from Beggars Bush car park. It is possible to walk west from here to Cissbury Ring too, but for Steep Down head east.

Crossing the road from the car park, the track leads across the edge of a field. In fact, fields are *the* habitat here – there is very little in the way of hedges or uncultivated downland, just big, big fields. But many of the farmers here grow wildlife as well as crops, taking part in agri-environment schemes that allow them to retain field margins, plant some of the crops in spring, leave over-winter stubbles etc.

As a result, the skies are alive with Sky Larks from March onwards. Corn Buntings, which

tend to breed quite late in the season, are also likely anywhere along the route from May onwards, singing from prominent perches and even from the top of the crops.

Steep Down itself is quite a prominent lump of downland, with footpaths that completely circumnavigate and cross the top. The eastern flank in particular does have excellent slopes of unfertilised grass with a few small bushes, perfect for Yellowhammers, Linnets and Corn Buntings, with the chance of Stonechats, too.

This is also a good vantage point from which to hear Quails deep in the waving crops below. July and August seem to be good months, though the tendency for males to stop singing, once paired, means a bad year for birdwatchers (or rather 'birdlisteners') although it may be good for the Quails. Don't expect to see one – ever!

Lancing Ring or Clump (the same thing, but the Ring referring to archaeological interest, the Clump to the trees on top of it) is a ten-minute walk on from Steep Down, or can be approached more easily from the car park on the Lancing side.

The Clump's trees are rather too dense, dark and tall to easily locate any birds in them. The scrub on the southern slope can be more productive, though everywhere here is prone to disturbance.

Early morning from August to October gives you the best birding here with the kind of diurnal movement you get at Beachy Head – pipits, wagtails, hirundines, finches – repeated here on a smaller scale and occurring because this is the first high ground in from the sea.

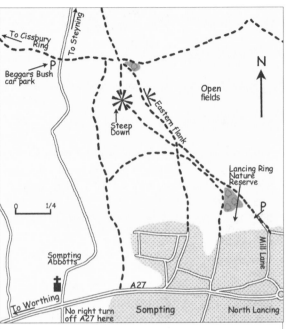

Other nearby sites

Less than 5 miles: Adur Estuary, Shoreham Harbour.
Less than 10 miles: Cissbury Ring to Chanctonbury Ring, Henfield Levels.

Access details

(4 miles NNE of Worthing)

For Steep Down access is from minor road between A27 (mid-way between Lancing and Sompting) and Steyning.

The turn (signed Sompting Abbotts) is only possible travelling E, so if coming W, continue to traffic lights at Sompting Sainsbury's and U-turn.

Beggars Bush car park (TQ161079) is a good-sized roadside bay 2 miles up the minor road at brow of hill.

Travelling from Steyning, the road is signed Sompting via Bostal and is very narrow.

For Lancing Ring/Clump: turn N off A27 at the only roundabout in Lancing. After

50 yards, turn R into Mill Lane opposite Sussex Potter pub. Drive all the way to the top of Mill Lane where there is a large Sussex Downs Conservation Board car park (TQ182062).

BY TRAIN: Just over 1 mile walk from Lancing Station to Lancing Ring. *BY BUS:* No.9 hourly Littlehampton-Portslade service travels through North Lancing.

Key points

- Allow 1-plus hours
- Expect 20-35 species
- Part of Arundel Park SSSI
- Rights of way open every day, except March 24
- Roadside free parking opposite, but can get busy.
- Café;toilets (20p)
- Western side in particular can get muddy
- Wheelchair access up east side of lake, but strong pusher needed
- No dogs (or horses!)
- No telescope needed!
- Expect lots of people at weekends

NESTLING deep in a steep wooded valley on the outskirts of Arundel, and only a stone's throw from the WWT Arundel reserve, the medieval Swanbourne Lake feels a strange mix of urban duck pond and woodland country park. Alongside the hordes of shrieking gulls clamouring for bread, there can be astonishing numbers of wintering Gadwalls and diving ducks plus breeding Mandarins, all giving very good views.

Target birds
All year – **Mandarin (75%)**. *Winter* – Chiffchaff (20%), Firecrest (10%).

Other likely bird species

All year	Buzzard	*Breeding season*
Wildfowl	Kestrel	Garden Warbler
Scrub birds	Moorhen	
Woodland birds	Coot	*Winter*
Shelduck	Grey Wagtail	Gulls
Gadwall	Marsh Tit	
Pochard		*Occasional*
		Common Sandpiper

Background information and birding tips

STARTING at Swanbourne Lodge, the broad paved water's edge gives all the access needed for large numbers of people to toss copious amounts of sliced bread into the shallow green waters. Genuinely wild Pochards and Tufted Ducks are ridiculously tame here, along with Canada Geese, Mallards (and Mallard-derivatives), Coots and Moorhens with even the chance of a Mandarin or Shelduck pitching up for a share.

Watching the diving ducks is great – the water is fantastically clear as they pump their way down the few feet to the bottom and bounce back up to the surface. Gulls have a year-round presence, thanks both to the bread and to the Black-headed breeding colony just over the road at WWT Arundel. The echoing mews of Common Gulls in winter seems somehow out of place in this shady valley.

It is often easy to leave the people behind - they thin out quickly 50 yards into the park. The track climbs up away from the water's edge, but still with great views down to dozens of Gadwalls. Meanwhile, Long-tailed Tit flocks wander along the wooded path edge, dragging a few Blue, Great and Marsh Tits with them, plus Treecreepers and the occasional Firecrest.

At the top end of the lake there are rights of way into Arundel Park. Ahead is what looks like a dark woodland but turns out to be a hidden grassy hollow. Grazed short, it is not bad for butterflies and above the wooded slopes expect to see Buzzards and Sparrowhawks, the latter displaying in spring. It might be here that you see your first Mandarins, yapping as they fly up into the trees.

On the walk back down the western side of the lake (yes, a nice circular route is possible), we have always been successful with Mandarins, especially tucked away under the tangle of trees that emerge from the water.

The sheer volume of people that visit Swanbourne can be off-putting and you don't want to be here birdwatching when the rowing boats take to the water in summer. The upside is that many of the birds are so tame - the wildfowl, the Jackdaws, even the Robins - so it's a great place for photographing birds in almost natural surroundings. It's a place for either a weekday, early morning, or with the family.

A short drive up the road from Swanbourne towards South Stoke gives good panoramas from the verge over the Arun Valley, one of the best vantage points for finding Bewick's Swans in winter.

The steep wooded riverbank just upstream from South Stoke is also notable for its tree-roost of Cormorants which can be seen wheeling in from late afternoon. Parking at South Stoke however, is very limited.

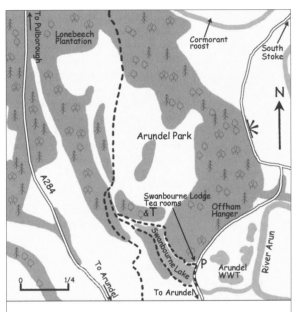

Access details

(0.5 mile NE of Arundel)

Follow the duck and castle symbols into Arundel off A27. After R-turn at a mini-roundabout in town centre, you pass the castle on your L. Drive on through a wonderful arbour of beech trees. In less than 0.5 mile, you will cross a large hump-back bridge, with castle trout pools immediately on your L. The bottom of Swanbourne Lake abuts the road again to your L. Just around the next R bend, there is parking for about 40 cars on the R side of the road

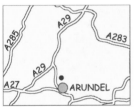

(TQ161079) just before WWT Arundel car park.

BY TRAIN: 1 mile walk from Arundel Station.
BY BUS: Both No.702 Brighton-Arundel and No.55 Arundel-Chichester hourly or more (not Sundays).

Other nearby sites

Less than 5 miles: Arundel WWT.
Less than 10 miles: Climping; Amberley Wild Brooks, Pulborough Brooks

Key points

- Allow 4-plus hours

- Expect 45-65 species

- Part of Chichester & Langstone Harbours SPA, Ramsar site and SSSI; both Thorney Deeps and Pilsey Island are LNRs, the former called Eames Farm

- Island is MoD and interior is strictly out of bounds - never stray off the path, no matter how good a bird you've seen!

- Rights of way open at all times, unless Army dictates otherwise

- Be prepared for a long exposed walk, with no facilities (bar one hide) and no means of short-cutting back

THORNEY ISLAND is not an island these days but a large peninsula jutting into the sheltered tidal basin of Chichester Harbour. It is famed for the largest Little Egret roost in the UK but also has a host of other great species on offer from Ospreys on passage to Bearded Tits, Short-eared Owls and big numbers of waders, including near annual Kentish Plovers. It is also one of the most awkward Sussex sites to visit. Be aware that the access is not straightforward and facilities are poor. If you are prepared to put in the effort however, the rewards are some of the most superb and quiet estuary birding in southern England.

Target birds

All year - Little Egret (95%), Black-tailed Godwit (90%), Cetti's Warbler (hear 70%, see 10%), Bearded Tit (hear 50%, see 20%), Mediterranean Gull (25%), Peregrine (20%), Grey Partridge (10%).

Passage - Osprey (60%), Hobby (40%).

Spring - Whimbrel (60%).

Autumn - Little Stint (40%), Curlew Sandpiper (40%).

Breeding season - Little Tern (80%), Turtle Dove (80%).

Winter - Knot (90%), Red-breasted Merganser (85%), Sanderling (80%), Greenshank (80%), Spotted Redshank (60%), Short-eared Owl (75%), Barn Owl (50%), Avocet (40%), Eider (30%), Corn Bunting (30%), Kingfisher (30%), Merlin (15%), Slavonian Grebe (10%), Long-tailed Duck (5%).

Other likely bird species

All year	*Passage*	*Winter*
Waterbirds	Hirundines	Brent Goose
Wildfowl	Warblers	Wigeon
Coastal waders	Wheatear	Gadwall
Inland waders	Whinchat	Shoveler
Gulls		Rock Pipit
Scrub birds	*Breeding season*	
Farmland birds	Sandwich Tern	*Occasional*
Garden birds	Common Tern	Kentish Plover
Shelduck	Cuckoo	Little Gull
Stonechat	Yellow Wagtail	Twite

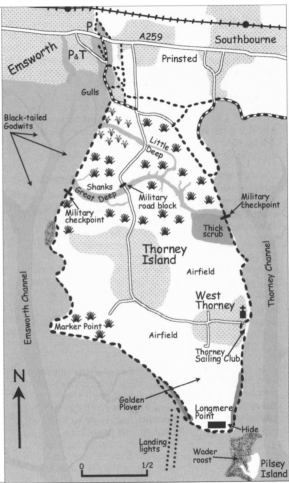

Access details

(7 miles W of Chichester)

From E, take A259 off A27 roundabout just W of Chichester and follow for 6 miles to Emsworth. Follow signs into small town centre.

Coming W from Havant, turn off A27 at junction after the Hayling Island turn towards Southbourne. At roundabout in Emsworth, turn R into town centre.

Pay and display parking with toilets, plus shops and cafes nearby is at SU749057.

BY TRAIN: 0.5 mile walk from Emsworth station to estuary.

BY BUS: No.700 Brighton-Southsea passes through Emsworth. Alternative is 2-hourly No.11 Chichester-Thorney service.

Background information and birding tips

THORNEY WAS ONCE a true island in Chichester Harbour, linked at low tide to the mainland by a causeway. In 1870, two straight sea walls about a mile apart were built out to the island and the area of estuary in between was drained. Thorney became a peninsula.

Public access to the island is now via these sea walls only, as the Island has been in Ministry of Defence hands since 1936. The interior of the island remains firmly off-limits and the access road is blocked by a military checkpoint. However, in bird terms this is of little consequence as the coast path circumnavigating the island gives six miles of glorious estuary-edge birdwatching, if your legs can take it!

Continues overleaf

Key points

- **Nearest facilities and designated car parking in Emsworth**

- **Some of the coastal path is tricky to negotiate**

- **Shorter visits just to the Deeps are just about possible for wheelchairs**

- **Respect the access restrictions to Pilsey Island they are in place to prevent disturbance to roosting waders**

- **A telescope is useful, if you can bear to carry it six miles!**

Contacts

Chichester Harbour Conservancy

01243 512301

We usually start at Emsworth, as there are very few places to park any closer to the Island. A short walk around the Marina brings you out onto the seawall, with the open mud of the upper estuary to your right. Gulls lounge here, with a high chance of a Mediterranean. In among the yachts in the channel are likely to be Red-breasted Mergansers, but most notable are passage Whimbrels and large numbers, often three figures, of Black-tailed Godwits, even in summer.

Over to your left is 'The Deeps'. Now managed as a Local Nature Reserve by Chichester Harbour Conservancy, the land has never been ploughed and is still managed using traditional farming practices of grazing and hay cutting, ideal for wildlife. The two deep channels would once have been tidal; the larger southerly channel is called the Great Deep, the smaller reed-fringed northerly one is, yes, Little Deep.

The wet scrub on the approach to Little Deep is reliable for Cetti's Warblers, or at least to hear them! The Little Deep itself still has much open water with a wide fringe of reed, where Little Grebes, Coots and Tufted Ducks breed and Shovelers and Gadwalls are likely in winter. The reeds inevitably host Reed Warblers, but are also good enough for a few pairs of Bearded Tits. The sea wall is a good vantage point for looking across the reed tops, checking too for Merlins and Hobbies zooming through.

Half a mile further on is the Great Deep. The banks here near its western sluice are renowned for their roost of shanks. All three species over-winter, and there is an incredible build-up of more than 100 Greenshanks in August.

Other freshwater waders such as Common Sandpipers are regular here on passage, and Shelducks and Little Egrets are year-round fixtures. The scrub at this end of the Great Deep is the site of the impressive Little Egret roost, where 281 were recorded in late-summer 1999.

Just beyond Great Deep, barbed-wire fences loom ominously. The Army operates the gates by remote control - smile sweetly into the camera, say your name, and access will generally be granted, though very occasionally access is denied for security reasons.

The seawall zigzags along the estuary edge, with Brent Geese and waders plentiful throughout the winter. The deep waters of the Emsworth Channel to your right, are the best place in Sussex for wintering Goldeneyes and are also the county's top spot for Long-tailed Ducks, though the latter are far from reliable. Common, Sandwich and Little Terns fish along here in summer. The wet fields inside the seawall should not be ignored either; they retain winter Snipe plus breeding Turtle Doves and Grey Partridges. Remember not to wander from the sea wall though.

It's a long slog then from Marker Point past the southern edge of the RAF's disused airfield to Longmere Point, an important high tide roost. The airfield, if undisturbed, is great for Golden Plovers, Short-eared Owls and Brent Geese in winter, and Wheatears on passage. There is also some scrub along this section, attracting Whinchats and warblers on passage, plus tits.

Check across the reed bed fro Hobbies chasing through on passage. (John Davis)

Some aircraft landing lights on wooden stilts lined up across the mud should also be checked. Perching among the Cormorants is sometimes an Osprey. These magnificent birds are annual here on spring and autumn migration, with often more than one lingering somewhere around the Island.

At Longmere Point there is a small basic hide overlooking the RSPB's Pilsey Island LNR. At low tide, vast areas of sand are exposed and waders are spread thinly, but at high tide the birds congregate at Pilsey Island in impressive numbers. Here are the largest congregations of Bar-tailed Godwits in Sussex, a couple of hundred Sanderlings in early spring, and a real chance in May of seeing a Kentish Plover among the Ringed. This is the best place to find Corn Buntings in winter, though their once-healthy breeding population on the Island is now struggling.

In autumn, Curlew Sandpipers and Little Stints are regular and there will undoubtedly be Oystercatchers, several thousand Dunlins and several hundred Knot throughout the winter. Beyond, in the deeper water, you should find Great Crested and occasional Slavonian Grebes in winter, along with more Red-breasted Mergansers and probably Eiders too, but a scope is essential, and afternoon watching can be directly into the sun.

The walk back along the eastern side of the island starts off through some dense bushes, with glimpses over the Chichester Channel to the east of the Island. Views then open over the east end of the airfield and the path then deviates into the edge of the village of West Thorney and back out again at the church.

Once past the village, the footpath becomes narrow and is very muddy after rain. It is difficult going particularly when you are tired after several miles' walking.

Once through the security gate on this eastern sea wall, there are still waders to be seen in the Prinsted Channel. The changing tides bring plenty of wader movement, with lots of Dunlins, Ringed Plovers, Redshanks and Grey Plovers. Recently, Avocets have also taken to wintering here, and we've seen Kingfishers on the sluice gates.

The seawall can then be followed around towards Prinsted or, for the shortest route back to Emsworth, take the track along the north side of the Deeps back towards Emsworth.

The meadows are excellent here for Barn Owls and for wintering Short-eared Owls - to see them simultaneously is to be expected near to dusk. We once watched three Short-eareds at the same time here - it may be enough reward to ease the final mile back to Emsworth!

Key points

- Allow 1.5-plus hours
- Expect 30-40 species
- Local Nature Reserve
- Only open Thurs - Sun, 10 til 6
- Free access to 20-minute trail
- Cheap permits for sale for longer trail
- Free car park with 6ft 6" entrance barrier
- Excellent little visitor centre with café and good toilets; open weekends
- Generally flat terrain, some paths a little muddy at times
- Wheelchair access in dry conditions, including two hides
- No dogs allowed

Contacts

Horsham District Council:
Countryside Service Unit
01403 256890

HEMMED IN BY Horsham, a bypass and a golf course, you wouldn't expect much from this little Local Nature Reserve, and yet you can clock up 35 species here quite easily in an hour. Willow Tit hangs on, Cetti's Warblers may just be establishing themselves, and there are plenty of common woodland and waterbirds in this well-managed little reserve. But take good note of those opening times!

Target Birds

Range of common water and woodland birds, including - *All year* – Willow Tit (20%). *Winter* – Siskin (50%); Redpoll (30%); Water Rail (10%).

Other likely bird species

All year	Goldcrest	Thrushes
Waterbirds		Pochard
Wildfowl	*Passage*	Grey Wagtail
Woodland birds	Hirundines	
Great Crested Grebe	Warblers	*Occasional*
Kestrel	Common Sandpiper	Lesser Spotted Woodpecker
Nuthatch	*Winter*	Cetti's Warbler
Treecreeper	Gulls	

Background information and birding tips

WARNHAM LOCAL NATURE Reserve is focused around a large 15th Century mill pond. The pond is surrounded by beds of reedmace and willow scrub and there are small areas of woodland, hedgerow and marsh to explore.

The Visitor Centre by the car park, is only open at weekends (April-September), and Sundays (October-March), although the toilets are open year-round. A short 20-minute trail is open free of charge, but if you intend to try the longer trail of one hour or more, which we recommend, there is a small permit fee payable in the Centre or the honesty box. There is plenty of free literature to pick up, and a good sightings board.

As soon as you venture out onto the reserve, there is a hide tucked away to your right giving views over the water's edge, but if you've been cooped up in the car or bus, there are just as good views over the Pond from the little meadow. In winter, flights of gulls spiral down to bathe. Scan the water for common wildfowl - both grebes are present year-round and there are usually a few Pochards and Teal in winter. All the ducks tend to congregate over towards the far side.

The long footbridge across a reed-filled inlet is only for those who have paid a permit, but anyone can walk left past the pond-dipping stations to Walnut Tree Plantation. This little copse holds woodland birds such as Treecreepers.

If you've paid your money, you can head on up the lake. A second well-built hide gives good views out across and up the lake, although you are often looking into the sun. Straight across from the hide there is a small heronry in some of the mature trees, with birds coming down to the water's edge to fish. The hedgerows and pond-side trees typically hold tits, including maybe a pair each of Willow and Marsh Tits, plus Greenfinches and Great Spotted Woodpeckers. The paths are well-tended, although they can get a little sticky in winter.

A boardwalk leads out over the vegetation-choked top of the lake, where there is still the slim chance of Lesser Spotted Woodpeckers and, from the far end of the boardwalk, a circular walk leads up a slope into a little quiet plantation, largely birch but with some mature conifers too. In particular, the northern end of the wood overlooks a private larch wood, where we have had wonderful views of the trees alive with Redpolls and Siskins.

Warnham isn't going to be the kind of place you travel far to see, but you will see birds (132 species have been recorded here), and it is somewhere that you can easily have to yourself on a Thursday or Friday afternoon, just as the poet Shelley used to do in his youth!

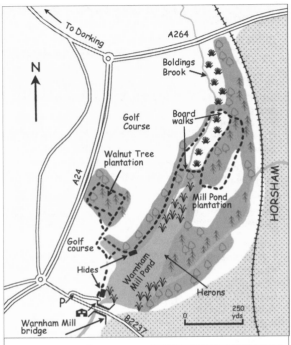

Access details

(1mile W of Horsham town centre)

From the A24 Horsham bypass on W-side of Horsham, turn E at roundabout along B2237 (**Warnham Road**) towards Horsham, following the large brown Nature Reserve duck signs. The entrance is only 100-yards along on N side of road, under 6' 6" height barrier (TQ166323).

BY TRAIN: 1 mile walk from Horsham Station along Hurst Road, and turn R onto Warnham Road.

BY BUS: No.61 Tillingbourne bus leaves 'Carfax' in Horsham town centre hourly Mon-Sat. Get off in Redford Ave, and walk N to Warnham Road, turn L, and reserve is 100-yards on R.

Other nearby sites

Less than 5 miles: St Leonard's Forest.
Less than 10 miles: Buchan Country Park

Key points

- Allow 1 hour
- 25-35 species
- SSSI and LNR
- Small car park and good wheelchair-friendly hide open 24 hours
- Hide faces north, so light good
- No other facilities
- Walks along LNR are along road edge, so no wellies required; some muddy paths on north shore
- Difficult by public transport
- Roadside watching not ideal but Legsheath Lane generally quiet
- Telescope helpful but not essential

Contacts

Friends of Weir Wood Reservoir
http://surf.to/weirwood
01342 326714

THIS MEDIUM-SIZED reservoir attracts some great birds – regular Ospreys on passage, breeding Mandarins, an active heronry, Common Terns, loads of Great Crested Grebes, and passage waders when water levels are right. The nature reserve end of the reservoir, in particular, is well worth a visit, with not only most of the birds but an excellent car park, bird feeders and hide.

Target birds *All year* – Mandarin (80%); Lesser

Spotted Woodpecker (5%). *Breeding season* - Grey Herons in heronry (100%); Common Tern (90%). *Passage* – Osprey (10%); Kingfisher (autumn – 30%). *Winter* – Redpoll (20%).

Other likely bird species

All year	Dunlin	*Occasional*
Waterbirds	Common Sandpiper	Rarer grebe or diver
Gulls		Goosander
Marsh Tit	*Winter*	Water Rail
Nuthatch	Pochard	Greenshank
	Tufted Duck	Green Sandpiper
Passage	Snipe	Little Stint
Hirundines	Siskin	Curlew Sandpiper
		Willow Tit

Background information and birding tips

AS YOU TURN into the little free car park off Legsheath Lane, a cloud of small birds is likely to fly up from the bounty of seed feeders and fat balls dangling in the bushes. These are courtesy of the 'Friends of Weir Wood Reservoir' and are generally stocked October to April. They are superb at drawing in Reed Buntings, Siskins, Great Spotted Woodpeckers, Nuthatches, Marsh Tits or even Willow Tits among the legions of commoner tits and finches.

The sturdy hide nearby, with great wheelchair access and up-to-date sightings chalk board inside, gives views over the top end of the reservoir, the Local Nature Reserve. Here, the reservoir is shaped like a U'-bend,

and most of the broader open block of the reservoir is out of sight, but most of the birding interest is concentrated up here anyway.

A dry summer will see water levels dropping to expose mud which attracts, for an inland reservoir, a fine chance of passage waders. Little Stints and Curlew Sandpipers are almost annual and tend to stick around for a few days, with maybe Greenshanks or Green Sandpipers. This is a also great time to see Ospreys and one or more will usually hang about in August or September. Maybe the platform to your right will encourage breeding one day. Already the provision of Common Tern rafts have done the trick, with a few pairs of these now present in summer.

Throughout the year, this western

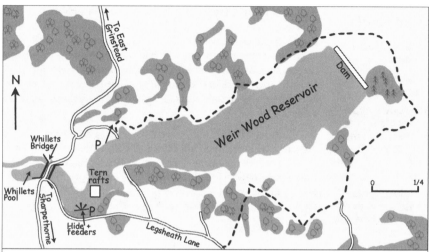

Access details

(2 miles south of East Grinstead)

From East Grinstead, take minor road S towards Sharpthorne. One mile beyond Sharp Hill, road turns sharply L over Whillets Bridge, turn immediately L into Legsheath Road. Car park is 0.5 mile on L (TQ382341). Two lay-bys before then allow views over reservoir. Alternatively from A22, turn W off at Wych Cross traffic lights.

At the crossroads by Ashdown Forest 'Goat' car park cross straight over. Weir Wood car park is just over a mile down on the R.

For car park N of the Reservoir, head from Whillets Bridge towards East Grinstead. After 300 yards, turn R down narrow lane (Admirals Bridge Road) on sharp L bend. Car park at bottom of hill (TQ386347). Car park not suitable for disabled (although marked as such on maps).

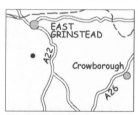

BY TRAIN: No direct access.
BY BUS: No.84 East Grinstead-Crawley passes over Whillets Bridge three services a day each way (Mon-Sat).

end of the reservoir attracts waterfowl. Great Crested Grebes are regular, with maybe twenty pairs displaying in front of the hide in early spring. The other wildfowl often tuck themselves away under the overhanging willows which skirt this end of the lake. A walk along the road edge can give better views. Expect a few Teal, Pochards and Tufted Ducks, but watch out for elusive Mandarins which are on the increase. The willows on the far side also support a fairly new but prospering heronry. The hide is also a good place to see Kingfishers, particularly July to November.

Where the road meets a T-junction, it is possible to walk right, along the verge, and look over Whillets Pool and then Whillets Bridge. Lesser Spotted Woodpeckers are occasionally seen here, but the road edge is narrow and dangerous and you will need to retrace your steps back to the reservoir.

It is also possible to walk the north bank of the reservoir. It looks promising on the map, but high fencing keeps you well away from the reservoir edge. Plenty of vegetation will block much of your views of the water so it can be frustrating compared to some sites. However, some passerine migrants use the hedges (including Wryneck in 2002!), and the open vista over the water after about 300 yards is the best vantage point for seeing Ospreys.

161

Key points

- Allow 3-plus hours

- Expect 20-35 species

- Mostly private woodland, but there is a small SSSI and SWT reserve (permit only)

- Public rights of way open at all times – keeping to them is imperative

- No facilities bar small rough car park

- Mud likely

- Not suitable for wheelchairs

- Very difficult by public transport

- Night walks are recommended only for those who know the woods well

- Taking a map is advisable – these woods are vast!

Contacts

For the SWT reserve only:
Sussex Wildlife Trust
01273 492630

NORTH OF CHICHESTER, vast tracts of private woodland cloak the South Downs. West Dean Woods are the birdwatchers' favourite. The management for shooting helps create the wide variety of habitats for birds, with elusive targets such as Hawfinches, Firecrests, Hen Harriers and Grasshopper Warblers. Rights of way are few but perfectly adequate for good long walks in search of the bounty of good birds.

Target birds

All year – Buzzard (80%), Siskin (50%, higher in winter), Crossbill (20%), Raven (15%), Willow Tit (10%). *Breeding season* – Turtle Dove (75%), Spotted Flycatcher (60%), Tree Pipit (30%), Grasshopper Warbler (10%), Firecrest (10%). *Winter* – Hen Harrier (20%), Redpoll (20%), Hawfinch (5%), Brambling (10%).

Other likely bird species

All year	Nuthatch	*Winter*
Woodland birds	Treecreeper	Thrushes
Red-legged Partridge	*Breeding season*	*Occasional*
Marsh Tit	Garden Warbler	Golden Pheasant

Background information and birding tips

SUSSEX WILDLIFE TRUST'S little car park at West Dean Woods *can* produce a wide range of woodland birds, but we all know how fickle they can be, especially in winter, so some long circular walks from here should allow you to catch up with a good suite of species.

Head west up the lane and, at the first left-bend in the road, turn right up the rough track. The SWT reserve is soon on your right. Tits (including Marsh), Great Spotted Woodpeckers and summer warblers are all likely in the mature trees and coppice. At the far end of the SWT reserve, the beds of wild daffodils are glorious in early spring. Note there is no access actually *into* the reserve.

The wood then opens out into

the privately owned and managed areas. Bold 'Private' signs at every possible side-track inhibit you from wandering randomly – you MUST stick to rights of way.

The age of the trees is crucial to the birds you will see. After clearing and replanting, they are good for Linnets, Nightjars, Tree Pipits and Whitethroats, and even Grasshopper Warblers. Within a few years, the trees become too high and dense, and are now more suited to Garden Warblers, Willow Warblers, Bullfinches and Turtle Doves. Eventually, they become tall enough for Blackcaps and Chiffchaffs.

Active woodland management like this soon makes books such as this out of date, so as a new clearing opens up, look for the key species moving in. What *will* probably be present and unchanged for many years is the large stand of dark mature conifers up beyond the SWT reserve, full of Goldcrests and Coal Tits. Siskins almost certainly breed here, and don't forget to check for Firecrests and Crossbills.

A hundred yards into the conifers, you reach a five-way junction. If you turn sharp left here, the long slope down through the conifer belt alongside Linchball Wood reaches a sunny woodland valley leading back south to the road near Yewtree Cottage. The fairly young hornbeams at the track's end consistently attract Hawfinches to roost in winter, although numbers are low (up to five). Walk left down the lane back to the car park past Staple Ash Farm, where a large Chaffinch flock in winter is worth sifting through for Bramblings.

If at the five-way junction in the wood you turn right, narrower footpaths lead through a mosaic of plantations of varying ages, up towards the edge of the scarp. The route continues through Venus Wood and down a wide but muddy ride, past a charcoal burner. It eventually comes out on the road 400-yards east of the car park. Again, a wide range of woodland species is likely, with even Golden Pheasants possible in the thickest conifer plantations. It's a long walk though and the OS Landranger is useful to keep you on course.

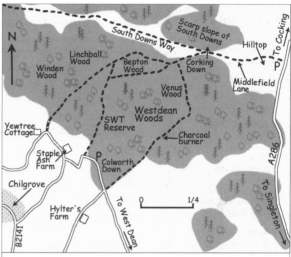

Access details

(6.5 miles NNW of Chichester)

For SWT Car park (SU844150):
From Chichester/A27, take the A286 north towards Midhurst and turn L after the village of Lavant on the B2141 towards Petersfield. After 2.5 miles, turn R into the narrow Hylters Lane for 1mile to a T-junction. Turn L and drive 0.5 mile to small rough car park on R under beech trees. Approaching on the B2141 from Petersfield, turn L in Chilgrove and wind round narrow lanes, with SWT car park 0.5 mile beyond Staple Ash Farm (SU844152).

Alternative good parking is possible on W-side of A286 on

the brow of the hill just S of Cocking (SU873166). This starting point adds about 2 miles to the walk, and includes a significant climb up the scarp of the downs to Venus Wood.

BY TRAIN: No direct access.
BY BUS: No.60 Bognor-Midhurst passes half-hourly along A286 – alight near car park.

Other nearby sites

Less than 10 miles: Iping and Stedham Commons, Kingley Vale, Chichester Gravel Pits

Key points

- Allow 1.5-plus hours
- Expect 15-25 species
- SSSI and National Trust site
- Open free access at all times
- Parking but no other facilities
- Some moderate slopes to climb, but paths generally dry
- Viewpoint but little else accessible for wheelchairs
- Very difficult by public transport
- Keep strictly to paths and keep dogs under control to protect ground-nesting birds
- Heathland is at high risk of fire in all seasons - take every precaution not to cause them

Contacts

National Trust,
West Sussex Downs
(West) 01730 816638

WOOLBEDING COMMON is one of those delightful hidden places that few know about. It is a heath on a hill, far more bracken-dominated than Iping and Stedham Commons way down below it, and bursting with Tree Pipits in summer. This National Trust site is also good for Wood Larks, Dartford Warblers and lovely views!

Target birds *All year* - Dartford Warbler (25%). *Breeding season* - Tree Pipit (95%), Wood Lark (40%), Nightjar (at dusk hear 80%, see 40%), Woodcock (at dusk 80%.

Other likely bird species

All year	Stock Dove	Swallow
Scrub birds	Stonechat	
Woodland birds	Mistle Thrush	*Winter*
Kestrel		Winter thrushes
Pheasant	*Breeding season*	
	Cuckoo	

Background information and birding tips

EVEN ONCE you've managed to find the National Trusts's car park for Woolbeding Common, tucked away in the back of beyond up single-track lanes, the main area of heath is still hidden from view behind the trees, like a well-kept secret.

First though, cross the road and go the few steps to the viewpoint (1). No wonder there's a bench there, you'd think that you were back in untamed Medieval England to look at the fabulous panorama laid out in front of you - mile after mile of wooded ridge and vale, and barely a house in sight. You'd also think that you might see a Buzzard hanging somewhere in the air, but though their numbers are good on the Downs over to your left, they don't seem to be too frequent here yet.

The steep bracken-filled slopes in front of the viewpoint (2) are excellent for Tree Pipits. In fact, Woolbeding Common as a whole is probably now the best place for them in Sussex. If you wish, you can walk down the slope to some of the wet woodlands below, though they are not exceptional for birds.

Much better is to walk back past your car, take the track out of the back right-hand corner of the car park, and then head up the slope towards the line of pylons. This track then follows underneath the wires out across the upper Common and then dog-legs down the hill, mirroring the long thin shape of the Common.

The top of the Common (3) is best for Dartford Warblers, as this is where most of the gorse is. Because the Common is narrow, whatever gorse you can see is what there is, and you can tailor your walk accordingly to check it out, though the dense bracken means that the Common has rather few paths across it.

Wood Larks sometimes sing from the wires, while Tree Pipits are possible anywhere where there are

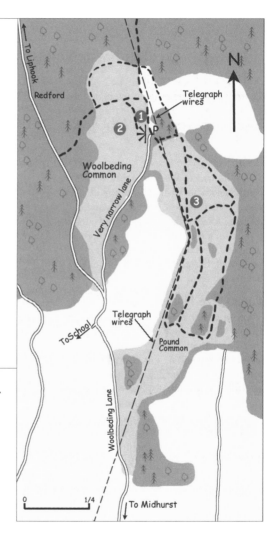

Access details

(3 miles NNW of Midhurst)

One mile out of Midhurst on A272 to Petersfield, turn N on minor road signed to Woolbeding and Redford. The road climbs through some narrow cuttings. After 2.5 miles, just after St Cuthman's School, a very narrow rough track (with grass growing in the middle) leads off right, signed Older Hill. Pass Pigeon Hill House and climb on up for 0.5 miles to National Trust car park (SU869260).

BY TRAIN: **No direct access.**
BY BUS: **Very difficult - No.93 Midhurst-Petersfield passes through Redford daily!**

isolated bushes in among the bracken. Nightjars of course need a dusk visit - the shorter flatter walk at Iping is much easier in this respect.

We cannot lie - we have had some pretty birdless experiences up here. But we've had good ones too, and generally we've seen very few people which, combined with the views, makes for a pleasurable escape.

Other nearby sites

Less than 5 miles: Iping and Stedham Commons.
Less than 10 miles: Chapel Common.

165

Sites with excellent wheelchair access and facilites

Arlington Reservoir

There is a disabled toilet in the main toilet block, and advance parking is then possible around by the dam, from which there is wheelchair access to the hide.

Arundel

The Wildfowl & Wetland Trust reserve is completely wheelchair-friendly, with parking near to the visitor centre and a disabled toilet; The visitor centre is on one level with a big picture window; there are wide metalled paths around reserve; the boardwalk has passing places; the hides have wheelchair bays.

Cuckmere Haven

There are disabled toilets at Seven Sisters Country Park visitor centre. The long metalled path all the way down the eastern side of valley is flat, and affords good views over the meanders and the wet grassland. The only difficulties are the shingle beach at the southern end of the track, which makes access to the sea difficult; and there is no opportunity to climb the riverbank to see into river channel itself or onto the western side of valley.

Pagham Harbour (Sidlesham Ferry only)

A disabled toilet, operated by a RADAR key, is at the Visitor Centre. A broad flat track then leads through to the hide, with a wheelchair bay, overlooking Sidlesham Ferry Pool. The track can then be followed almost to the 'Dragon' (see site text if you are baffled at this point!), but turn left along the west bank of the harbour rather than down the side of Ferry Long Pool. This track circles back around to the Visitor Centre, a route of a little under a mile. Access is just possible at Church Norton down to the harbour edge.

RSPB Pulborough Brooks

There are designated parking bays next to the visitor centre, and from here there is flat access to the centre, tea-room, and disabled toilet. Two electric scooters are available on loan, which permit a complete circuit of the nature trail to be undertaken. The moderate slope down the hill has a zigzag track cut into the grass, and a new wheelchair path is under construction (2003) down to Nettley's Hide. All hides are designed for wheelchair access.

Rye Harbour

There is a disabled toilet near the main car park. A metalled track leads from car park all the way to beach, with excellent access to the first hide overlooking the wader scrape and Flat Beach. The track then leads all the way to Winchelsea Beach along the Beach Reserve, giving good views of the Little Tern colony. There is unfortunately no wheelchair access to the hides overlooking Ternery Pool, nor to Castle Water or the Bittern viewpoint. Access onto the shingle beach is understandably difficult, though views over the sea are possible from by the Old Lifeboat House.

Sites with some wheelchair access and facilities

Adur Estuary
Limited views from Old Shoreham Bridge

Ardingly Reservoir
There is a car park for the disabled up to the left side of the dam, giving elevated views over the reservoir. Wheelchair access is then possible across the dam itself and into the first hide, with some further access around the reservoir margin in dry weather.

Beachy Head
Short 'Peace Path'for wheelchairs around Beachy Head itself, plus disabled toilets

Brighton-Newhaven Cliffs
Access via underpasses to undercliff walk at Saltdean and Ovingdean, and directly at Brighton Marina and Rottingdean

Buchan Country Park
Disabled toilet, plus paths that are accessible, if a little steep and bumpy/ muddy in places

Chidham and Cobnor
Well-made Cobnor disabled footpath leads from disabled car park (with disabled toilet accessible by RADAR key) for 400 yards with excellent views

East Head and West Wittering
Metalled access road gives good views over fields used by Brent Geese and Golden Plover, and around back of Snowhill Marsh, plus toilets, but otherwise access difficult

Newhaven Tidemills
No facilities, but concrete track gives access to and along beach

Northpoint Pit: Roadside birdwatching

Scotney Court: Roadside birdwatching

Selsey Bill
Major car park at SZ850923, 400 yards west of 'The Wall', gives good elevated watching from car

Shoreham Harbour
Flat metalled path along Widewater

Splash Point and Seaford Head
Flat metalled promenade leads right to Kittiwake colony and easy seawatching; toilets nearby

Warnham Mill Pond: Hides and much of track accessible in dry weather, with toilets

Weir Wood Reservoir: Great hide with wheelchair bay adjacent to car park

USEFUL CONTACTS

Disabled toilets leaflet
Available from RADAR, 12 City Forum, 250 City Road, London EC1V 8AF. tel: 02071 250 3222

Disabled Birders Association
Bo Boelens, 18 St Mildreds Road, Margate, Kent CT9 2LT. www.disabledbirdersassociation.org.uk

BEST SITES VIA PUBLIC TRANSPORT

A LMOST EVERY SITE in this book is accessible by public transport. That does not mean, however, that access is easy - many sites are served by limited timetables and/or require a considerable walk once you have alighted.

We do have friends, however, who will gladly travel from north London for the day to Pulborough Brooks, Pagham Harbour or Rye Harbour, showing that much is possible given the will-power.

The following are some of the best sites that are readily accessible by train or bus from some of the major train stations. Understanding that travellers by public transport need facilities close at hand (no chance to nip off in the car to the nearest petrol station for emergency supplies!), we have also indicated below the proximity of facilities on foot.

NB: CHECK ALL DETAILS BEFORE YOU TRAVEL - Traveline 0870 608 2 608/ Rail enquiries 08457 484950

From Chichester railway station

No.51 bus (incl. Sundays) to **Chichester gravel pits** (journey eight minutes), **Pagham Harbour** (15 minutes), **Selsey Bill** (30 minutes). Toilets at Pagham Harbour; all facilities in Selsey

No.53 bus (incl. Sundays) to **East Head and West Wittering** (16 minutes). Toilets and café facilities at East Head.

From Brighton railway station

Adur Estuary – 10 minutes on the Brighton–Worthing train, with 0.5 mile walk from Shoreham station. All facilities in Shoreham

Arlington Reservoir – though trains to Berwick station on Eastbourne line are infrequent, it is only a 0.5 mile walk to the reservoir, with toilets there and a pub near the station

Brighton Marina and **Sheepcote Valley** – several bus services (journey 10 minutes), and all facilities in Brighton Marina village

Brighton to Newhaven Cliffs – Nos.14 and 712 buses (journey 30 minutes), and facilities in the coastal towns

Castle Hill to Swanborough Hill – good circuit is No.22 to Castle Hill, and walk across Downs through to Peacehaven, catching the No.14 or 712 back to Brighton

Cuckmere Haven – No.712 (journey 50 minutes), with good facilities at Seven Sisters Country Park
Hollingbury Camp – by rail or bus (journey 10 minutes) – facilities back in Brighton

From Lewes railway station

Lewes Brooks – train to Southease station drops you right next to the riverbank. Alternatively, take the train to Newhaven and walk back up the river to Lewes. Facilities in Newhaven and Lewes
Newhaven Tidemills – train to Newhaven station, and short walk from there. Facilities in Newhaven
Splash Point and Seaford Head – train to Seaford, and 0.5 mile walk from there. All facilities in Seaford

From Hastings railway station

Combe Haven – a whole range of buses pass along from Hastings towards Bexhill – alight at The Bulverhythe pub.
Hastings Country Park – either take No.344 bus out to Fairlight and walk back, or vice versa. All facilities in Hastings

From Rye railway station

Rye Harbour – No.325 bus to Rye Harbour (journey eight minutes, not Sundays). Toilets and pubs in Rye Harbour

From Arundel railway station

1.5 mile walk to **Arundel WWT** and **Swanbourne Lake**. All facilities at WWT

From Brighton –Southsea railway line

Chidham and Cobnor – alight at Nutbourne station and walk from there. Limited facilities but good pub (The Old House at Home) in Chidham
Thorney Island – alight at Emsworth and walk from there. All facilities in Emsworth, though none around Thorney Island

From Pulborough railway station

Pulborough Brooks – No.100 bus from Pulborough station stops at reserve entrance. All facilities at RSPB.

THE SUSSEX BIRD LIST

**Firecrests
are rare
passage
migrants in the
Sussex area.**
(John Davis)

INCLUDES ALL species recorded in Sussex to 2003, with their current status according to the Sussex Ornithological Society. With scarce and rarer birds we have given an indication of the time of year and type of location in which they may occur. Don't expect to see those species that have only been seen a few times since records began!

Some species have been given new names by the British Ornithologists' Union. Where these differ from the names used in the text, the alternative name is given in brackets. Note that the main text avoids using terms such as 'Common', 'Eurasian' and 'European' where the convention in British birdwatching is to just use the bird name without. However, we recognise that for birdwatchers from other countries, these are often important to avoid ambiguity.

The status of each species is defined as follows:

Status	Breeding pairs	Winter / Passage
Very rare		1-10 records in totals
Rare	Less than annual	Less than annual
Very scarce	1-10 per year	1-20 per year
Scarce	11-100	21-200
Fairly common	101-1,000	201-2,000
Common	1,001-5,000	2,001-10,000
Very common	5,001-30,000	10,001-60,000
Abundant	30,000 +	60,000 +

County list: 388 species
Average number of species seen in the Sussex each year: 262 species
Average number of species breeding regularly in Sussex: 131 species
Record day count: 138 (set in 2002 by the Selsey Scorchers)

.........Red-throated Diver	*Gavia stellata*	Fairly common winter visitor and passage migrant offshore. Rare inland.
.........Black-throated Diver	*Gavia arctica*	Scarce winter visitor and passage migrant offshore. Rare inland. Easiest to see on seawatches in May
.........Great Northern Diver	*Gavia immer*	Very scarce winter visitor and passage migrant offshore. Rare inland. Top site – Selsey Bill
.........White-billed (Yellow-billed) Diver	*Gavia adamsii*	Very rare vagrant offshore. Just a small handful of recent records.
.........Little Grebe	*Tachybaptus ruficollis*	Scarce resident, passage migrant and winter visitor. Inland waters.
.........Great Crested Grebe	*Podiceps cristatus*	Fairly common resident, passage migrant and winter visitor.
.........Red-necked Grebe	*Podiceps grisegena*	Scarce winter visitor and passage migrant, usually offshore
.........Slavonian Grebe	*Podiceps auritus*	Scarce winter visitor and passage migrant offshore. Top site – Pagham Harbour.
.........Black-necked Grebe	*Podiceps nigricollis*	Very scarce winter visitor and passage migrant, usually seen on inland waters. Top sites - Scotney Court and Rye Harbour best.
.........(Northern) Fulmar	*Fulmarus glacialis*	Fairly common breeding visitor (to seacliffs) and passage migrant offshore.
.........Cory's Shearwater	*Calonectris diomedea*	Rare vagrant offshore. Less than annual.
.........Sooty Shearwater	*Puffinus griseus*	Very scarce autumn vagrant offshore. A few individuals recorded annually, Sep-Oct.
.........Manx Shearwater	*Puffinus puffinus*	Scarce passage migrant offshore.
.........Balearic Shearwater	*Puffinus mauretanicus*	Rare vagrant offshore, mainly Jul-Sep. A few individuals recorded annually.
.........(European) Storm Petrel	*Hydrobates pelagicus*	Rare vagrant offshore. Several recorded annually, mostly June-Nov. Top site – Selsey Bill
.........Leach's Storm-Petrel	*Oceanodroma leucorhoa*	Rare vagrant, vast majority offshore after storms. Occurs almost annually.
.........(Northern) Gannet	*Morus bassanus*	Fairly common passage migrant and summer (non-breeding) visitor offshore
.........(Great) Cormorant	*Phalacrocorax carbo*	Scarce resident (breeds at Rye Harbour) and common winter visitor.
.........(European) Shag	*Phalacrocorax aristotelis*	Scarce winter visitor and passage migrant. Top site - Brighton Marina.
.........Bittern	*Botaurus stellaris*	Very scarce winter visitor to inland and coastal reedbeds. Top site - Rye Harbour.
.........American Bittern	*Botaurus lentiginosus*	Very rare vagrant, no records for almost a century.
.........Little Bittern	*Ixobrychus minutus*	Rare vagrant, less than annual. Mostly recorded Apr-Jun, not necessarily by water.
.........(Black-crowned) Night Heron	*Nycticorax nycticorax*	Rare vagrant, less than annual but sometimes two or three in a year. Most records Apr-May at coastal sites, though has been recorded at Pulborough Brooks and Arlington Res.
.........Squacco Heron	*Ardeola ralloides*	Very rare vagrant – a small handful of records in the last 20 years, all in June. Ditches and reeds both at coastal and inland sites.
.........Cattle Egret	*Bubulcus ibis*	Very rare vagrant, but annual since 1998. Individuals may linger – one at Ovingdean stayed Jan-May.
.........Little Egret	*Egretta garzetta*	Fairly common passage migrant and winter visitor to most estuaries. May now breed. Roosts at Thorney have reached almost 300.
.........Great (White) Egret	*Egretta alba*	Very rare vagrant, but now annual and increasing. Mainly coastal, but recently recorded on Pevensey Levels and Ashdown Forest.
.........Grey Heron	*Ardea cinerea*	Fairly common resident.
.........Purple Heron	*Ardea purpurea*	Rare vagrant, just about annual, usually Apr-May. Mainly coastal.
.........Black Stork	*Ciconia nigra*	Very rare vagrant, just a few records at spring and autumn migration. Sightings both at inland and coastal sites
.........White Stork	*Ciconia ciconia*	Rare vagrant, occurring annually in recent years at spring and autumn migration. Fields, inland as well as on the coast.
.........Glossy Ibis	*Plegadis falcinellus*	Very rare vagrant, usually coastal. Recent records occurred Apr and Sep-Oct.

..........(Eurasian) Spoonbill	*Platalea leucorodia*	Very scarce passage migrant, usually coastal but sometimes inland. Several individuals recorded each year.
..........Mute Swan	*Cygnus olor*	Fairly common resident.
..........Bewick's (Tundra) Swan	*Cygnus columbianus*	Scarce winter visitor. Top site - Amberley Wild Brooks
..........Whooper Swan	*Cygnus cygnus*	Very scarce winter visitor and passage migrant, rarely reaching double figures each year. Usually inland.
..........Bean Goose	*Anser fabalis rossicus (tundra Bean Goose)*	Very scarce winter visitor and passage migrant, recorded most years but in very small numbers. Top site - Scotney Court.
....	*Anser fabalis fabalis (taiga Bean Goose)*	Rare winter visitor and passage migrant
..........Pink-footed Goose	*Anser brachyrhynchus*	Very scarce winter visitor and passage migrant, not recorded every year. Inland as well as coastal. Top site – Scotney Court.
..........(Greater) White-fronted Goose	*Anser albifrons*	Scarce winter visitor and passage migrant. Top site – Scotney Court, where winter flock numbers three-figures
..........Greylag Goose	*Anser anser*	Fairly common resident and winter visitor.
..........Snow Goose	*Anser caerulescens*	Very rare winter visitor, usually thought to be escapes. One thought to be wild was at Scotney Court Feb-Mar 1999.
..........Canada Goose	*Branta canadensis*	Fairly common resident and passage migrant.
..........Barnacle Goose	*Branta leucopsis*	Very scarce winter visitor. Small numbers each year, mostly Dec-Feb, but many feral or escaped. Scotney Court is a favoured site.
..........Brent Goose	*Branta bernicla bernicla (dark-bellied Brent Goose)*	Very common winter visitor and passage migrant. Mostly in the western estuaries and harbours.
....	*Branta bernicla hrota (pale-bellied Brent Goose)*	Very scarce winter visitor.
....	*Branta bernicla nigricans (black brant)*	Very rare winter visitor
..........Red-breasted Goose	*Branta ruficollis*	Very rare winter visitor. Possibly only two authentic records, Arun Valley (1958) and Pagham Harbour (1986/7).
..........Egyptian Goose	*Alopochen aegyptiacus*	Rare vagrant, recorded most years often on levels.
..........Ruddy Shelduck	*Tadorna ferruginea*	Very rare vagrant. Annual records of escapes.
..........(Common) Shelduck	*Tadorna tadorna*	Fairly common resident and common winter visitor.
..........Mandarin (Duck)	*Aix galericulata*	Scarce resident. Top sites - Arundel WWT, Swanbourne Lake and Weir Wood Reservoir.
..........(Eurasian) Wigeon	*Anas penelope*	Common winter visitor and passage migrant.
..........American Wigeon	*Anas americana*	Very rare vagrant. One was at Pagham (Oct 1996- Feb 1997).
..........Gadwall	*Anas strepera*	Very scarce resident and fairly common winter visitor and passage migrant. Top site – Chichester Gravel Pits
..........(Eurasian) Teal	*Anas crecca*	Scarce resident and common winter visitor and passage migrant.
..........Green-winged Teal	*Anas crecca carolinensis*	Very rare vagrant with only a handful of records. Mostly Jan-Apr, usually inland.
..........Mallard	*Anas platyrhynchos*	Common resident and winter visitor.
..........(Northern) Pintail	*Anas acuta*	Fairly common winter visitor and passage migrant, has bred
..........Garganey	*Anas querquedula*	Scarce passage migrant and rare breeding visitor and summer visitor. Top site - Pulborough Brooks.
..........Blue-winged Teal	*Anas discors*	Very rare vagrant. Recent records have been at Church Norton and Splash Point.
..........(Northern) Shoveler	*Anas clypeata*	Very scarce resident and fairly common winter visitor and passage migrant.
..........Red-crested Pochard	*Netta rufina*	Rare winter visitor and passage migrant, has bred. Several records annually, mainly inland lakes and gravel pits.
..........(Common) Pochard	*Aythya ferina*	Rare resident & fairly common winter visitor and passage migrant.
..........Ring-necked Duck	*Aythya collaris*	Very rare vagrant, usually Dec-Mar. Small handful of recent records including at Warnham Mill Pond
..........Ferruginous Duck	*Aythya nyroca*	Rare vagrant, less than annual. Recent long-stayer at Rye Harbour gravel pits, also recorded at inland waters such as Weir Wood Res.
..........Tufted Duck	*Aythya fuligula*	Fairly common resident and winter visitor.
..........(Greater) Scaup	*Aythya marila*	Scarce winter visitor and passage migrant. Top site – Scotney Court
..........(Common) Eider	*Somateria mollissima*	Scarce winter visitor and passage migrant.

..........Long-tailed Duck	*Clangula hyemalis*	Scarce winter visitor and passage migrant. The Emsworth Channel off Thorney Island is a good site to try.
..........(Black) Common Scoter	*Melanitta nigra*	Common passage migrant and fairly common winter visitor.
..........Surf Scoter	*Melanitta perspicillata*	Very rare vagrant, with a handful of recent records, all at the coast. Mainly Dec-Apr.
..........Velvet Scoter	*Melanitta fusca*	Scarce winter visitor and passage migrant. Easiest to see during spring seawatching, or in Rye Bay.
..........(Common) Goldeneye	*Bucephala clangula*	Fairly common winter visitor
..........Smew	*Mergellus albellus*	Very scarce winter visitor. Top sites – Northpoint Pit and Rye Harbour
..........Red-breasted Merganser	*Mergus serrator*	Fairly common winter visitor and passage migrant. Top site – Thorney Island
..........Goosander	*Mergus merganser*	Scarce winter visitor and passage migrant. Top sites - Weir Wood Reservoir and Rye Harbour.
..........Ruddy Duck	*Oxyura jamaicensis*	Very scarce resident and scarce winter visitor.
..........(European) Honey Buzzard	*Pernis apivorus*	Very scarce passage migrant. Several records annually, though the 500 in the year 2000 was a one-off! High proportion of sightings at coast during migration, esp Sep.
..........Black Kite	*Milvus migrans*	Rare vagrant, recently recorded more years than not. Most records Apr-May, nearly always by the coast.
..........Red Kite	*Milvus milvus*	Rare vagrant, but now regularly recorded each year. Downland and the coast.
..........White-tailed Eagle	*Haliaeetus albicilla*	Very rare vagrant. Over 50 records to 1961, but none since.
..........(Eurasian) Marsh Harrier	*Circus aeruginosus*	Scarce passage migrant and rare winter visitor.
..........Hen Harrier	*Circus cyaneus*	Scarce winter visitor and passage migrant. Top site - Amberley Wild Brooks.
..........Montagu's Harrier	*Circus pygargus*	Very scarce passage migrant, formerly bred and some individuals recently attempted to establish territories on the downs. Most records are during migration.
..........(Northern) Goshawk	*Accipiter gentilis*	Very scarce resident and winter visitor.
..........(Eurasian) Sparrowhawk	*Accipiter nisus*	Fairly common resident and passage migrant.
..........(Common) Buzzard	*Buteo buteo*	Rare resident and scarce passage migrant – breeding numbers and range increasing in county.
..........Rough-legged Buzzard	*Buteo lagopus*	Rare winter visitor and passage migrant, recorded on average two or three times per decade. Recent long-staying bird at Lewes Levels.
..........Osprey	*Pandion haliaetus*	Scarce passage migrant. Top sites – Thorney Island and Weir Wood Reservoir.
..........(Common) Kestrel	*Falco tinnunculus*	Fairly common resident and passage migrant.
..........Red-footed Falcon	*Falco vespertinus*	Rare vagrant, recently recorded most years. Usually May-Jun.
..........Merlin	*Falco columbarius*	Scarce winter visitor and passage migrant. Top site – Beachy Head (in October)
..........(Eurasian) Hobby	*Falco subbuteo*	Scarce breeding visitor and passage migrant.
..........Gyr Falcon	*Falco rusticolus*	Very rare vagrant. One 20th century record on the downs between Cissbury and Chanctonbury Rings (Mar 1972).
..........Peregrine (Falcon)	*Falco peregrinus*	Scarce resident, passage migrant and winter visitor.
..........Black Grouse	*Tetrao tetrix*	Extinct resident. Last recorded in Ashdown Forest in 1937.
..........Red-legged Partridge	*Alectoris rufa*	Common resident.
..........Grey Partridge	*Perdix perdix*	Fairly common resident, but much declined. Top site - Climping
..........(Common) Quail	*Coturnix coturnix*	Scarce breeding visitor to Downs, but fluctuating numbers. Top site – Steep Down
..........(Common) Pheasant	*Phasianus colchicus*	Very common resident.
..........Golden Pheasant	*Chrysolophus pictus*	Scarce resident, perhaps now nearly extinct.
..........Water Rail	*Rallus aquaticus*	Scarce resident, winter visitor and passage migrant. Top site – Arundel WWT
..........Spotted Crake	*Porzana porzana*	Very scarce passage migrant, now several records annually. Most are of birds trapped at Pett Levels.
..........Sora	*Porzana carolina*	Very rare vagrant, one at Pagham Lagoon (Oct-Dec 1985).
..........Little Crake	*Porzana parva*	Very rare vagrant, two post war records at Beachy Head (Apr 1968) and Cuckmere (Mar 1985).
..........Baillon's Crake	*Porzana pusilla*	Very rare vagrant, one record of a bird trapped at Pett Levels (Aug 1992).
..........Corn Crake	*Crex crex*	Rare passage migrant, bred until about 1945. Recent records are less than annual, usually autumn.

(Common) Moorhen	*Gallinula chloropus*	Very common resident and winter visitor.
(Common) Coot	*Fulica atra*	Common resident and winter visitor.
(Common) Crane	*Grus grus*	Rare vagrant, less than annual. As likely on the levels as on the coast. All recent records Sep-Apr.
Little Bustard	*Tetrax tetrax*	Very rare vagrant. None since 1925.
Great Bustard	*Otis tarda*	Extinct resident and very rare vagrant. Last seen (and shot) in the late nineteenth century!
(Eurasian) Oystercatcher	*Haematopus ostralegus*	Scarce resident and fairly common passage migrant and winter visitor.
Black-winged Stilt	*Himantopus himantopus*	Rare vagrant, averages two or three records each decade. Inland as well as coastal.
(Pied) Avocet	*Recurvirostra avosetta*	Scarce winter visitor and passage migrant., has bred. Top site – Pagham Harbour.
Stone-curlew	*Burhinus oedicnemus*	Rare summer visitor and passage migrant, has bred. Now recorded most years on migration, usually on the coast.
Collared Pratincole	*Glareola pratincola*	Very rare vagrant, three post war records at Rye Harbour (Jun 1978) and Pagham Harbour (Jul 1987 and May 2001).
Oriental Pratincole	*Glareola maldivarum*	Very rare vagrant. One on Pevensey Levels (Aug 1993).
Black-winged Pratincole	*Glareola nordmanni*	Very rare vagrant. One at Sidlesham Ferry (Oct 1981).
Little (Ringed) Plover	*Charadrius dubius*	Rare breeding visitor and scarce passage migrant.
Ringed Plover	*Charadrius hiaticula*	Fairly common resident, passage migrant and winter visitor.
Killdeer	*Charadrius vociferus*	Very rare vagrant. One post war record at Sidlesham Sewage Farm (Mar1974).
Kentish Plover	*Charadrius alexandrinus*	Very scarce passage migrant, formerly bred. Now recorded annually at the coast, predominantly Mar-May. Top sites – Thorney Island and Rye Harbour
Lesser Sand Plover	*Charadrius mongolus*	Very rare vagrant. The bird at Pagham (Aug 1997) was the first British record.
Greater Sand Plover	*Charadrius leschenaultii*	Very rare vagrant. The bird at Pagham (Dec 1978-Jan 1979) was the first British record. Since seen at Pilsey (Jul 1998).
(Eurasian) Dotterel	*Charadrius morinellus*	Very scarce passage migrant. Annual records in spring (Apr-May) and autumn (Aug-Sep). Top site – Castle Hill to Swanborough Hill.
American Golden Plover	*Pluvialis dominica*	Very rare vagrant. One post war record at Church Norton (Sep 1988).
Pacific Golden Plover	*Pluvialis fulva*	One record – Rye Harbour (Apr 2003)
(European) Golden Plover	*Pluvialis apricaria*	Common winter visitor and passage migrant.
Grey Plover	*Pluvialis squatarola*	Common winter visitor and passage migrant.
Sociable Plover	*Vanellus gregarius*	Very rare vagrant. Just a small handful of post war records.
(Northern) Lapwing	*Vanellus vanellus*	Fairly common resident and winter visitor.
(Red) Knot	*Calidris canutus*	Common winter visitor and fairly common passage migrant. Top site – Thorney Island
Sanderling	*Calidris alba*	Fairly common winter visitor and passage migrant. Top sites – Climping and Thorney Island
Semipalmated Sandpiper	*Calidris pusilla*	Very rare vagrant. Just a handful of records near the coast.
Little Stint	*Calidris minuta*	Scarce passage migrant.
Temminck's Stint	*Calidris temminckii*	Very scarce passage migrant, recorded most years. Vast majority are found at coastal sites, far more frequent in May than in autumn. Top site – Pagham Harbour
Least Sandpiper	*Calidris minutilla*	Very rare vagrant. Two records, at Pett Pools (Jul 1984) and Sidlesham Ferry (Jul 1995).
White-rumped Sandpiper	*Calidris fuscicollis*	Very rare vagrant. Only a few post war records, all but one at Pagham or Chichester Harbours, all Aug-Nov.
Baird's Sandpiper	*Calidris bairdii*	Very rare vagrant. Mainly coastal Jul-Sep.
Pectoral Sandpiper	*Calidris melanotos*	Very rare vagrant, now recorded most years Jul-Oct. Inland waters as well as coastal.
Curlew Sandpiper	*Calidris ferruginea*	Scarce passage migrant.
Purple Sandpiper	*Calidris maritima*	Scarce winter visitor and passage migrant. Top sites - Newhaven Harbour, Shoreham Harbour and Brighton Marina.
Dunlin	*Calidris alpina*	Abundant winter visitor and common passage migrant.
Broad-billed Sandpiper	*Limicola falcinellus*	Very rare vagrant, recent records at Pett Levels (May 1988) and Sidlesham Ferry (May 1993).
Stilt Sandpiper	*Micropalama himantopus*	Very rare vagrant. Three records Jul-Sep at Pagham, Chichester GP and Chichester Harbour

Buff-breasted Sandpiper	*Tryngites subruficollis*	Very rare vagrant with a handful of post war records, all Sep-Oct. Three of these were at Sidlesham Ferry.
Ruff	*Philomachus pugnax*	Scarce winter visitor and passage migrant.
Jack Snipe	*Lymnocryptes minimus*	Scarce winter visitor and passage migrant.
(Common) Snipe	*Gallinago gallinago*	Fairly common resident and common winter visitor.
Great Snipe	*Gallinago media*	Very rare vagrant, very few post war autumn records. The last one at Bodiam (1975) was shot.
Long-billed Dowitcher	*Lymnodromus scolopaceus*	Very rare vagrant, with just a small handful of post war records of which two Thorney,two at Sidlesham.
(Eurasian) Woodcock	*Scalopax rusticola*	Fairly common resident and winter visitor.
Black-tailed Godwit	*Limosa limosa*	Common winter visitor and passage migrant.
Bar-tailed Godwit	*Limosa lapponica*	Common winter visitor in west of county and passage migrant. Top site – Thorney Island
Whimbrel	*Numenius phaeopus*	Common passage migrant and very scarce summer visitor and winter visitor. Top site – Rye Harbour
(Eurasian) Curlew	*Numenius arquata*	Common winter visitor and passage migrant, formerly bred.
Upland Sandpiper	*Bartramia longicauda*	Very rare vagrant. One post war record at Bracklesham (Dec 1979).
Spotted Redshank	*Tringa erithropus*	Scarce winter visitor (eg Pagham, Thorney) and passage migrant. Top site – Pagham Harbour (in winter)
(Common) Redshank	*Tringa totanus*	Fairly common resident, passage migrant and winter visitor.
Marsh Sandpiper	*Tringa stagnatilis*	Very rare vagrant. Mainly at Pett Level and Pools, Rye and Pagham Harbours, most sightings Jul-Aug.
(Common) Greenshank	*Tringa nebularia*	Fairly common passage migrant and scarce winter visitor. Top site (autumn/winter) - Thorney Island
Lesser Yellowlegs	*Tringa flavipes*	Very rare vagrant, with a handful of post war records. Most ecently seen at Pett Pools and Cuckmere Haven.
Green Sandpiper	*Tringa ochropus*	Fairly common passage migrant and very scarce winter visitor.
Wood Sandpiper	*Tringa glareola*	Scarce passage migrant. Top site – Pagham Harbour
Terek Sandpiper	*Xenus cinereus*	Very rare vagrant, two post war records. Midrips (May 1951) was the first British record. Also Pagham (May 1969).
Common Sandpiper	*Actitis hypoleucos*	Fairly common passage migrant and very scarce winter visitor, has bred. Top site – Lewes Brooks (on River Ouse)
Spotted Sandpiper	*Actitis macularia*	Very rare vagrant. Two post war records, at Weir Wood (Aug 1974) and Barcombe (Nov 1977) reservoirs.
(Ruddy) Turnstone	*Arenaria interpres*	Fairly common winter visitor and passage migrant, and scarce summer visitor.
Wilson's Phalarope	*Phalaropus tricolor*	Very rare vagrant with a handful of post war records. Most were Aug-Oct sightings at Pagham and Rye Harbours.
Red-necked Phalarope	*Phalaropus lobatus*	Rare passage migrant, less than annual with most being Sep juveniles. Sidlesham Ferry is the top spot.
Grey Phalarope	*Phalaropus fulicarius*	Very scarce autumn and rare winter visitor, recently occurring annually. Mostly after storms at coastal sites, but a few records inland.
Pomarine Skua	*Stercorarius pomarinus*	Scarce passage migrant in spring at seawatching sites and very scarce winter visitor.
Arctic Skua	*Stercorarius parasiticus*	Fairly common passage migrant and rare winter visitor.
Long-tailed Skua	*Stercorarius longicaudus*	Rare vagrant, one or two recorded offshore most years. Most occur Aug-Sep, fewer in May.
Great Skua	*Catharacta skua*	Scarce passage migrant and very scarce winter visitor.
Mediterranean Gull	*Larus melanocephalus*	Scarce resident, passage migrant and winter visitor, has bred
Laughing Gull	*Larus atricilla*	Very rare vagrant, two records. The one at The Crumbles (Jul 1923) was the first British record. Also seen between the Adur and Splash Point (Apr 1991).
Franklin's Gull	*Larus pipixcan*	Very rare vagrant. Recorded at Arlington Res. (Jul 1970) and at Brighton Marina and Newhaven Tidemills (one bird, Dec 1990- Jan 1991).
Little Gull	*Larus minutus*	Scarce passage migrant.
Sabine's Gull	*Larus sabini*	Rare autumn visitor, now occurring most years. A lot of records after the 1987 hurricane. All records offshore, except one at Arlington Res.
Bonaparte's Gull	*Larus philadelphia*	Very rare vagrant. Three post-war records, at Newhaven, Langney Point and Pagham Lagoon.
Black-headed Gull	*Larus ridibundus*	Common resident and abundant winter visitor and passage migrant.

175

Slender-billed Gull	*Larus genei*	Very rare vagrant. Two post war records, at Langney Point (Jun-Jul 1960) and Rye Harbour gravel pits (Apr 1963).
Ring-billed Gull	*Larus delwarensis*	Very rare vagrant, a small handful of records 1984-7 all Nov-Feb. Two of these were at Weir Wood Res.
(Mew) Common Gull	*Larus canus*	Common winter visitor and passage migrant, has bred.
Lesser Black-backed Gull	*Larus fuscus*	Fairly common passage migrant and winter visitor, and scarce breeding visitor.
Herring Gull	*Larus argentatus*	Common resident, passage migrant and winter visitor.
	Larus argentatus cachinnans	(Caspian Gull) Very rare vagrant. One record, by the R.Adur at Shoreham Airport (Sep 1997).
	Larus argentatus michahellis	(Yellow-legged Gull) Scarce passage migrant and summer visitor, and very scarce winter visitor.
Iceland Gull	*Larus glaucoides*	Very scarce winter visitor and passage migrant, recorded annually. Vast majority of sightings near the coast.
Glaucous Gull	*Larus hyperboreus*	Very scarce winter visitor and passage migrant. Top site – Pagham Harbour
Great Black-backed Gull	*Larus marinus*	Common winter visitor and passage migrant, now breeding in very small numbers.
(Black-legged) Kittiwake	*Rissa tridactyla*	Common winter visitor, passage migrant and breeding visitor. Top site – Splash Point
Ivory Gull	*Pagophila eburnea*	Very rare vagrant. One apparently genuine post war record, at Cuckmere Haven (Nov 1954).
Gull-billed Tern	*Sterna nilotica*	Rare vagrant, less than annual offshore and coastal sites.
Caspian Tern	*Sterna caspia*	Rare vagrant, less than annual offshore and coastal sites.
Lesser Crested Tern	*Sterna bengalensis*	Very rare vagrant. A small handful of recent sightings at or passing Rye Harbour and all in May.
Sandwich Tern	*Sterna sandvicensis*	Scarce breeding visitor, and common passage migrant.
Roseate Tern	*Sterna dougallii*	Very scarce passage migrant and summer visitor. Top site – Rye Harbour
Common Tern	*Sterna hirundo*	Scarce breeding visitor and common passage migrant.
Arctic Tern	*Sterna paradisaea*	Fairly common passage migrant.
Bridled Tern	*Sterna anaethetus*	Very rare vagrant. One at Rye Harbour (May 1993).
Sooty Tern	*Sterna fuscata*	Very rare vagrant. One recent record, Rye Harbour (Jul 1984).
Little Tern	*Sterna albifrons*	Scarce breeding visitor and fairly common passage migrant, breeding at Rye Harbour.
Whiskered Tern	*Chlidonias hybrida*	Very rare vagrant, with just a handful of records. Coastal (but one record at Darwell Res.) mostly May-Jun.
Black Tern	*Chlidonias niger*	Fairly common passage migrant.
White-winged Black Tern	*Chlidonias leucopterus*	Rare vagrant, less than annual. Most records from coastal sites, but recently at Chichester GP. Mainly autumn.
(Common) Guillemot	*Uria aalge*	Fairly common winter visitor and passage migrant.
Razorbill	*Alca torda*	Fairly common winter visitor and passage migrant.
Black Guillemot	*Cepphus grylle*	Rare vagrant offshore, can go a decade between sightings. Recent long-staying bird at Brighton Marina.
Little Auk	*Alle alle*	Very scarce autumn and winter visitor offshore. Recorded most years, predominantly Nov.
(Atlantic) Puffin	*Fratercula arctica*	Very scarce passage migrant offshore, recorded most years. Regular records from Selsey Bill.
Pallas's Sandgrouse	*Syrrhaptes paradoxus*	Very rare vagrant, not recorded since 1889.
Rock Dove (Feral Pigeon)	*Columba livia*	Common resident.
Stock Dove	*Columba oenas*	Common resident and winter visitor.
Common Woodpigeon	*Columba palumbus*	Abundant resident and winter visitor.
Collared Dove	*Streptopelia decaocto*	Very common resident.
Turtle Dove	*Streptopelia turtur*	Common but declining summer visitor and passage migrant.
Ring-necked Parakeet	*Psittacula krameri*	Very scarce resident, perhaps now extinct as breeding species.
Great Spotted Cuckoo	*Clamator glandarius*	Very rare vagrant. Two post war records, at Bognor Regis (Aug 1967) and North of Shoreham Airport (Apr 1990).
(Common) Cuckoo	*Cuculus canorus*	Fairly common summer visitor.
Yellow-billed Cuckoo	*Coccyzus americanus*	Very rare vagrant. Two fairly old records of dead birds, at Eastbourne (Nov 1952) and Middleton-on-Sea (Dec 1960).
Barn Owl	*Tyto alba*	Scarce resident. Amberley Wild Brooks is best.
Snowy Owl	*Nyctea scandiaca*	Very rare vagrant. No truly genuine records.

Little Owl	*Athene noctua*	Fairly common resident. Top site – Pulborough Brooks
Tawny Owl	*Strix aluco*	Fairly common resident
Long-eared Owl	*Asio otus*	Rare resident and very scarce passage migrant and winter visitor.
Short-eared Owl	*Asio flammeus*	Scarce winter visitor and passage migrant, has bred. Top sites – Amberley Wild Brooks, Thorney Island
(European) Nightjar	*Caprimulgus europaeus*	Fairly common breeding visitor.
(Common) Swift	*Apus apus*	Common breeding visitor and passage migrant.
Alpine Swift	*Apus melba*	Rare vagrant, less than annual. Usually spring overshoots, most sightings are at Beachy Head.
(Common) Kingfisher	*Alcedo atthis*	Fairly common resident and winter visitor.
(European) Bee-eater	*Merops apiaster*	Rare vagrant, less than annual, has bred. Mostly seen at coastal sites, esp. Beachy Head.
(European) Roller	*Coracias garrulus*	Very rare vagrant, not recorded since 1977. Nearly all records from inland localities.
Hoopoe	*Upupa epops*	Vary scarce passage migrant, now annually, has bred. Inland as well as coastal sites, Apr-May and Aug-Sep.
(Eurasian) Wryneck	*Jynx torquilla*	Very scarce passage migrant, several records annually, mainly at coastal sites. Has bred. Majority Aug-Oct (try Beachy Head) but some also Apr-May.
Green Woodpecker	*Picus viridis*	Fairly common resident.
Great Spotted Woodpecker	*Dendrocopos major*	Common resident.
Lesser Spotted Woodpecker	*Dendrocopos minor*	Fairly common resident. Top sites – Pulborough Brooks, Burton Mill Pond and Amberley Wild brooks
White-winged Lark	*Melanocorypha leucoptera*	Very rare vagrant. No acceptable records since the first British record at Brighton in 1869.
(Greater) Short-toed Lark	*Calandrella brachydactyla*	Very rare vagrant, only a small handful of post war coastal records.
Crested Lark	*Galerida cristata*	Very rare vagrant, no records since 1881.
Wood Lark	*Lullula arborea*	Very scarce resident and passage migrant.
Sky Lark	*Alauda arvensis*	Common resident, passage migrant and winter visitor.
Shore (Horned) Lark	*Eremophila alpestris*	Rare winter visitor Nov-Mar, less than annual. Always near the coast, most at the Rye Harbour area.
Sand Martin	*Riparia riparia*	Fairly common breeding visitor and very common passage migrant.
(Eurasian) Crag Martin	*Ptyonoprogne rupestris*	Very rare vagrant. Two records, both at Beachy Head, including only the second British record in 1988.
(Barn) Swallow	*Hirundo rustica*	Common breeding visitor and abundant passage migrant.
Red-rumped Swallow	*Hirundo daurica*	Rare vagrant, less than annual, usually Apr-May. Predominantly coastal sites, most in Beachy Head area.
Cliff Swallow	*Hirundo pyrrhonota*	Very rare vagrant
House Martin	*Delichon urbica*	Common breeding visitor and scarce passage migrant.
Richard's Pipit	*Anthus novaeseelandiae*	Rare vagrant, less than annual. Usually near the coast, Sep-Oct.
Blyth's Pipit	*Anthus godlewskii*	Very rare vagrant. One 1882 record, misidentified until the 1960's when it was declared the first British record.
Tawny Pipit	*Anthus campestris*	Very scarce vagrant, one or two recorded most years. Majority seen at the coast, Aug-Sep. Top sites – beachy Head and Climping
Olive-backed Pipit	*Anthus hodgsoni*	Very rare vagrant. One record, at Beachy Head (Oct 1987).
Tree Pipit	*Anthus trivialis*	Fairly common but declining breeding visitor and passage migrant.
Meadow Pipit	*Anthus pratensis*	Common resident and very common passage migrant.
Red-throated Pipit	*Anthus cervinus*	Very rare vagrant. Just a handful of records, usually Oct on the coast.
Rock Pipit	*Anthus petrosus*	Very scarce resident and fairly common winter visitor and passage migrant.
	Anthus petrosus littoralis	(Scandinavian Rock Pipit) Very scarce passage migrant, recorded most years on the coast. Often Feb-Mar. Top site – Brighton-Newhaven Cliffs
Water Pipit	*Anthus spinoletta*	Scarce winter visitor and passage migrant – Combe Haven is perhaps top site in UK.
Yellow Wagtail	*Motacilla flava flavissima*	Fairly common breeding visitor and passage migrant.

177

....	*Motacilla flava flava* (Blue-headed Wagtail)	Very scarce vagrant.
....	*Motacilla flava thunbergi* (Grey/Ashy-headed Wagtail)	Very rare vagrant. Only a handful of records, usually near the coast May-Jun.
..........Grey Wagtail	*Motacilla cinerea*	Fairly common resident, passage migrant and winter visitor.
..........Pied Wagtail	*Motacilla alba yarelli*	Common resident, passage migrant and winter visitor.
....	*Motacilla alba alba* (White Wagtail)	Very scarce passage migrant.
..........(Bohemian) Waxwing	*Bombycilla garrulus*	Vary scarce winter visitor, irruptive and some years not recorded. Often seen in towns, Oct-Apr.
..........(White-throated) Dipper	*Cinclus cinclus*	Very rare vagrant. Just a couple of post-war records.
..........(Winter) Wren	*Troglodytes troglodytes*	Abundant resident.
..........Dunnock (Hedge Accentor)	*Prunella modularis*	Abundant resident.
..........Alpine Accentor	*Prunella collaris*	Very rare vagrant. One post war record, on the cliffs at Telscombe (Apr 1955).
..........Rufous-tailed Scrub-Robin	*Cercotrichas galactotes*	Very rare vagrant. One post war record, at The Wicks (Sep 1951). This was the sixth British record.
..........(European) Robin	*Erithacus rubecula*	Abundant resident, passage migrant and winter visitor.
..........Thrush Nightingale	*Luscinia luscinia*	Very rare vagrant. Two records, at Beachy Head (Aug-Sep 1984) and a juvenile trapped at Pett (Sep 1998).
..........(Common) Nightingale	*Luscinia megarhynchos*	Fairly common breeding visitor. Top sites – Pulborough Brooks, Ebernoe Common, Amberley Wild Brooks, Ditchling Beacon to Ashcombe Bottom, Powedermill to Darwell
..........Bluethroat	*Luscinia svecica*	Very scarce passage migrant, less than annual. Majority are at coastal sites Aug-Oct.
..........Black Redstart	*Phoenicurus ochruros*	Rare resident, fairly common passage migrant and scarce winter visitor. Top sites – Beachy Head (passage), Brighton Marina, Brighton-Newhaven Cliffs and Shoreham Harbour (winter)
..........(Common) Redstart	*Phoenicurus phoenicurus*	Scarce breeding visitor and fairly common passage migrant. Breeds in Ashadown Forest.
..........Whinchat	*Saxicola rubetra*	Rare summer visitor and fairly common passage migrant, used to breed
..........Stonechat	*Saxicola torquata*	Scarce resident, passage migrant and winter visitor.
..........(Northern) Wheatear	*Oenanthe oenanthe*	Very scarce breeding visitor and common passage migrant.
..........Pied Wheatear	*Oenanthe pleschanka*	Very rare vagrant. One record, at Newhaven (July 1990) following unseasonal strong cold southerly winds.
..........Black-eared Wheatear	*Oenanthe hispanica*	Very rare vagrant. Two post war records, one at Beachy Head (May 1987) and one at Bewl Water dam (May 1988).
..........Desert Wheatear	*Oenanthe deserti*	Very rare vagrant, four post war records. Two were at Selsey, two at Beachy Head.
..........(Rufous-tailed) Rock Thrush	*Monticola saxatilis*	Very rare vagrant. One record, inland in West Sussex (May 1996).
..........White's Thrush	*Zoothera dauma*	Very rare vagrant, only one acceptable record in 1898.
..........Ring Ouzel	*Turdus torquatus*	Scarce passage migrant. Top site - Beachy Head.
..........(Common) Blackbird	*Turdus merula*	Abundant resident and winter visitor.
..........Black-throated (Dark-throated) Thrush	*Turdus ruficollis*	Very rare vagrant, just one record. This was the first British record and was shot near Lewes in 1868.
..........Fieldfare	*Turdus pilaris*	Common passage migrant and winter visitor.
..........Song Thrush	*Turdus philomelos*	Abundant resident and very common passage migrant and winter visitor.
..........Redwing	*Turdus iliacus*	Abundant passage migrant and very common winter visitor.
..........Mistle Thrush	*Turdus viscivorus*	Very common resident, passage migrant and winter visitor.
..........Cetti's Warbler	*Cettia cetti*	Very scarce resident, passage migrant and winter visitor. Top site - Arundel WWT.
..........(Common) Grasshopper Warbler	*Locustella naevia*	Very scarce but declining breeding visitor and fairly common passage migrant. Top site – Beachy Head (passage), Amberley Wild Brooks (breeding season)
..........Savi's Warbler	*Locustella luscinioides*	Rare vagrant, probably has bred. Less than annual and rarely seen, as most records are of trapped birds.
..........Aquatic Warbler	*Acrocephalus paludicola*	Very scarce autumn visitor, now recorded annually though almost all records are from traps.
..........Sedge Warbler	*Acrocephalus schoenobaenus*	Fairly common breeding visitor and very common passage migrant.
..........Paddyfield Warbler	*Acrocephalus agricola*	Very rare vagrant. One record, trapped at Pett Levels (Oct 1992).

Marsh Warbler	Acrocephalus palustris	Rare breeding visitor and passage migrant. The majority of records are trapped birds at Pett Levels.
(Eurasian) Reed Warbler	Acrocephalus scirpaceus	Common breeding visitor and passage migrant.
Great Reed Warbler	Acrocephalus arundinaceus	Rare vagrant, less than annual. Near to the coast, May-Jun.
Booted Warbler	Hippolais caligata	Very rare vagrant, just a small handful of recent coastal records.
Sykes's Warbler	Hippolais rama	Very rare vagrant, just a small handful of recent coastal records.
Icterine Warbler	Hippolais icterina	Rare vagrant, less than annual. Most records near the coast, Aug-Sep, rarely May-Jun.
Melodious Warbler	Hippolais polyglotta	Rare vagrant, less than annual. All records near the coast, most in the Beachy Head and Pagham areas. Usually Aug-Sep, rarely May-Jun.
Dartford Warbler	Sylvia undata	Scarce resident, passage migrant and winter visitor.
Subalpine Warbler	Sylvia cantillans	Very rare vagrant, less than annual. Most records from Beachy Head area Apr-Jun.
Sardinian Warbler	Sylvia melanocephala	Very rare vagrant. Just a small handful of post war records, all coastal.
Barred Warbler	Sylvia nisoria	Very scarce autumn visitor. Recently recorded annually. Coastal Aug-Oct.
Lesser Whitethroat	Sylvia curruca	Common breeding visitor and passage migrant.
(Common) Whitethroat	Sylvia communis	Very common breeding visitor and passage migrant.
Garden Warbler	Sylvia borin	Very common breeding visitor and passage migrant.
Blackcap	Sylvia atricapilla	Very common breeding visitor and passage migrant, and scarce winter visitor.
Greenish Warbler	Phylloscopus trochiloides	Very rare vagrant. Two acceptable post war records, both at Beachy Head (May 1981 and Sep 1995).
Pallas's (Leaf) Warbler	Phylloscopus proregulus	Very scarce autumn visitor, recently recorded annually. Usually coastal, Oct-Nov. Top site - Belle Tout area of Beachy Head.
Yellow-browed Warbler	Phylloscopus inornatus	Very rare vagrant, now recorded annually on the coast Oct-Nov. Top site - Belle Tout area of Beachy Head.
Hume's (Leaf) Warbler	Phylloscopus humei	Very rare vagrant. Just a small handful of post war records, all near the coast.
Radde's Warbler	Phylloscopus schwarzi	Very rare vagrant, with a handful of recent records. All Sep-Nov, near the coast.
Dusky Warbler	Phylloscopus fuscatus	Very rare vagrant, three post war records, at Beachy Head (Oct 1974 and Oct 1991) and Combe Haven (Oct 1992).
Western Bonelli's Warbler	Phylloscopus bonelli	Very rare vagrant, a handful of post war records, all at Beachy Head.
Wood Warbler	Phylloscopus sibilatrix	Very scarce summer visitor and passage migrant.
Chiffchaff	Phylloscopus collybita	Very common breeding visitor and passage migrant, and scarce winter visitor.
Willow Warbler	Phylloscopus trochilus	Abundant breeding visitor and passage migrant.
Goldcrest	Regulus regulus	Very common resident, and common passage migrant and winter visitor.
Firecrest	Regulus ignicapilla	Rare breeding visitor and scarce passage migrant and winter visitor. Top sites – Beachy Head, Pagham Harbour, Arundel WWT
Spotted Flycatcher	Muscicapa striata	Fairly common but much declined breeding visitor and passage migrant.
Red-breasted Flycatcher	Ficedula parva	Rare autumn visitor, less than annual. Majority of sightings are at Beachy Head.
Collared Flycatcher	Ficedula albicollis	Single record, Pagham, June 2002
Pied Flycatcher	Ficedula hypoleuca	Scarce passage migrant, has bred.
Bearded Tit	Panurus biarmicus	Very scarce resident and scarce passage migrant and winter visitor. Top sites – Thorney Island and Combe Haven
Long-tailed Tit	Aegithalos caudatus	Very common resident.
Marsh Tit	Parus palustris	Fairly common resident.
Willow Tit	Parus montanus	Scarce and declining resident.
Crested Tit	Parus cristatus	Very rare vagrant. Two records in gardens in 1997 of birds of unknown origin.
Coal Tit	Parus ater	Very common resident.

179

Blue Tit	*Parus caeruleus*	Abundant resident.
Great Tit	*Parus major*	Abundant resident.
(Wood) Nuthatch	*Sitta europaea*	Very common resident.
Wallcreeper	*Tichodroma muraria*	Very rare vagrant, three records being the 3rd, 6th and 9th British records. The last was at Hastings in Apr 1977.
(Eurasian) Treecreeper	*Certhia familiaris*	Very common resident.
(Eurasian) Penduline Tit	*Remiz pendulinus*	Rare autumn visitor, less than annual. Most records are of trapped birds at Pett Level, but some seen at Pagham Harbour's Long Pool. Usually Oct-Nov.
(Eurasian) Golden Oriole	*Oriolus oriolus*	Very scarce passage migrant and summer visitor, may have bred. Vast majority of records in May-early Jun, with most sightings at Beachy Head and Pagham Harbour.
Isabelline Shrike	*Lanius isabellinus*	Very rare vagrant, one record at Pagham Harbour (Mar-Apr 1975). It was only the 6th British record.
Red-backed Shrike	*Lanius collurio*	Very scarce passage migrant, formerly bred. Recorded most years, May-Jun but mostly Aug-Oct. Seen mainly at coastal sites, especially Beachy Head and Pagham Harbour.
Lesser Grey Shrike	*Lanius minor*	Very rare vagrant, with a handful of post war records at the coast.
Great Grey Shrike	*Lanius excubitor*	Very scarce winter visitor and passage migrant, with several records annually. Predominantly heaths and commons, top site undoubtedly Ashdown Forest.
Woodchat Shrike	*Lanius senator*	Rare vagrant, less than annual. Not recorded winter.
(Eurasian) Jay	*Garrulus glandarius*	Very common resident, passage migrant and winter visitor.
(Black-billed) Magpie	*Pica pica*	Very common resident.
(Spotted) Nutcracker	*Nucifraga caryocatactes*	Very rare vagrant with a small handful of post war records. Last recorded at Beachy Head (Aug 1970).
(Red-billed) Chough	*Pyrrhocorax pyrrhocorax*	Extinct resident and very rare vagrant. Bred until about 1830. One flew over Beachy Head in Oct 1996.
(Eurasian) Jackdaw	*Corvus monedula*	Very common resident.
Rook	*Corvus frugilegus*	Very common resident.
Carrion Crow	*Corvus corone*	Very common resident.
Hooded Crow	*Corvus cornix*	Very scarce vagrant, less than annual.
(Common) Raven	*Corvus corax*	Very scarce breeding resident and vagrant. Breeding again after an absence of over 50 years.
(Common) Starling	*Sturnus vulgaris*	Abundant resident, passage migrant and winter visitor.
Rose-coloured (Rosy) Starling	*Sturnus roseus*	Very rare vagrant, less than annual.
House Sparrow	*Passer domesticus*	Abundant resident but declining.
Tree Sparrow	*Passer montanus*	Scarce resident, passage migrant and winter visitor, much declined.
Chaffinch	*Fringilla coelebs*	Abundant resident, passage migrant and winter visitor.
Brambling	*Fringilla montifringilla*	Fairly common winter visitor and passage migrant.
(European) Serin	*Serinus serinus*	Very scarce passage migrant, has bred. Several individuals recorded annually, mostly Mar-May at coastal sites. Top sites – Beachy Head and Selsey Bill
(European) Greenfinch	*Carduelis chloris*	Very common resident passage migrant and winter visitor.
(European) Goldfinch	*Carduelis carduelis*	Common resident passage migrant and winter visitor.
(Eurasian) Siskin	*Carduelis spinus*	very scarce breeding visitor and common winter visitor and passage migrant
(Common) Linnet	*Carduelis cannabina*	Very common resident passage migrant and winter visitor.
Twite	*Carduelis flavirostris*	Scarce winter visitor and passage migrant, several records annually mostly Oct-Jan, now much less frequent than previously. Rarely seen inland.
(Lesser) Redpoll	*Carduelis cabaret*	Fairly common breeding visitor, passage migrant and winter visitor.
Mealy Redpoll	*Carduelis flammea*	Very rare winter visitor, less than annual.
(Common) Crossbill	*Loxia curvirostra*	Scarce winter visitor, periodically breeds in irruption years
Parrot Crossbill	*Loxia pytyopsittacus*	Very rare vagrant, one record in St. Leonard's Forest in 1870. It was shot.
Trumpeter Finch	*Bucanetes githagineus*	Very rare vagrant. One at Church Norton (May 1984).
Common Rosefinch	*Carpodacus erythrinus*	Rare vagrant. Less than annual, most in Beachy Head area.
Bullfinch	*Pyrrhula pyrrhula*	Very common resident.
Hawfinch	*Coccothraustes coccothraustes*	Scarce resident and very scarce passage migrant.
Black-and-White Warbler	*Mniotilta varia*	Very rare vagrant. One record, at Beachy Head (Oct 1996).
Blackpoll Warbler	*Dendroica striata*	Very rare vagrant. One record, at Bewl Water (Dec 1994).

White-throated Sparrow	*Zonotrichia albicollis*	Very rare vagrant. One record, at Beachy Head (Oct 1968) which was the seventh British record.
Slate-coloured (Dark-eyed) Junco	*Junco hyemalis*	Very rare vagrant. One at Winchelsea Beach (Feb 1972),was sixth British record.
Lapland Bunting (Longspur)	*Calcarius lapponicus*	Very scarce passage migrant and winter visitor, mostly to the coast. Recorded most years Sep-Feb.
Snow Bunting	*Pletrophenax nivalis*	Scarce winter visitor and passage migrant, fewer records than in past.
Yellowhammer	*Emberiza citrinella*	Very common resident.
Cirl Bunting	*Emberiza cirlus*	Extinct resident, very rare vagrant. Bred until the early 1980's. Just a small handful of sightings since then on the Pagham/Selsey peninsula.
Rock Bunting	*Emberiza cia*	Very rare vagrant. Two netted near Shoreham in 1902 were the first British records. No acceptable record since.
Ortolan Bunting	*Emberiza hortulana*	Very scarce autumn visitor., less than annual. Mostly coastal records Aug-Sep.
Rustic Bunting	*Emberiza rustica*	Very rare vagrant. One record. Roedean had the first British record in 1867. Since then just a small handful of acceptable post war records.
Little Bunting	*Emberiza pusilla*	Very rare vagrant. A handful of records including the first for Britain at Roedean in 1864. Most records near the coast.
Reed Bunting	*Emberiza schoeniclus*	Common resident, passage migrant and winter visitor.
Pallas's (Reed) Bunting	*Emberiza pallasi*	Very rare vagrant. One record, trapped at Pett Level (Oct 1990). It was not seen in the field.
Black-headed Bunting	*Emberiza melanocephala*	Very rare vagrant, with the first British record at Brighton racecourse in 1868. Two post war records, at Rye Harbour (Sep 1971) and Birling gap (Jun 1994).
Corn Bunting	*Miliaria calandra*	Fairly common resident, but declining.
Northern Oriole	*Icterus galbula*	Very rare vagrant. One record, at Beachy Head (Oct 1962), which was the second British record.

SUSSEX BREEDING MILESTONES

First breeding records

1945	Little Ringed Plover
1960	Collared Dove
1971	Mandarin (f)
1973	Firecrest
1975	Cetti's Warbler
1976	Fulmar
1976	Gadwall
1976	Kittiwake
1977	Greylag Goose (f)
1987	Mediterranean Gull
1989	Siskin
2000	Great Black-backed Gull

Last breeding records

1878	Razorbill
19th C	Black Grouse
1904	Guillemot
1938	Montagu's Harrier
1944	Wryneck
1945	Corncrake
1956	Kentish Plover
1963	Common Gull
1968	Red-backed Shrike
1980s	Cirl Bunting
1980s	Stone Curlew
1991	Curlew

BIRD GROUP DEFINITIONS

An explanation of collective bird groupings used in this book

Wildfowl – *commonplace swans, geese and ducks on Sussex pools, lakes and reservoirs*
Mute Swan, Canada Goose, Mallard, Teal (winter), Tufted Duck

Waterbirds – *birds other than wildfowl seen regularly on or by fresh water*
Little Grebe, Cormorant, Grey Heron, Moorhen, Coot, Sedge Warbler (breeding season), Reed Warbler (breeding season), Reed Bunting

Coastal waders – *regularly-seen wading birds of the seashore and tidal waters, mostly in winter*
Redshank, Oystercatcher, Dunlin, Turnstone, Curlew, Ringed Plover, Grey Plover

Inland waders – *regularly-seen wading birds at the muddy margins of freshwater pools*
Snipe (now very rare in summer), Common Sandpiper (passage; rare in winter), Green Sandpiper (passage; infrequent in winter), Lapwing, Redshank

Gulls – *commonplace gulls in Sussex*
Common Gull (winter), Herring Gull, Black-headed Gull, Great Black-backed Gull, Lesser Black-backed Gull (in small numbers)

'White-winged' gulls – Glaucous, Iceland and Mediterranean Gulls

Auks - here taken to mean just Guillemot and Razorbill

Hirundines - here taken to mean Swallow, House Martin, Sand Martin (restricted during breeding season), with Swift included, though not actually part of the *hirundinidae* family.

Woodland birds – *commonplace birds in deciduous woodland in Sussex*
Sparrowhawk, Woodpigeon, Tawny Owl (rarely seen), Green Woodpecker, Great Spotted Woodpecker, Wren, Robin, Blackbird, Song Thrush, Blackcap (breeding season), Chiffchaff (breeding season), Willow Warbler (breeding season), Goldcrest, Long-tailed Tit, Coal Tit, Blue Tit, Great Tit, Jay, Jackdaw, Crow, Chaffinch, Greenfinch, Bullfinch

Scrub birds – *commonplace birds in scrubby habitats in Sussex*
Woodpigeon, Green Woodpecker, Wren, Dunnock, Robin, Blackbird, Song Thrush, Whitethroat, Willow Warbler (breeding season), Long-tailed Tit, Blue Tit, Great Tit, Magpie, Chaffinch, Greenfinch, Goldfinch, Linnet, Bullfinch, Yellowhammer

Farmland birds – *commonplace birds on Sussex farmland, hedgerows and scrub*
Kestrel, Sparrowhawk, Pheasant, Red-legged Partridge, Lapwing (winter), Gulls (winter), Stock Dove, Woodpigeon, Collared Dove, Sky Lark, Swallow, Meadow Pipit (mainly winter), Pied Wagtail, Wren, Dunnock, Robin, Blackbird, Song Thrush, Mistle Thrush, Whitethroat, Blue Tit, Great Tit, Long-tailed Tit, Corvids, Starling, Chaffinch, Greenfinch, Goldfinch, Linnet, House Sparrow, Yellowhammer

Garden birds – *commonplace birds around habitation in Sussex*
Woodpigeon, Collared Dove, House Martin, Wren, Dunnock, Robin, Blackbird, Song Thrush, Blue Tit, Great Tit, Magpie, Jackdaw, Crow, Starling, House Sparrow, Chaffinch, Greenfinch

Corvids – here taken to mean Crow, Rook, Magpie, Jackdaw

Thrushes – used as a cover-all term in winter for Song Thrush, Blackbird, Redwing and Fieldfare

Warblers – used as a cover-all term for Chiffchaff, Willow Warbler, Blackcap, Garden Warbler, Lesser Whitethroat and Whitethroat

BIBLIOGRAPHY

Birds of Sussex [Sussex Ornithological Society 1996] edited by Paul James. ISBN 0 9528466 0 8

A History of Sussex Birds [Witherby 1938] J. Walpole-Bond

Sussex Nature Reserves [Sussex Wildlife Trust 2002] edited by Richard Cobden

Where to Watch Birds in Kent, Surrey & Sussex [3rd edition, Helm 1997] Taylor, Wheatley & Burges. ISBN 0 7136 4544 X

The Sussex Bird Report [Sussex Ornithological Society, published annually. Contact SOS]

The Shoreham District Ornithological Society Report [SDOS, published annually]

The Birds of Selsey Bill and the Selsey Peninsula [Owen Mitchell, published 2003. For copies, contact Owen at 4 Lodge Close, Middleton, Bognor Regis, West Sussex, PO22 6NF.]

Pagham LNR – Wardens Report [WSCC, published annually. Available from Pagham Harbour Visitor Centre]

Friends of Rye Harbour LNR Report [ESCC, published annually. Available from Lime Kiln Cottage at Rye Harbour.]

A Natural History of the Cuckmere Valley [Book Guild 1997] Patrick Coulcher. ISBN 1 85776 158 8

USEFUL WEBSITES

See also 'Key Birdwatching Contacts' pp186-187

ashdownforest.co.uk – wide ranging info on Ashdown Forest.

birdguides.com – all you could wish for in a birdwatcher's site, but you have to subscribe.

eurobirding.co.uk – general birding site including some detailed info on several Sussex sites.

findon.com – fascinating info about Cissbury and Chanctonbury Rings and the Downs in general.

Homepage.ntlworld.com/ sussex.birder/ - Ian Barnard's excellent up-to-date website about Sussex birds and birding

sevensisters.org.uk – all about the Seven Sisters country park.

sussexnatureweb. btinternet.co.uk – interesting portraits of lots of Sussex reserves.

westwitteringbeach.co.uk – useful info on West Wittering and East Head.

yates.clara.net/lnr – website for Rye Harbour LNR

HOW TO FIND OUT WHAT'S BEEN SEEN

www.susos.org.uk/sightings. Updated daily, this excellent website is the place where most active birdwatchers in Sussex post their sightings. E-mail records to **sightings@susos.org.uk**

BirdLine South East 09068 700 240. To report sightings to this telephone hotline, tel 08000 377 240 or 07626 966 966

Birdwatching e-groups in Sussex - This Sussex Birds E-group is for e-mail discussion of all birding and bird related matters in Sussex. No postings allowed on: caged birds and falconry, rare breeding birds or winter raptor roosts in sensitive areas; anything that could be deemed libellous. To subscribe to the list, send a blank e-mail to: **SussexBirds-subscribe@ yahoogroups.com**

GLOSSARY

Birdwatching has developed a bit of a language of its own; conservation has created yet another (dominated by acronyms). The following terms crop up in text:

BIRDRACE: A competition, usually between teams of four people, to see how many species can be seen (and heard) in a day in the county, and hopefully raise money for charity in the process. Start at 3am if you want to win!

BTO: British Trust for Ornithology.

CARR: Woodland growing on soils with permanently high water levels. These are often dominated by willow and alder.

COMMIC TERN: A tern that is too distant to be firmly identified as either Common or Arctic

DIURNAL: Taking place during the day.

ESCC: East Sussex County Council.

FALL: A sudden arrival of a large number of migrant birds in one location. Often occurs during fog or misty rain, or follows poor weather the night before. The birds are often tired, can even land on your head, but may only hang around for a short time.

FERAL: Populations of a species that were once domesticated but are now living in a wild state.

ID: Identification, used as in 'Did you get an ID on that bird?'

LNR: Local Nature Reserve – LNRs are both for people and wildlife. They are places with wildlife or geological features that are of special interest locally, and give people opportunities to study, learn and enjoy nature.

LOAFING: Some birds, such as gulls, spend time idly during the day, sometimes preening, often just hanging about. This is called 'loafing', not to be confused with 'roosting'.

LOCAL PATCH: A frequently-visited site close to the birdwatcher's home.

MIGRANT: A bird that undertakes migration.

MIGRATION: A journey undertaken by birds, principally between their breeding grounds and wintering areas, almost always along predictable routes and at predictable times of year. En route, birds may linger for considerable whiles at favoured staging posts.

NNR: National Nature Reserve - managed, on behalf of the nation, by English Nature or other approved bodies. They are places for important wildlife and natural features in England, and there are about 200 NNRs nationally. There is a presumption against development, but no legal protection.

PASSAGE: Effectively synonymous with 'migration', can be an adjective (eg 'passage migrant', taken to mean a migrant that is only seen in that location en route to breeding or wintering grounds), or a noun (eg 'the Scoters were on passage').

184

PASSERINE: Any bird of the order *passeriformes*; perching birds, having feet with three toes pointing forward and one back. Includes a wide range of bird families from larks and pipits to finches.

POM: Affectionate or syllable-saving term for Pomarine Skua.

RAMSAR SITE: A wetland site of international importance as defined at, and protected by, the international convention in Ramsar, Iran in 1971. Is written 'Ramsar', not 'RAMSAR'.

RAPTORS: A cover-all term for birds of prey, can sometimes include owls.

RARITIES & SEMI-RARITIES: British rarities are those birds which are seen, on average, 150 times or less in the entire country each decade. Semi-rarities are a less well-defined group of species that are seen infrequently and generate excitement among birdwatchers, and may require descriptions at county level to be accepted. Includes Temminck's Stint, Wryneck, Hoopoe, Tawny Pipit etc.

RODING: The display flight of the Woodcock, whereby males make wide-ranging level flight at dusk over their 'territory' making distinctive snorting noises.

ROOSTING: The (in)activity when birds rest and sleep, often in groups and at established roosting sites.

RSPB: Royal Society for the Protection of Birds.

SEABIRDS: A loose term to describe birds which are seen only exceptionally away from the open sea or their coastal nesting areas – includes Gannet, shearwaters, Fulmar, petrels.

SPA: Special Protection Area – site of international importance for migrant or wintering birds, protected under the European Union's Birds Directive.

SSSI: Site of Special Scientific Interest – English legal designation for a site with special interest for its flora, fauna, geological or physiographical features.

SWT: Sussex Wildlife Trust.

WADERS: Generic term for a large family of long-legged bird species, usually found near water along shores or on bogs and marshes, sometimes occurring in huge numbers on the coast. Includes Redshank, Curlew, Dunlin and Lapwing.

WeBS COUNT: A count of birds made during The Wetland Bird Survey, a joint scheme of the BTO, WWT, RSPB and Joint Nature Conservation Committee to monitor non-breeding waterbirds in the UK.

WSCC: West Sussex County Council.

WWT: Wildfowl and Wetlands Trust.

YEARLIST: A record of the number of bird species seen (and heard) in your chosen geographical area in a calendar year.

Sussex Bird Recorder
John Hobson, 23 Hillside Road, Storrington, RH20 3LZ.
Tel: 01903 740155. Email: janthobson@aol.com

Ashdown Forest Conservators'
Manage the Forest as an amenity and place of resort, protect the rights of common; and protect the Forest from encroachment and to conserve it as a quiet area of outstanding natural beauty. There is also a Society of Friends of Ashdown Forest.
Contact: The Ashdown Forest Centre, Wych Cross, Forest Row, Sussex, RH18 5JP. Tel: 01342 823583

British Trust for Ornithology (BTO)
Formed in 1933, is an independent, scientific research trust, investigating the populations, movements and ecology of wild birds in the British Isles. Specialising in volunteer wild bird surveys, this work makes a direct and vital contribution to bird conservation, by enabling both campaigners and decision-makers to set priorities and target resources. It also provides a unique insight into the state of our environment. Anyone interested in birds can get involved, from beginner to expert.
Contact: BTO, The Nunnery, Thetford, Norfolk, IP2 2PU
Tel: 01842 750050 www.bto.org.uk

Chichester Harbour Conservancy (CHC)
Is an independent statutory body managing Chichester Harbour and an amenity area of land surrounding, with the powers of a County Council for nature conservation. Friends of Chichester Harbour is a group concerned with sustaining and improving the environment of the harbour for the benefit of all users - both the people and the wildlife.
Contact: The Harbour Office, Itchenor, Chichester Harbour, West Sussex, PO20 7AW
Tel:01243 512301 Fax: 01243 513026
www.conservancy.co.uk

English Nature (EN)
This is the Government-funded body whose purpose is to promote the conservation of England's wildlife and natural features.
Contact: English Nature Sussex and Surrey Team, 31 High Street, Lewes, East Sussex, BN7 2LU. Tel: 01273 476595 www.english-nature.org.uk

Environment Agency
Is the leading public body responsible for protecting and improving the environment in England and Wales. They have an important role in conservation and ecology, especially along rivers and in wetlands.
Contact: EA, Sussex Area Office, Saxon House, Worthing, West Sussex, BN11 1DH Tel: 01903 215835

Friends of Weir Wood Reservoir
Works to help manage the Weir Wood Local Nature Reserve. Members receive three newsletters a year, and help with enhancing the biodiversity of the site (work parties every Tues, 10.30am-3pm, tools provided!). Subscription min. £2/year. Send you Weir Wood bird

records to: Barbara Mortlock, 37 Barnmead, Haywards heath, West Sussex, RH16 1UY. Contact the Friends via Bob Johnson (Hon Secretary), Leven, Pilmer Road, Crowborough, TN6 2UG.

Friends of Widewater Lagoon (FOWL)
Is a group dedicated to enhancing the beauty of Widewater. Their aim is to make people aware of the natural beauty of what is a unique conservation area.
Contact: http://freespace.virgin.net/martino.marcaz/fowl/index.htm

Henfield Birdwatch
Was set up by Mike Russell in 1998 under a Millennium Fellowship Award. A comprehensive survey of birds in the parish was carried out during 1999 and the results published in a 68-page book Henfield Birdwatch 2000. The group aims to repeat this every five years, with specific species surveyed annually. Walks, mainly local, are organised, there is a March AGM and a November talk open to all.
Contact: Mike Russell, C/o Woods Mill, Henfield Tel: 01273 492630.

National Trust (NT)
Was founded in 1895 to preserve places of historic interest or natural beauty for people to enjoy. It is best known for its stately homes but it also owns some 40,000 acres of land in the south-east across 155 different sites. Much of this land is of high wildlife interest and the Trust is working to maximise its value for wildlife whilst balancing the issues of public access, archaeology and landscape.
www.nationaltrust.org.uk.

Royal Society for the Protection of Birds (RSPB)
Founded in 1889 and has since grown into Europe's largest wildlife conservation charity with more than a million members. Work ranges from conservation policy to education, wildlife law enforcement to land purchase. Work in Sussex is coordinated from the South East Regional Office, with a major reserve in the Arun Valley based at Pulborough Brooks, and smaller reserves on the Adur Estuary and at Fore Wood. RSPB Local Groups in Sussex, open to all and organising field trips and indoor meetings, are based in: Battle; Brighton & District; Chichester & SW Sussex; Crawley & Horsham; East Grinstead; Eastbourne & District; Hastings & St Leonards; and Heathfield.
Contact: RSPB, 42 Frederick Place,Brighton, BN1 4EA. Tel: 01273 775333 Fax:01273 220236
www.rspb.org.uk

Shoreham District Ornithological Society (SDOS)
Founded in 1953, is the oldest birdwatching society in

Sussex, covering Shoreham, Brighton, Worthing, Steyning and Storrington. The Society holds monthly indoor meetings from October to April, and arranges a programme of field outings throughout the year. Members receive three newsletters a year as well as a comprehensive annual bird report.
Contact: The Honorary Secretary, Mrs Brianne Reeve, The Old Rectory, Coombes, Lancing, West Sussex BN15 0RS.

South East Water
Supplies 400 million litres of top quality drinking water every day, to 1.5 million people in the South East. In conservation terms, it looks after 19 SSSIs and two LNRs, working extensively in partnership with wildlife organisations and local groups.
Contact: South East Water, The Lodge, Arlington Reservoir, Berwick, Polegate, East Sussex BN26 6TF. Egoddard@southeastwater.co.uk. Tel: 01323 870810

Southern Water
Balances running an efficient, value for money service with protecting some of the finest natural assets in Sussex. Its reservoirs and treatment works are often located on secluded sites and they provide a rich, natural habitat for birds, wildlife and plants, with some have been designated as SSSIs.
Contact: Southern House, Yeoman Road, Worthing, BN13 3NX Tel: 0845 278 0845
www.southernwater.co.uk

Sussex Biodiversity Record Centre, a partnership project,
Acts as a focus for environmental information in Sussex. It gathers, processes and stores information on species and habitats in Sussex, and provides information for environmental decision-makers and the general public.
Contact: Sussex Biodiversity Record Centre, Woods Mill, Henfield, West Sussex, BN5 9SD. Tel: 01273 - 497553/554 E-mail: sxbrc@sussexwt.org.uk

Sussex Downs Conservation Board (SDCB)
Established in 1992, aims to protect, conserve and enhance the natural beauty of the Sussex Downs Area of Outstanding Natural Beauty; to encourage people's quiet enjoyment of the Downs; and to promote sustainable economic and social development.
Contact: SDCB, Stanmer Park, Lewes Road, Brighton, BN1 9SE Tel: 01273 625242

Sussex Ornithological Society (SOS)
With a membership exceeding 1600, provides a focal point in the county for all those interested in birding, from those preparing detailed scientific papers to those merely trying to identify what they have seen

on their bird table. Members receive the Annual Bird Report, quarterly newsletter, and have the chance to take part in the annual conference and field outings.
Contact: Secretary, Beavers Brook, The Thatchway, Angmering, West Sussex, BN16 4HJ.
Email:secretary@susos.org.uk www.susos.org.uk

Sussex Wealden Greensand Heath Project (SWGHP)
Is a five-year partnership between EN, DEFRA, NT, SDCB and WSCC, financially supported by the Heritage Lottery Fund, to conserve and enhance the heaths of the Wealden area. The project will assist landowners to carry out conservation work to help safeguard the future of the many rare species dependent on these heaths.
Contact: SWGHP, Bepton Road, Midhurst, West Sussex GU29 9QX. Tel: 01730 812134

Sussex Wildlife Trust (SWT)
Uses its knowledge and expertise to help people and organisations in Sussex to enjoy, understand and take action to conserve the Sussex environment and its wildlife. It has over 13,500 members and looks after 3400 acres in 37 nature reserves, has an extensive schools programme, speaks out on all major environmental issues in Sussex, and works with landowners to achieve a better environment.
Contact: SWT, Woods Mill, Henfield, West Sussex, BN5 9SD. Tel: 01273 492630; Fax: 01273 494500; Email: enquiries@sussexwt.org.uk Conservation Careline: 01273 494777 www.sussexwt.org.uk

West Sussex County Council
Helps maintain and improve the natural environment for future generations. It manages prestigious countryside such as Pagham Harbour, offers an environmental education service at Buchan Country Park, and provides wildlife advice, grants and practical help to West Sussex residents, planners and developers. The Council is responsible for running the West Sussex Sites of Nature Conservation Importance (SNCI) Project.
Contact: WSCC, County Hall, Chichester, PO19 1RQ Tel: 01243 777100

Wildfowl and Wetlands Trust (WWT)
Founded in 1946 by artist and naturalist Sir Peter Scott to conserve wetlands and their biodiversity, maintains a network of wetland nature reserves as integral parts of nine conservation-led visitor centres across the UK. The 60-acre Arundel centre attracts significant numbers of native and migratory water birds. These, and the hundreds of resident wildfowl, enable people to get closer to wetland birds and enjoy wetland landscapes in a welcoming and unchallenging environment.
Contact: WWT Tel: 01903 883355 Fax: 01903 884834 E-mail:info@arundel.wwt.org.uk www.wwt.org.uk

INDEX

This index lists all the site names, other relevant places and all birds listed in the 'target' or 'other likely species' lists in the site guide section. They are also indexed from other sections where relevant. The number of entries listed under each species should not be seen as an indication of how common or otherwise the bird is in Sussex. (**Bold** numbers indicate page number for a Featured Site).

191

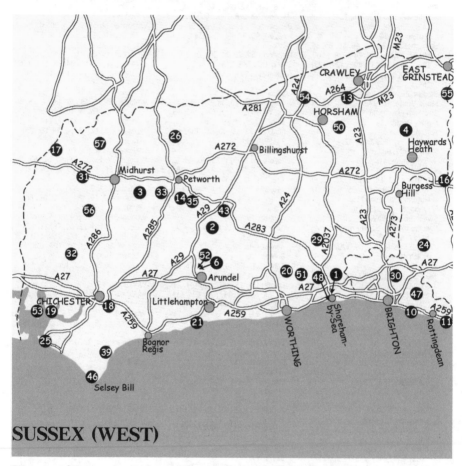

SUSSEX (WEST)

Key to sites - numbers refer to site numbers in text

1 Adur Estuary
2 Amberley Wild Brooks
3 Ambersham Common
4 Ardingly Reservoir
5 Arlington Reservoir
6 Arundel WWT
7 Ashdown Forest
8 Beachy Head
9 Bewl Water
10 Brighton Marina
11 Brighton to Newhaven Cliffs

12 Broadwater Forest
13 Buchan Country Park
14 Burton Mill Pond
15 Castle Hill to Swanborough Hill
16 Chailey Common
17 Chapel Common
18 Chichester Gravel Pits
19 Chidham
20 Cissbury to Chanctonbury
21 Climping

22 Combe Haven
23 Cuckmere Haven
24 Ditchling Beacon to Ashcombe Bottom
25 East Head & West Wittering
26 Ebernoe Forest
27 Fore Wood RSPB
28 Hastings Country Park
29 Henfield Levels
30 Hollingbury Camp
31 Iping & Stedham Commons

192